MOSCOW
— and the —
COMMUNIST
PARTY OF INDIA

TECHNOLOGY PRESS BOOKS
IN THE SOCIAL SCIENCES

MOSCOW

——— and the ———

COMMUNIST
PARTY OF INDIA

**A Study in the Postwar Evolution of
International Communist Strategy**

JOHN H. KAUTSKY

THE M.I.T. PRESS
Massachusetts Institute of Technology
Cambridge, Massachusetts

To
Cathy and Peter

ACKNOWLEDGMENTS

I should like to record my deep indebtedness to Messrs. Morris Watnick and Bernard S. Morris, with whom it was my good fortune to be associated in research on international Communism for some time before I undertook this study. Their valuable counsel and suggestions greatly aided me in its preparation, and both deserve credit, Morris Watnick in particular, for having been the first to call my attention to the essential novelty of the Communists' present strategy.

In the present work I have used and refined this broad concept of a new Communist strategy as the basis of my research, and in this process I believe I have proved its usefulness. I owed the opportunity to do this to my appointment as a research associate at the Center for International Studies at the Massachusetts Institute of Technology in 1953–1954. I am grateful to Professor Max F. Millikan, the Director of the Center, and, particularly, to Professor Walt W. Rostow, the Director of its China Project, for having made it possible for me to pursue my research under ideal conditions.

Dr. Toshio G. Tsukahira, then of Harvard University, my colleague at the Center for International Studies and the author of a study of the postwar evolution of Communist strategy in Japan, contributed to the clarification of my concepts of Communist strategy both through his application of them in his own work and through many conversations.

Professor Benjamin I. Schwartz of Harvard made valuable suggestions for the initial research plan for this study.

Mr. Gene D. Overstreet of Michigan State College, whose unpublished Master's Thesis proved helpful at one stage of my work, very kindly sent me some important material from India.

Both the reader and I owe much to Mr. Richard W. Hatch of the Center for International Studies, who used his editorial talents to make this study much more readable than it would otherwise have been.

It goes without saying that none of the above-named persons is in any way responsible for the form or the conclusions of this book or for any interpretations or errors contained in it.

I wish to thank the publishers of the *American Political Science Review* and of *Pacific Affairs* for their permission to reprint here some material that first appeared in two articles of mine published in the June 1955 issues of these two journals, and the publishers of the *Current Digest of the Soviet Press* for allowing me to use their translations of a number of passages quoted from the Soviet press.

JOHN H. KAUTSKY

Rochester, New York
July 1956

CONTENTS

Contents

INTRODUCTION

My principal purposes in this investigation are to assess the role played by the Soviet and, at least by implication, the Chinese Communists in the formation of the strategy of the Communist Party of India and to present a case study in the postwar development of international Communist strategy in general. The method employed is to analyze in detail the twists and turns of the Indian Communist Party line since 1945 and statements relevant to Indian Communist strategy emanating from Moscow and, secondarily, Peking in order to detect and, as far as possible, explain the degree of correspondence between them.

This approach does not require any evaluation of the Party line either to test its adherence to Marxist or Leninist doctrine or to examine the extent to which it is likely to lead to Communist success in the existing Indian environment. One of the assumptions on which this study is based is that in the last analysis shifts in a Communist party line are due to corresponding earlier shifts in Moscow and perhaps Peking rather than to the interpretation of Marxism or Leninism by local Communist leaders or the internal conditions of a given country. This study therefore does not deal with all types of relations between Moscow and the Indian Communists, for example, those in the propaganda field. Nor is this a history of the Communist Party of India.[1] It is not concerned with the strength and composition of the Party, its organization, leadership, and many different activities, or with its successes, failures, and prospects except as they illustrate the application of various strategies. It is limited to the analysis of one decisive aspect of that Party's history—the development of its party line.

Given the basic uniformity of Communist strategy throughout the non-Communist world and the similarity of the relationships between Moscow and the various Communist parties, it follows that this essay is as much a case study of the process by which a Communist party line is formulated and finally adopted as it is an analysis of Indian Communism.

The Indian rather than any other Communist party was chosen for

1

my investigation for a number of reasons. Among these are, of course, both the importance of India as the most powerful non-Communist nation in Asia and the most populous one in the world, and India's significance in the area in which Communism has made its greatest advances in recent years. Equally important was the hope that indirectly some light might be thrown on one element in Sino-Soviet relations, since both Moscow and Peking could be presumed to have some interest in Indian Communist strategy. To these must be added the very practical reason of the availability of sources, usually a severely limiting factor in research in this field. No other important Asian Communist party draws up all its major documents in English, and few of them engage to the extent that the Indian Party does in the type of public discussion and the publication of the type of documents on which my analysis is largely based; nor does the relevant Soviet literature pay as much attention to most of the other Asian Communist parties as it does to the Indian one. Finally, the Indian Communist Party, probably more than any other in Asia, has been subject in the postwar years to a number of very sharply marked turns in strategy, most of them accompanied by the kind of internal upheaval and "self-criticism" that throws much light on the inner workings of a Communist party, making it an ideal subject for this kind of investigation.*

Since my interest centers on the development of Communist strategy after World War II, this study does not, except in a very few paragraphs, deal with the evolution of the Indian Party line in the prewar and war periods. The switches in international Communist strategy, paralleling the sharp changes in the international relations of the Soviet Union, in these periods are too familiar to require documentation or recounting here. The story of the corresponding strategy changes of the Indian Communist Party is less widely known, but enough of it, supported by many quotations from Communist documents, emerges in a recent book by M. R. Masani[2] to make it unnecessary to piece it together from the original sources. The present study, with its detailed analysis of such sources, is confined to the period from the end of World War II to the Third Congress of the Communist Party of India held at the beginning of 1954. It thus covers fully the period when, partly under the influence of the victories of the Chinese

* Nehru once called it "the most stupid among the Communist parties of the world." Quoted in Frank Moraes, "Can Communism Conquer India?" *United Nations World*, VII, No. 7 (July 1953), 24–27 and 63, on p. 24. And Chester Bowles wrote that "the whole history of the party is a series of major mistakes and somersaults." *Ambassador's Report* (New York: Harper & Brothers, 1954), p. 137.

Communists, the most significant strategy changes were made in Moscow and subsequently applied in India.

Documentation and distinction of strategies. It has been clear to me from the outset that two requirements would have to be met by my investigation if its results were to be both reliable and meaningful. The first of these is thorough documentation.

The subject of Communism seems to lend itself peculiarly to speculation, which, though it cannot be proved correct, often cannot be disproved either. In order to avoid raising the question of such speculation I have limited myself to the interpretation of data that could be presented in the study itself. What are appropriate data for the study of Communist party strategy? The party's activities, it might appear, are its strategy put into action. However, and especially in the case of a weak, poorly organized, and widely scattered party such as the Indian, strategy as envisaged by the top leadership is likely to be translated into action but imperfectly and at best belatedly. Furthermore, not having observed Indian Communist activities at first hand, I would have to rely for their description on the conflicting interpretations of varying reliability offered by many writers. An analysis of the party's day-to-day propaganda might provide a better clue to its strategy, but propaganda is but an application of strategy and not strategy itself; and I am interested here only in the latter, regardless of whether and how it is applied in practice, since I use the Indian Party's strategy and especially changes in its strategy merely as an index of its relation with Moscow.

It is my conviction that strategy itself, as distinguished from its application, can best be discovered in the official documents of the party's top leadership and, in the case of Soviet expressions on this subject, in the so-called "scientific" analyses of some of the members of the USSR Academy of Sciences and in other so-called "international documents," by which delicate term Communist party leaders themselves often quite frankly refer to Soviet statements whose policy guidance they follow. It is on these sources that this study is almost exclusively based. While their language often appears obscure at first sight, I hope to demonstrate that it is by no means impenetrable and that the Communists' own official and published words can be used to reveal the answers to the questions asked here. Careful study of Communist pronouncements can prove far more rewarding than search for the secret channels of communication of international Communism, a search which, even if successful, can tell us nothing about the content of the communications. To pursue this more fruitful but less spectacular approach, it is necessary to engage in rather detailed

analysis of some documents and to use extensive verbatim quotations
—a procedure that both preserves the original flavor of Communist
writing and thinking and permits the reader to check for himself the
data on which my interpretations are based, data that can, in many
cases, be obtained only with some difficulty in the United States.

The second requirement that must be met is the consistent adherence to a clear set of criteria for the distinction of various Communist
strategies. It is manifestly impossible to know which strategy a Communist party is following at any time, to detect changes from one
strategy to another, and to determine which strategies are advocated
by various factions if we are not absolutely clear in our minds as to
what constitutes the distinguishing characteristics of the various strategies and what are the elements common to two or more strategies.
Terms used to describe strategies must be well defined. The indis-
criminate use of such phrases as "united front," "popular front," revolutionary," "militant," "hard," "soft," "radical," and "moderate"
simply will not do, for all of these can, as will be seen, be entirely
meaningless or even grossly misleading. My first chapter is devoted
to the setting up of a rigorous taxonomic scheme designed to isolate
the essential features of each Communist strategy. If these are set
down rather pedantically and without much evidence or proof, it is
because all the subsequent chapters of this study furnish ample supporting illustrations. The pattern established and the terminology
used* in the first chapter will be used, often without further explanation, throughout the book, and some familiarity with them is therefore
a prerequisite for understanding it.†

Notes for the Introduction

1. The most useful histories of the Communist Party of India are M. R. Masani,
The Communist Party of India, A Short History (London: Derek Verschoyle, 1954;

* It may be noted that to a large extent Communist terminology is used in the
following discussion, since it is both derived from and applied to the analysis of
Communist writings. Though quotation marks will generally be omitted for the
sake of simplicity, it must be remembered that the meaning to be attached to such
terms as imperialism, feudalism, bourgeoisie, socialism, or national liberation is
that given to them by the Communists.

† While this scheme is tested in the present study only in its application to the
strategy of the Indian Communist Party and the Moscow line for Asian Communism, it is my conviction, arrived at on the basis of other research on international Communism, that it is applicable to Communist strategy throughout the
non-Communist world. It is therefore suggested that this classification of Communist strategies may serve as a useful tool of analysis for the study of the strategy
of any Communist party not in power or that of any Communist international
organization.

New York: Macmillan, 1954) and Madhu Limaye, *Communist Party, Facts and Fiction* (Hyderabad: Chetana Prakashan, February 1951). See also M. R. Masani, "The Communist Party in India," *Pacific Affairs*, XXIV, No. 1 (March 1951), 18–38, and, for the post-1946 period, Madhu Limaye, "Indian Communism: The New Phase," *ibid.*, XXVII, No. 3 (September 1954), 195–215, and Morton Schwartz, "The Wavering 'Line' of Indian Communism," *Political Science Quarterly*, LXX, No. 4 (December 1955), 552–572. Less satisfactory historical treatments are the brief pamphlet, S. R. Mohan Das, *Communist Activity in India (1925–1950)* (Bombay: Democratic Research Service, 1950), and also Ruth Fischer, "The Indian Communist Party," Russian Research Center, Harvard University, Minutes of the Seminar Meeting, July 11, 1952 (mimeographed), as well as her article by the same title, based on this lecture, in *Far Eastern Survey*, XXII, No. 7 (June 1953), 79–84. Useful data on the postwar period also appear in Jean A. Curran, Jr., "Dissension Among India's Communists," *Far Eastern Survey*, XIX, No. 13 (July 12, 1950), 132–136; W. Gordon Graham, "Communism and South Asia," *The Pacific Spectator*, V, No. 2 (Spring 1951), 215–231; and Chester Bowles, *Ambassador's Report* (New York: Harper & Brothers, 1954), ch. 10. This chapter appeared in somewhat different and briefer form as "The Odds on Communism in India," *Harper's Magazine*, Vol. 208, No. 1244 (January 1954), 41–48. An Indian Communist view of the war and postwar period may be found in "Review of the Second Congress of Communist Party of India," *People's Age* (Bombay), March 21, 1948, Supplement, while a Soviet view of the period to 1947 is represented by A. M. Dyakov, "Crisis of British Rule in India and the Liberation Struggle of her Peoples," *Crisis of the Colonial System* (Bombay: People's Publishing House, 1951), pp. 1–48. The present study is briefly summarized in John H. Kautsky, "Indian Communist Party Strategy Since 1947," *Pacific Affairs*, XXVIII, No. 2 (June 1955), 145–160.

2. M. R. Masani, *The Communist Party of India*, Chapters II–V.

THE THREE STRATEGIES OF COMMUNISM

I. THE "LEFT" AND "RIGHT" STRATEGIES

The central problem of Communist strategy has always been to determine who should, at any given time, be considered the main enemy and consequently what classes should be accepted as allies of Communism and what type of alliance should be entered into with them. These three factors, and especially the latter two, furnish the crucial distinctions between different Communist strategies. Two alternative solutions of this problem formed the bases of the two strategies followed by international Communism during its first thirty years as an organized movement (except in China, where they were both abandoned after twenty or twenty-five years). In the Communists' own terminology,* we may refer to them here simply as the "left" and the "right" strategies.

The "left" strategy. The "left" strategy, which can perhaps be called the classical strategy of Communism and is often erroneously thought to be still in effect, considered capitalism as its main enemy. Even in underdeveloped areas the native bourgeoisie was looked upon as an enemy on a par with foreign imperialism and native feudalism, that is, the landlords and the nobility. This strategy envisaged the socialist revolution as its immediate goal. Even in societies which, according to the Marxian scheme of historical stages, had not yet traversed the capitalist stage, the next revolution was presumed to lay the basis for socialism and to merge with or even skip some of the phases of the so-called bourgeois-democratic revolution.

The "left" strategy was an attempt to form a "united front from below." It was based on appeals to workers and also poor peasants,

---

* Used particularly while one strategy was in effect to condemn as deviationists the followers of the other one.

and petty bourgeois elements, both as individuals and as members
of local organizations affiliated with socialist or "bourgeois" parties
or, in the underdeveloped countries, so-called bourgeois-nationalist
movements. These appeals were designed to induce the rank and file
to leave such parties and join the Communists, either directly or by
cooperating with them in "united action." Such appeals were therefore always coupled with violent denunciations of the top leaders of
the other parties as servants of the bourgeoisie and of imperialism and
as traitors to the interests of their rank-and-file followers. Similar
tactics were followed in the trade-union field in pursuance of this
"left" strategy.

The "right" strategy. The "right" strategy of Communism regarded
as its main enemy not capitalism but Fascism and similar movements
and, in underdeveloped areas, feudalism and foreign imperialism.
The professed immediate aim of this strategy was the establishment
or defense of democracy or national liberation, to which social revolution had to be subordinated. It therefore looked forward to a revolution in two stages: first a bourgeois-democratic revolution directed
against Fascism or imperialism and feudalism, followed later by a
proletarian-socialist revolution directed against the bourgeoisie and
capitalism, with the Communists participating in the first as well as
in the second.

Not being anti-capitalist, the "right" strategy called for an alliance
of the Communist party with other parties which were recognized
as anti-Fascist or anti-imperialist and anti-feudal, and which might
include both labor and bourgeois parties.* Its most important characteristic, which easily distinguished the "right" strategy from the
other Communist strategies, was, thus, that it involved a united front
"from above," a "top alliance" with other parties arrived at in agreement with their national party leadership. Similar alliances or even
mergers of Communist trade unions with socialist and nationalist
trade unions were also advocated as part of this policy.

It is clear, then, that the "left" and "right" strategies were designed

* The "popular front" was broad enough to embrace both of these, whereas the
"united front from above," in the narrower sense of this term, was an alliance of
the Communist party only with a labor or socialist party. In practice this distinction is not too important, for the really difficult decision for Communists was to
ally themselves with any strong party and particularly with their most hated
enemies, the democratic socialists. Since these latter are, in any case, regarded as
lackeys of the bourgeoisie, once this decision was made, it was easy and usual to
extend the alliance to at least some left-wing bourgeois parties. We may therefore
overlook the distinction here and refer to both the popular front and the united
front from above by the latter term.

for diametrically opposite objectives: the united front from below was intended to weaken and split the very groups with which the Communists sought to enter an alliance when they were committed to a united front from above. The unfortunate fact that the Communists referred to both these strategies as "united front" policies has given rise to much confusion and can obscure shifts from one to the other. It is all too often overlooked that, in a sense, Communists always follow a united front policy and that to state no more than this, as is frequently done, without distinguishing between the united fronts from above and below, is merely to inform us that they, like all political parties, seek to increase their strength.

Different as the two strategies were, it must be emphasized that in both of them the Communist party insisted that it was a proletarian party, representing the interests of the workers and secondarily of the poor peasantry and petty bourgeoisie but not of the capitalists. It remained basically anti-bourgeois even when it entered into alliances with certain bourgeois parties and groups in a united front from above.

Until after the Second World War the "left" and the "right" strategies were essentially the only ones pursued by international Communism. Both found application during the early 1920's. Then the "left" strategy was in effect throughout the late twenties and early thirties. It was replaced about 1935 by the "right" strategy, which remained in use until 1947, interrupted only by a return to the "left" strategy during the period between the conclusion of the Stalin-Hitler Pact in August 1939 and the Nazi invasion of Russia in June 1941.

II. THE NEO-MAOIST STRATEGY

During the Second World War, the Chinese Communists under the leadership of Mao Tse-tung developed a strategy that is fundamentally different from the two traditional ones although it unites certain of their features. During and immediately after the war, when the Chinese Communists seemed to be relatively isolated from the international Communist movement, this strategy was apparently not understood in Moscow and was largely unknown among the Communist parties of the world. However, with the onset of the cold war, a period coinciding with the growing victories of the Chinese Communists beginning in 1947 and the emergence of Communist China as a second power in the Communist world in 1949, the new Maoist strategy gradually came to be appreciated by Moscow as best meeting its foreign policy requirements. It was consequently applied by international Communism until it has by now become the one accepted strategy for Communism—first in the countries of the Far East and South and Southeast Asia, secondly in the other under-developed countries in the Near East, Africa, and Latin America, and finally even in the West[1] to the extent that the Communists depict its countries as colonial spoil of "American imperialism."* We shall henceforth generally refer to this new strategy, as we define it below, as the "neo-Maoist strategy."†

The appeal to the bourgeoisie "from below." Like the "right" strategy, the neo-Maoist strategy singles out foreign imperialism and, where applicable, feudalism as its main enemy. Also like the "right" strategy, therefore, it expects the revolution to take place in two stages,‡ first as an anti-imperialist struggle for national independence or an anti-feudal bourgeois-democratic revolution and only later as a socialist revolution.[2] The range of forces to be united under Communist leadership consequently also corresponds to that grouped in

---

* "In view of the policy of expansion pursued by the American monopolies, the struggle for national independence and economic development has now become a necessity not only for the peoples of the colonial and semi-colonial countries but also for those in the developed capitalist countries." "Decisions of Third World Trade Union Congress," *For a Lasting Peace, for a People's Democracy!* (organ of the Cominform), October 30, 1953, p. 2.

† The use of the simple term "Maoist" to characterize this new strategy would be entirely justifiable, primarily because Mao must be credited with its original development and incidentally also because it was recommended to the Asian Communist parties by both Peking and Moscow as "the Chinese path" (see pp. 96–98 and p. 103, below). The term might, however, be taken to indicate that a Communist party follows Chinese Communist as distinguished from Soviet guidance or consciously follows the Chinese example. It might also imply that Chinese Communist practice furnishes the best example of the Maoist strategy. Finally, the term "Maoist strategy" is often associated with the Chinese Communist tactics of reliance on the peasantry and on guerrilla warfare in rural areas. Since all these implications and associations do not necessarily accord with our definition of and our findings on the new strategy, it was thought best to forego the use of the simple term "Maoist" for it and to distinguish it from the two traditional Communist strategies by referring to it as "neo-Maoist." It is hoped that this term will stress the first appearance of the strategy in China and its basic similarity with the fundamental features of Maoism as well as the fact that it has spread among the parties of international Communism in part independently of Chinese Communist influence and that it may use tactics quite different from the specific Chinese Communist ones.

‡ The Communist attempt, by *ex post facto* rationalizations, to fit the Eastern European "People's Democracies" and the Chinese "New Democracy" into the Marxian scheme of two revolutions has resulted in the expectation of varying numbers of stages or substages of the revolution, but of always more than one stage under the neo-Maoist strategy.

the united front from above and particularly the popular front, embracing the so-called "bloc of four classes" of the proletariat, the peasantry, the petty bourgeoisie, and the anti-imperialist sections of the bourgeoisie.[3]   To some extent this union is to be attained by the methods of the united front from above, that is, by a "top alliance" with other parties, but these are generally parties weaker than the Communist party and frequently fronts set up by the Communists. Principally, the neo-Maoist strategy follows the method of the united front from below of the "left" strategy.   The large parties, more or less actually representing the classes to be united, with which the Communist party would be allied in a united front from above, under the "right" strategy, are denounced as traitors to the interests of these classes (for example, the socialists as traitors to the workers, the nationalist parties as traitors to the anti-imperialist bourgeoisie) and as servants of imperialism.   The same policy is applied by the Communist trade unions.

The Communist party itself (or in conjunction with its "united front" of subsidiary and front-parties) now claims to represent the interests of the entire peasantry and the anti-imperialist capitalists as well as those of the proletariat, the poor peasantry, and the petty bourgeoisie.   Having, under both traditional strategies, confined their appeal to these latter three "exploited" groups, the Communists were able to attract sections of only these groups through the united front from below; but—and this is crucial—they could seek the support also of sections of the bourgeoisie and of the entire peasantry only through the united front from above.   It is because of the radical innovation of appealing directly to the interests of all four classes that the neo-Maoist strategy can apply the method of the united front from below to a range of groups so wide that it could formerly be encompassed only in the united front from above.[4]

We need not be concerned with the theories according to which the bourgeoisie is divided into a pro-imperialist and an anti-imperialist wing.*   What matters is merely that the dividing line between the potential friends and the enemies of the Communist party is now drawn not short of the bourgeoisie but bisecting it.   In practice, of

---

* The terminology used in Communist literature to describe the various sections of the bourgeoisie is not always consistent.   Those capitalists who are only slightly or not at all tied to imperialism and can thus help form the "bloc of four classes" are generally called the "national," "medium," "middle," or "liberal" capitalists or bourgeoisie (although the term "national" may also be used simply as a synonym for "native") , while that section of the bourgeoisie which is regarded as a firm ally of imperialism is referred to variously as "comprador," "bureaucratic," "big," or "monopolistic."

course, the division is not made so much along economic or socio-
logical lines, as is implied by the terms used to describe the two sections, but along political lines. Those businessmen who, for whatever
reasons, are willing or likely to be willing to follow the lead of the
Communist party are considered anti-imperialist capitalists. Those
who are or are likely to remain opposed to the Communists, even if
they have no ties with foreign interests and have only small busi-
nesses, are condemned as allies and servants of imperialism. Just as
in the case of the working class, whose character as a true proletariat
is determined by its adherence to Communism, the Marxist materialist conception of history is turned upside down; class affiliation is
deduced from ideology rather than vice versa.

Reliance on the peasantry. As the neo-Maoist strategy was developed in China and more recently in some countries of Southeast Asia,
its most important characteristic appeared to be not the appeal "from
below" to the bourgeoisie but reliance on the peasantry rather than
the industrial working class as a mass base in the struggle for power.[5]
This is indeed the logical culmination of a development that began
when Lenin departed from Marxism by divorcing the party from the
actual proletariat and by more and more defining the proletariat in
terms of its relationship to the party. Under neo-Maoism, the party—
to Marxism a mere means to the ends of the proletariat—now itself
becomes the end and can therefore use any suitable class, not just the
proletariat, to help it attain power.[6]

However, in considering the differences between the two traditional
Communist strategies and the neo-Maoist one this actual reliance on
the peasantry is not crucial. In China the peasants were the Communist Party's main target; elsewhere other groups can be substituted,
as has been the case in Japan and to some extent also in India and,
of course, in Western Europe. On the other hand, some reliance on
the peasantry is not a new Communist policy. In practically none
of the underdeveloped countries have the Communists in any real
sense of the word been a working-class party. Rather, they have
largely been intellectuals seeking a popular base where they could
find it. In this search, even under the old "right" and "left" strategies, they have never looked exclusively to the industrial working
class (which, in its Marxian sense of an urban stratum cut off from
its rural moorings, has, at least until recently, been virtually nonexistent in most underdeveloped countries). Instead they have also
sought out the petty bourgeoisie and at least some sections of the
peasantry, both of which can easily be characterized as exploited
classes in underdeveloped countries. They have attempted to conceal

this fact, just as Maoism has in China, by speaking of working-class hegemony, which always means their own hegemony; that is, they substituted themselves for the working class by a process of mental transposition.

Thus chief reliance on the peasantry is not absolutely essential to the neo-Maoist strategy as here defined; on the other hand, Communists in underdeveloped countries have always and under all strategies to some extent—though rarely as exclusively as the Chinese Communists were forced to—looked to the peasantry to furnish their mass base; and, finally, Maoism and its new strategy do not frankly admit this fact in their theory. For these reasons reliance on the peasantry is not a characteristic by which the neo-Maoist strategy can always be clearly distinguished from the traditional "right" and "left" strategies.

The end of the class struggle. The essential and unique characteristic of the neo-Maoist strategy is its direct appeal "from below," that is, not through bourgeois parties, to sections of the bourgeoisie. This appeal is made openly and defended on theoretical grounds, and, unlike reliance on the peasantry, it is startlingly new to Communists. Programs to protect national industries against foreign competition and especially to guarantee the industrialists' profits and interests[7]—in brief, the proposition that the Communist party, the party of the exploited toilers, represents also the interests of the capitalists, who are, by Marxian definition, the exploiters, and that the two classes between which the class struggle is supposed to be raging can be united in the Communist party—are hardly in keeping with traditional Communist doctrine. They can, however, be considered an extraordinary but logical extension of "proletarian internationalism," that is, the identification of the interests of the proletariat everywhere with those of the Soviet Union: the party of the proletariat is to unite all classes, regardless of their class interests, provided they are opposed to imperialism, meaning the United States.* In short, the class struggle has been replaced by the cold war.

---

* The only conceivable further extension of this anti-imperialist alliance could be made by adding feudal elements to the bloc of four classes. Since the immediate goal is presumably an anti-feudal, though not an anti-capitalist revolution, this is an even more extraordinary step than the inclusion of capitalists. Yet even it has been taken: "The scale of this national united front (of the Chinese people) embraces workers, peasants, intellectuals, the petty-bourgeoisie, the national bourgeoisie and even the progressive gentry." Liu Shao-chi, *Internationalism and Nationalism* (Peking: Foreign Languages Press; written November 1948). See also the quotation from Mao Tse-tung on p. 54, below, and the following Vietnamese Communist statements: "The motive forces of the Viet-Nam revolution at present are the people comprising primarily the workers, peasants, petty-bourgeoisie and national bour-

Although the acceptance of this strategy was quite possible for a movement the very essence of which is the quest for power by any available means and which has long used original Marxism as mere verbiage to cover its opportunism, it represents such a sharp departure from earlier strategies that it is the best point on which to focus an attempt to distinguish the neo-Maoist from the two older Communist strategies. Another such departure is the Communist appeal under the neo-Maoist strategy to all, not just part, of the peasantry, although this is not so clearly a distinguishing characteristic as the appeal to the bourgeoisie, since it does not involve the addition of a wholly new class to the range of potential supporters but merely that of the "middle" and to a lesser extent the "rich" peasantry to the "poor" peasantry.*

III. Violent and Peaceful Tactics

In view of the fact that Communist strategies are usually classified as either violent or peaceful the complete absence of this criterion from the discussion so far may appear odd. Important as it is, the use or absence of violent methods does not constitute a basic distinction between Communist strategies. The basic distinction, as we have seen, is to be found in the extent and type of the alliance made by the Communists with non-Communist elements. Attempts to identify one or the other of the three strategies with a "hard" or "soft" line, though frequently made, are therefore misleading. Thus it is often implied that the "right" strategy is necessarily coupled with a "soft" line. It is, of course, true that in many circumstances an alliance between the Communist party and labor and bourgeois parties is inconceivable where the Communist party engages in violent activities. But in other circumstances its allies may be engaged in or approve of such activities, as, for example, during the Spanish Civil

---

geoisie, followed by the patriotic and progressive personages and landlords." "Platform of the Viet-Nam Lao Dong Party," *People's China*, III, No. 9 (May 1, 1951), Supplement. "The right of patriotic landlords to collect land rent in accordance with law shall be guaranteed." "Manifesto of the Viet-Nam Lao Dong Party," *ibid.*

* A simple and perhaps oversimplified test to determine which of the three strategies the Communists pursue at any one time consists of the following one or two questions: Are the Communists making a serious attempt to form an alliance with the top leadership of the socialist party? If the answer is yes, they are following the "right" strategy; if it is no, a second question must be asked: Are there any capitalists among the groups to whose interests the Communists are appealing? If the answer to this question is no, they are following the "left" strategy; if it is yes, they are adhering to the neo-Maoist strategy.

War and the wartime resistance in Western Europe or in colonial revolts. On the other hand, the "left" strategy, while easily adaptable to armed violence, need not necessarily employ that tactic. Thus, with certain exceptions, it was used peacefully in Western Europe before 1935. Finally, the neo-Maoist strategy, although developed in China and long applied in Indo-China, Malaya, Burma, and the Philippines in conjunction with guerrilla warfare, can also be combined with a "soft" line, as is illustrated by the tactics pursued in the second half of the postwar decade by the Indian and Indonesian Communists and, for that matter, by those in Western Europe and Latin America. It follows that, since each of the three strategies can be applied in a violent or a peaceful manner, if violence is to be used as a criterion of classification at all, it can only subdivide each of the three strategies.

To the Communists, the use of armed force is a matter not of strategy but of tactics, which can be changed according to conditions while the strategy remains unchanged. Violence can be used in some localities of a country even while peaceful methods are applied in others at the same time, as was the case in India for some time. Furthermore, the distinction between policies of violence and of non-violence is only one of degree for the Communists. The extremes—parliamentary and propaganda activity on the one hand, and sabotage and civil war on the other—are, of course, clearly distinguishable; but certain intermediate tactics, for example, strikes and street demonstrations more or less intentionally leading to armed clashes and even riots, cannot be so easily classified. For all these reasons, the presence or absence of violence is not a useful principal criterion for the classification of Communist strategies.*

Having now established what we mean by the "right," the "left," and the neo-Maoist strategy, we are ready to trace the evolution, under Soviet and Chinese Communist influence, of the strategy of the Communist Party of India.

---

* The following Burmese Communist program, reproduced in full from Myat Htoo, "People's United Struggle Going Forward," *Cross Roads* (Delhi), April 19, 1953, pp. 8–9, may serve as a classical example of the new strategy, containing both its essential features (two-stage revolution, bloc of four classes, including capitalists) and its specifically Chinese but not universally applicable ones (main reliance on peasantry, armed struggle):

"Burma being a semi-colonial and semi-feudal country, the Party is to carry out a People's Democratic Revolution, the present main enemy being imperialism;

"To set up a dictatorship of the four classes, the workers, peasants, the petty bourgeoisie and the national bourgeoisie;

"The leadership of the working class will be based on a firm alliance with the peasantry;

Notes for Chapter 1

1. For documentation of the application of the new strategy in Latin American and Western countries, see the author's "The New Strategy of International Communism," *The American Political Science Review*, XLIX, No. 2 (June 1955), 478–486, on pp. 484–486. For an excellent documented discussion of the neo-Maoist strategy, see Bernard S. Morris and Morris Watnick, "Current Communist Strategy in Nonindustrialized Countries," *Problems of Communism*, IV, No. 5 (September–October 1955), 1–6.

2. See particularly Mao Tse-tung, *On the New Democracy* (January 19, 1940), extracts in Conrad Brandt, Benjamin Schwartz, and John K. Fairbank, *A Documentary History of Chinese Communism* (Cambridge: Harvard University Press, 1952), pp. 263–275. This important pamphlet is reprinted in full as *China's New Democracy* in U. S. Congress, House of Representatives, Committee on Foreign Affairs, Subcommittee 5, National and International Movements, *The Strategy and Tactics of World Communism*, Supplement III, Country Studies (House Document 154, 80th Congress, 2nd Session. Washington, U. S. Government Printing Office, 1949), C. China, Appendix, pp. 67–91.

3. Sections of the bourgeoisie are first explicitly included, and strikingly pro-capitalist statements appear in Mao Tse-tung, *On Coalition Government* (April 24, 1945), extracts in Brandt et al., *op. cit.*, pp. 295–318, especially pp. 303–306.

4. Numerous quotations from Soviet, Chinese, and Indian sources in the following chapters will illustrate the Communist attitude toward the bourgeoisie under the neo-Maoist strategy. For a useful summary of the Chinese Communists' attitude toward the anti-imperialist bourgeoisie, with several long quotations from Mao on the subject, see Yu Huai, "On the Role of the National Bourgeoisie in the Chinese Revolution," *People's China*, I, No. 1 (January 1, 1950), 7–10.

5. For an excellent discussion, see Benjamin I. Schwartz, *Chinese Communism and the Rise of Mao* (Cambridge: Harvard University Press, 1952), especially pp. 72–78 and 189–204.

6. This point is well made in Morris Watnick, "Continuity and Innovation in Chinese Communism," *World Politics*, VI, No. 1 (October 1953), particularly pp. 94–96. See also Morris Watnick's illuminating chapter, "The Appeal of Communism to the Underdeveloped Peoples," in Bert F. Hoselitz, ed., *The Progress of Underdeveloped Areas* (Chicago: The University of Chicago Press, 1952), pp. 152–172.

7. For examples, see Mao's statement quoted on pp. 31 and 63 and quotations from Indian Communist documents on pp. 135, 144, 161–162, 177, below.

"The main axis of the revolution is the agrarian revolution and the slogan land to the tiller;

"Capital will not be abolished, but there may be restrictions on it. It is a prerequisite for socialism;

"The main form of struggle is the armed struggle through the formation of an army; A protracted war will be carried out with revolutionary bases in rural areas;

"Foreign policy will be based on the maintenance of world peace; and

"The main weapons for victory will be the army, the People's Democratic Front and the Party."

CHAPTER
—— 2 ——————————————————

THE "RIGHT" STRATEGY AND ITS
ABANDONMENT (1945–1947)

I. THE "RIGHT" STRATEGY IN THE POSTWAR YEARS

"Left"—"right"—"left"—"right": From the beginning to 1945. Ever since its beginnings, the Communist Party of India (CPI) has sought to adhere to international Communist strategy as determined in Moscow, although it has not at all times been equally prompt or successful in making the changes required thereby. Organized, after some earlier unsuccessful efforts, as an all-India party only in 1933, the CPI began its career religiously following the "left" strategy of Communism as it had been laid down by the 6th Congress of the Communist International in 1928. Though it thereby isolated itself from the broad Indian nationalist movement, the CPI, according to this "left" strategy, denounced the National Congress as "a class organization of the capitalists" and concentrated its fire particularly on the left wing of the Congress led by Jawaharlal Nehru and on the Congress Socialist Party organized in 1934.[1]

When Moscow finally recognized the danger posed by German Fascism and changed its foreign policy and, correspondingly, the strategy of international Communism, the CPI, too, after some delays, obediently switched to the "right" strategy as it had been ordered to do at the 7th Comintern Congress of 1935. Accordingly, it now sought to join with the Indian Socialists and with the Congress which was to be transformed into the "Anti-Imperialist Front of the People."[2]

After the conclusion of the Hitler-Stalin Pact of August 1939 and the outbreak of World War II in September 1939 the Communist Party of India, performing the same manoeuvre as all Communist parties at that time, shifted back from the "right" to a "left" strategy. The fight against Fascism, which they had advocated for the past few years, was now called an imperialist war, and the erstwhile partners

16

in the anti-imperialist people's front, the Congress and the Congress Socialist Party, were now once again "unmasked" as reformists and agents of imperialism. The Communists alone claimed to be revolutionary anti-imperialists, and they sought to cripple war production by means of strikes.[3]

While this line proved not unpopular in India, where anti-war sentiment was widespread, the return from the "left" to the "right" strategy after the German invasion of Russia in June 1941, a shift that eventually resulted in such growth of Communist strength and prestige in the West and in Southeast Asia, proved disastrous for the CPI's reputation in India, for the Party's new ally was to be Britain, still widely regarded as India's main enemy. Only under severe pressure, especially from the Communist Party of Great Britain, long the CPI's mentor, could the Party be prevailed upon to shift from its "imperialist war" to the "people's war" line. Under it, the Communists did everything to discourage and discredit Gandhi's anti-British Quit India campaign and to increase production and oppose strikes.[4]

Weak guidance from Moscow in favor of the "right" strategy. As a result of its wartime policies, the CPI emerged from the war isolated and demoralized. Since such a state of the Party did not prevent its leadership from following a firm line at other times, we are safe in ascribing the marked absence of such a line during the next two years to the lack of firm guidance from abroad rather than to the internal condition of the CPI or even to the highly complicated situation in India during this period immediately preceding the attainment of her independence, although they were undoubtedly contributing factors. In 1945 the Chinese Communists were still as far removed from the minds of Indian Communists as were their armies from the borders of India, and the CPI looked to Moscow for inspiration (and to the British Communists, who, however, always merely did their best to interpret the Moscow line themselves). Moscow, however, was itself uncertain in its reaction to Indian developments in this period.

At the end of the war, the USSR, seeking to attain its objectives through cooperation among the great powers, stated that the colonial problem could be settled peacefully and gradually. In line with this view, the Communist parties in Asia, as in Europe, were working for coalition governments to strengthen their own positions and were willing to compromise with the colonial powers.[5] Soviet statements on India up to the time of the Cabinet Mission (February 1946) were relatively mild in their references to British policy and rather uncertain and noncommittal on internal developments.[6] A. M. Dyakov, one of the foremost Soviet writers on India, described the National Congress as a broad movement for national independence influencing all classes. He also spoke of a "national liberation movement," which, however, he seemed to identify with the Congress.[7]

United front from above with Congress and Muslim League, 1945–July 1946. Such voices from Moscow posed a dilemma for the Indian Communists: It was impossible not to be strongly anti-British and yet cooperate with the nationalist forces in practice, though in words they had already done so during the war.[8] Thus, when the nationalist movement resulted in another wave of mass demonstrations in 1945, the Communists were confused and remained largely opposed to them.[9] Furthermore, even if the CPI had met with any sympathy from Indian nationalists, it would have been impossible to form a united front from above with two organizations as opposed to each other as the Congress and the Muslim League. Yet this is what the party line called for.* The somewhat strange character of this united front from above is indicated by this statement in the draft election manifesto of the CPI for the elections to the Indian Provincial Assemblies to be held in April 1946: "Our Party is entering the electoral contest not to fight one or both of the Congress or the League, but to stand in the middle and fight the flames they both light by ourselves putting forward a plan of Indian freedom that embodies their just demands, but repudiates the unjust claims of both. . . ."[10]

Only early in 1946, when the nationalist mass demonstrations culminated in the February mutiny in the Royal Indian Navy, did the Communists finally join in these anti-British activities, and even then, as a later "self-critical" Communist report states, it was the rank and file rather than the leadership that participated.[11] Although the Congress had, in view of the CPI's wartime policy, disqualified Communists from holding office in Congress organizations, and the CPI had consequently asked its members to resign from membership in the Congress, the Party was at this time clearly following the "right" strategy aiming at a united front from above with the Congress and the League as was apparently expected of it by Moscow. The final version of the CPI election manifesto of January 1946 states that the

* Thus a CPI delegate admonished the Congress of the British Communist Party not to look down on the League: "While you rightly admire the National Congress as the premier organization of the freedom movement, you should not dismiss the differences with the Moslem League as merely the promptings of imperialist wire-pullers. The driving force and base of the Moslem League are the Moslem masses of various nationalities who have come to consciousness of their nationhood." "India. Speech of Comrade S. S. Mirajkar, delegate from the C.P.I.," *World News and Views,* XXV, No. 49 (December 15, 1945), 406.

Party's main endeavor would be to build a United Freedom Front. "The Communist Party concentrates all its fire against the Imperialist rulers of our common motherland and considers it a crime to waste one word or lose one comrade in internal factional warfare."[12] The manifesto culminates in the slogan "Vote Communist—For Congress-League-Communist united front for the final battle of Indian liberation."[13]

The election manifesto makes the traditional Communist class appeal, typical of the "right" as well as the "left" strategy, to the workers, peasants, the petty bourgeoisie, and the intelligentsia, but not to the bourgeoisie. Consequently its economic program contained such anti-capitalist planks as the banning of "private trade in people's food," "nationalization of all key industries," and "state control of all capital resources."[14]

That the united-front-from-above policy had at this time strong support from abroad and that it was to be pursued regardless of the realities of the situation, including the fact that the Congress wanted none of this alliance, are shown by this statement of Rajani Palme Dutt, the outstanding British Communist writer, who is himself of Indian descent:

> It is to be hoped that this breach may be overcome at the earliest possible moment, in view of the paramount importance of national unity in the coming period. The National Congress has a long tradition as the main uniting body of all sections of Indian progressive nationalism. The overwhelming majority of the Indian people look to the National Congress as the leader of their struggle for freedom. It is of the greatest importance that effective cooperation in the common national struggle should be established between the National Congress and the rising force of the political working class movement, as well as of younger radical opinion, represented by the Communist Party.[15]

The "left" August 1946 resolution. After the Cabinet Mission of February 1946 the Soviet view of the role of the British in India became more outspokenly hostile. The Mission's Plan was regarded as a device to strengthen the British position and to weaken the national liberation movement.[16] More important from our point of view, the Indian Communist Party was now considered as an independent force opposing the Plan, and the Congress leadership was treated as representing the interests of the Indian bourgeoisie. The right-wing leadership was said to represent the big bourgeoisie, which desired agreement with Britain, whereas Nehru represented the progressive wing and the Congress membership was drawn from all classes,[17] a view which by no means excluded the continuance of the united-front-from-above approach to the Nehru wing.

Possibly as a result of this change in Moscow and the interpretation placed on it by the Indian Communists, or perhaps simply because Moscow had not furnished sufficiently strong guidance to the CPI on the "right" strategy, a section of the CPI leadership, presumably headed by Balchand Trimbak Ranadive, gained the upper hand in the councils of the Party, which had been dissatisfied with the less than radical tactics against the British, and, above all, had no use for an alliance with the Congress and the Muslim League. At any rate, the Central Committee, meeting from July 23 to August 5, 1946, adopted a resolution[18] stating that the recent mutinies, strikes, and peasant unrest indicated a mounting revolutionary upsurge that must lead to the end of the imperialist-feudal regime. Like Moscow, the CPI rejected the British Plan as a manoeuvre to split the freedom movement and to perpetuate imperialist rule in a new form. Possibly encouraged by Moscow's characterization of the Congress leadership as representing bourgeois interest (though the particular article cited above as representing this Soviet view was published a month later), the resolution sharply turns from the "right" strategy of seeking an alliance with that leadership to the "left" strategy of a united front from below against it. The Congress and League leaderships (factional warfare against which the CPI had considered a crime half a year earlier) are denounced for bargaining with the imperialists and turning their backs on and sabotaging the people's movement. A "joint front of popular parties" is to be forged which is to draw in increasing numbers of the membership of the Congress and League.

A later official review of the Party's history, written during a "left" period, hails this sudden shift. It states that the August 1946 resolution "gave the line clear to our ranks to lead the great strike battles . . . to head the great struggles of the peasants . . . which enabled our comrades to unleash revolutionary struggles . . . against the autocracy of the Nizam in Hyderabad."[19] The Communists did, in fact, in this period try to seize the leadership of various, primarily economic rather than political, protest movements. Among these, the peasant uprising in the particularly poor Telengana districts of Hyderabad, which assumed the form of an armed rebellion and resulted in the establishment of a "liberated area," was destined to continue for five years and, as we shall see, to constitute an important part of the background of the discussions of CPI strategy during this period.

Return to the "right" strategy by the end of 1946. The August 1946 resolution did not result in a clear party line for long; the

Party remained confused and divided between those who supported the policy of the resolution and those who regarded it as a left-sectarian deviation. Moscow was apparently silent and perhaps itself uncertain as to what the relationship between the CPI and the Congress ought to be. When, by the end of 1946 and as a result of Communist-led violence, various provincial governments, especially in the South, took anti-Communist measures, a return on the part of the CPI to the "right" strategy became apparent. The peasant uprisings continued, probably because the Communists could no more stop them than they had started them, since they were essentially spontaneous outbreaks against economic hardships. However, they were now said by the Communists to be directed against "the British bureaucrats and reactionary Indian vested interests,"[20] that is, against imperialism and feudalism, rather than against the Congress, with which a united front from above was now once again sought. Even the anti-Communist measures taken by Congress ministries were blamed not on the Congress but on the "bureaucracy,"[21] which could be identified with the British. We know from the later "leftist" Communist criticism of this period that this was no coincidence but a definite policy; there it is also claimed that the "right reformist" leadership of the CPI of the time discouraged the uprisings, terming them "vanguardist actions," and tended to minimize strikes and to support the "bourgeois" slogan of national reconstruction.[22]

The "right" Mountbatten Resolution of June 1947. The Soviet reaction to the Mountbatten Plan of 1947 once again displayed a clear attitude toward the British but an ill-defined one toward the Congress. The Plan was pictured as a British attempt to retain actual power through the Balkanization of India and through reliance on the support of the princes and "definite sections of India's propertied classes" who feared social change. The Congress leadership was said to be under pressure from these groups to accept the Plan, but was not identified with them, while the Congress rank and file was described as opposed to the plan.[23] Similarly, the Indian Communist Party's resolution on the subject,[24] unanimously adopted at a meeting of the Central Committee in Delhi, June 10 to 20, 1947, stated that the sole purpose of the Mountbatten Plan was "to disrupt the people, strengthen reaction, get into an alliance with it and thus make Indian independence formal." "The strategy of British imperialism is . . . to forge a new alliance with the Princes, landlords and Indian Big Business . . ." and British Big Business was relying on "the great influence of Indian Big Business over the extreme Right wing of the Congress leadership."

Far from being another shift to the "left" strategy, however, this so-called Mountbatten Resolution of the CPI is a clear affirmation of its continued policy of a united front from above with the Muslim League and especially the Congress. The promise of dominion status is hailed as an important concession giving new opportunities for national advance. The governments of India and Pakistan are referred to as "the popular Governments," and "the Congress is the main national democratic organization." Ten months earlier the Congress leadership was accused of sabotaging the people's movement, but now "the Communist Party will fully cooperate with the national leadership in the proud task of building the Indian Republic on democratic foundations. . . ." Rather than leading strikes and peasant uprisings, the Central Committee now assures the Congress that "the Communist Party is fully conscious that the task of nation-building and the grim reality of economic crisis demands the continuity of production." In short, "The Communist Party realizes that the new situation demands the broadest Joint Front based on the principle of fullest cooperation between the popular Governments and all popular organizations. . . ." "Only the firm initiative of all progressives—the Communists, Left elements in the Congress and the League—can bring it about . . . to defeat communal, reactionary and compromising elements within the Congress and the League."*

The "right" strategy after Indian independence, August–December 1947. The CPI's Mountbatten Resolution had prepared the ground for a clearly pronounced application of the "right" strategy during the communal riots that followed the attainment of India's independence on August 15, 1947, and her partition into two dominions. The Indian Communists, regarding these riots as instigated by the British and supported by Indian reaction, including the right wing of the Congress represented particularly by Sardar Vallabhbhai Patel, said that they "were really the attack of the imperialists and feudal order on the popular advance."[25] The Party's strategy was based on a theory

---

* As we shall see shortly, it is doubtful that Palme Dutt was in this period, as he had probably been in Comintern days, an important transmitter of the party line between Moscow and India. However, the Indian Communists may well still have regarded him as such, and it is therefore important to note that, as in early 1946, he came out with strong backing for the "right" strategy adopted by the CPI leadership: "Now more than ever the situation reveals the urgent need, increasingly recognized on both sides, to endeavour to overcome the past phase of sharp divisions between the Congress and the Communist Party . . . in order to march forward together upon a common programme of democratic advance. . . ." R. Palme Dutt, "The Mountbatten Plan for India," *Labour Monthly*, XXIX, No. 7 (July 1947), 210–219.

of differences between Sardar Patel on the one hand and Nehru and his so-called progressive wing of the Congress on the other,[26] and the latter was to be strengthened against the former through the united-front-from-above policy.

The Party now came forward with such slogans as "Fight Communalism,"[27] "Increase Production," and "Don't Foment Strikes."[28] Even more characteristic of its "right" strategy of the period was a speech by Puran Chand Joshi, its General Secretary, to a mass meeting in Calcutta on October 8, 1947, which the Party's organ, under the banner headline "Nehru must not resign," described as "a stirring call to the people to rally behind Pandit Nehru."[29] Writing against the riots and communalists in the same period, Joshi exclaimed: "All support to the Government.   Reaction is threatening our two Governments and it is the duty of us all to rally whole-heartedly and enthusiastically behind them and pledge them all our support."[30] It is important to note that Joshi, the foremost advocate of the "right" strategy in the CPI,[31] was not the only one supporting this policy at that time.   In an article appearing as late as December 1947 B. T. Ranadive, Joshi's successor and later accuser, and generally regarded as the head of the "left" faction in the CPI Politburo, also spoke of Nehru's progressive foreign policy and democratic aspirations and declared that the people "must rally round Nehru" "to support Nehru's policy and push his government ahead, decisively against reaction."[32]

We find that Palme Dutt of the Communist Party of Great Britain, frequently one of the CPI's chief guides, was strongly behind the "right" strategy at this time.   In an interview with Madhu Limaye, Joint Secretary of the Indian Socialist Party, in November 1947, reported by the latter, he demanded the readmission of the Communists to the Congress so that they could support its progressive wing under Nehru against the reactionary bloc led by Sardar Patel.[33] At this point it is fairly clear, however, that Dutt spoke no longer as the voice of Moscow to India (if it is assumed that Moscow spoke with one voice on Indian affairs in this period), for by November 1947 there were several indications of the development of a new line in Moscow quite incompatible with Dutt's recommendation.   We turn to these changes in Moscow and to their reflections and results in India in the next two sections of this chapter.

This section has led us to the conclusion that for two years after the close of World War II Moscow favored the "right" strategy of cooperation "from above" with the bourgeois-nationalist movements of colonial areas.   However, Moscow probably had little knowledge of or even interest in conditions in India—or the rest of Asia—during this period of Soviet preoccupation with Europe. Moscow was, therefore, rather uncertain about the role of the Congress and could give little guidance to the Indian Communists on their paramount problem, their relations with the Congress. Thus, left with a good deal of independence, probably much to its regret, the CPI by and large followed the "right" strategy, seeking a united front from above both with the Congress, or at least its "progressive" wing, and with the Muslim League. It was, however, apparently so unsure of the proper course to take that at one point in 1946 it suddenly switched to the "left" strategy of the united front from below against these movements, only quickly to revert to the "right" one. Throughout, so far as we know, it was never repudiated or, for that matter, clearly encouraged in its course by Moscow.

II. The Shift from the "Right" Strategy in Moscow

Moscow's adherence to the "right" strategy had been dictated primarily by its relations with the West. During 1947 these relations deteriorated rapidly, as was indicated by such events as the failure of the Moscow Conference, the ouster of the French and Italian Communist Parties from the cabinets of their countries, the rejection of the Marshall Plan by the USSR, and the foundation of the Cominform. Clearly, the Soviet policy of cooperation with the Western powers had been definitely abandoned, and this change necessarily had to be followed by a change in the strategy of international Communism.

The meeting of the USSR Academy of Sciences of June 1947. The first indication of a shift in the Soviet attitude toward India came in a joint session on Indian studies held in Moscow, June 14–18, 1947, by the sections for history and philosophy, literature and language, and economics and law of the Academy of Sciences of the USSR. At the very same time at which the Indian Communist Party adopted its Mountbatten Resolution praising the Congress and offering its cooperation to the Congress government in a united front from above, this session was unanimous in sharply condemning the Congress. It thus marked a distinct change in Moscow's hitherto uncertain but never wholly hostile attitude toward the Congress and implied the necessity of a turn away from the "right" strategy on the part of the Indian Communists.

The four reports delivered at this meeting by E. M. Zhukov,[34] the head of the Academy's Pacific Institute and the most authoritative of

the Soviet "theoreticians" in this field, by V. V. Balabushevich[35] and
A. M. Dyakov,[36] the two chief Soviet academic experts on India, and
by the economist S. M. Melman[37] are far from unanimous, however,
in suggesting a strategy to replace the united front from above in
India. The differences in their approach may appear minor and
merely verbal in the context of the four reports. However, since they
were not overcome in Moscow for about two years and, above all, since
they furnish the first indication of a gradual and hesitant adoption
by Moscow of neo-Maoism as a new strategy for international Communism, they deserve close attention.

The reports of the June 1947 session of the Academy of Sciences
are distinguished from earlier Soviet discussion of Indian affairs by
greater reliance on class analysis. They emphasize that class conflicts
in India have grown in intensity and that the working class has become
the leading element among the anti-imperialist forces. They attach
relatively little importance to the peasant movement, which they
characterize as backward and definitely subordinate to the working
class. They agree in describing the Congress as reactionary and in
league with imperialism—an accusation that is made retroactive to
cover a period when the Soviet view of the Congress had been more
favorable and hopeful. Nehru, who had formerly been regarded as
"progressive," is expressly included in this condemnation. They thus
conclude that India is clearly divided into two camps, the so-called
imperialists and reactionary forces united in the Congress, opposed
by a supposedly growing popular movement for independence and
democracy led by the working class, meaning, of course, the Communist
Party.

The reports differ only in their class analysis of the reactionary
forces. Balabushevich and Dyakov include among these the bourgeoisie, which they denounce as having, out of fear of the rising
masses, made a treacherous deal with imperialism. They thus suggest
by implication a return from the "right" strategy of the united front
from above with the Nehru wing of the Congress to the old "left"
strategy of Communism which appeals to workers, and also peasants
and the petty bourgeoisie, but not to the bourgeoisie, to abandon non-
Communist parties for a united front from below with the Communists.[38] Zhukov, on the other hand—and in this he is followed by
Melman—is careful to include only the "big" bourgeoisie among the
reactionary forces cooperating with imperialism, clearly implying that
the "middle" as well as the petty bourgeoisie and the peasantry are
at least potential allies of the working class.

Small as the distinction between the entire bourgeoisie and the "big" bourgeoisie may be and as, indeed, it may at the time have appeared to be to the authors of these reports themselves, it constitutes the introduction of an element into Communist policy characteristic of a strategy hitherto unknown to international Communism but destined to become its virtually universally applicable line in the space of a few years. To be sure, the distinction between the "big" and the "progressive" bourgeoisie had, as we have seen, been frequently made before, but always in conjunction with the "right" strategy aiming at a united front from above, a "top-alliance" with the organization of the progressive bourgeoisie. Zhukov suggests no such alliance with the Nehru wing of the Congress any more than Balabushevich or Dyakov; like them, he condemns the entire Congress, but unlike theirs, his analysis permits the inclusion of a section of the bourgeoisie, the "medium" bourgeoisie, in the united front from below. This, however, is the chief characteristic distinguishing the neo-Maoist from the old "left" strategy.[39] We are thus justified in considering Zhukov, on this crucial point, as a follower of the neo-Maoist strategy and Balabushevich and Dyakov as adherents of the "left" strategy.*

Coexistence in Moscow of the "left" and the neo-Maoist strategies. It is conceivable that the differences we have emphasized indicate the existence or at least the development in Moscow at one and the same time of two party lines, which could in turn be symptomatic of a policy split on the advisability of adopting the neo-Maoist strategy.†

---

  * We may note that in his emphasis on the urban working class and his low estimate of the peasant movement Zhukov is no closer than his two colleagues to Maoism, the specific form of the neo-Maoist strategy first developed in China.

  † This type of speculation can be linked with the assumption of a division in Moscow on the question of the Soviet attitude toward the Chinese Communists, in which case the adherents of the "left" strategy tend to be regarded as opposed not only to the new strategy but also to Mao and the Chinese Communists and to be associated with a supposedly "left" and Europe-oriented group in the Kremlin usually identified with Zhdanov. We cannot affirm such an analysis, though neither can we absolutely deny that there are any elements of truth in it—in fact, we shall have to return to the subject at somewhat greater length in the next chapter, because it seems possible that some of the actions of the Indian Communist Party leadership were based on similar assumptions (see pp. 76–77, below). That unanimity of opinion does not always rule among the Soviet top leadership may be safely assumed and has at times become obvious. But unfortunately, with very few exceptions, of which this is not one, no evidence has reached us to indicate the lines along which any disagreements may run or even the subjects on which disagreements may exist. It will be wise for us, therefore, to shun this type of baseless speculation, fascinating as it is, and to confine ourselves to an area where the availability of some evidence permits the statement of at least informed guesses if not established facts.

The striking fact, however, is that the two analyses appear peacefully side by side and, as we shall see, continue to run concurrently for approximately two more years, without one side ever denouncing the other or so much as explicitly stating any disagreement with it. In view of the fact that on any matter of importance to Soviet policy only one view is considered "correct" and all others are regarded as not merely incorrect but also vicious, this suggests strongly that there was no real awareness of any difference or, at any rate, of the importance of the difference. It would no doubt be going too far to deduce from this attitude alone any Soviet indifference toward the fate of the Chinese Communists, but it is perhaps linked with a gross underestimation on Moscow's part of the Chinese Communist potential for victory at that time. The neo-Maoist strategy of a direct Communist appeal to the anti-imperialist sections of the bourgeoisie had obviously become known in Moscow by mid-1947, but its general strategic import was yet to be appreciated. Nor was it then recognized that it differed fundamentally from the older "left" strategy.

Thus, after a period of two years, from 1945 to 1947, when Moscow had no specific party line for the Indian Communists but generally favored the "right" strategy, there followed, to be sure, a definite shift in 1947; but it initiated a period of another two years with not one but two party lines. The two—the "left" and the neo-Maoist strategies—were not clearly distinguished, however, and resulted in a distinctly "anti-right" policy. Moscow's indecisiveness displayed in its failure to formulate a clear party line for the Indian Communists between 1945 and 1949 can be explained most easily by Soviet preoccupation with the West during this period. The composition of the Cominform, the reports made at its establishment at the end of September 1947, and the contents of its newspaper are clear evidence of the lack of attention devoted to Asian affairs by Moscow, an attitude of which disbelief in total Communist victory in China must have been a part. It cannot reasonably be contended that Moscow was incapable of deciding on a party line for the Indian Communists, but it was apparently not sufficiently interested in India to bother to formulate one—even at a time when the CPI would have greatly welcomed guidance from abroad. Only this lack of concern on the part of Moscow with Indian affairs can explain the fact that the CPI was, apparently without criticism and certainly without being repudiated, permitted to follow its "right" policy of cooperation with the Congress for six months after the session of the Soviet Academy of Sciences had heralded the change of policy in Moscow.* Nor can the developments

* The fact that Palme Dutt, too, adhered to the "right" strategy long after this session is another illustration of Moscow's lack of interest in the CPI.

of the next two years be explained satisfactorily either on the assumption that Moscow had by 1947 wholeheartedly accepted the neo-Maoist strategy or on the assumption that it was propounding strictly the old "left" line.   They are explicable only if we recognize that Moscow was undecided between the two and most probably not even conscious of this indecision.

Zhdanov's report at the first Cominform meeting, September 1947. Although the change of Moscow's general international line had been foreshadowed by the June session of the Academy of Sciences as well as other events in 1947, the chief signal for the switch was generally taken to be the report made by Andrei Zhdanov at the founding meeting of the Cominform in Poland at the end of September 1947.[40]   This speech sets forth the well-known doctrine of the division of the world into two camps, the imperialist, anti-democratic camp headed by the United States and the anti-imperialist, democratic camp headed by the Soviet Union.   The speech is concerned almost wholly with the role of the United States and the situation in Europe.   Although it deals extensively with the growing strength of the anti-imperialist camp and its composition, it strikingly omits any mention of the Chinese Communists.   Apart from some remarks such as that the Soviet-dominated camp "has the sympathy of India, Egypt and Syria" and is backed "by the fighters for national liberation in the colonies and dependencies," only the following brief paragraph out of over two closely printed newspaper pages is devoted to the colonial areas:

> World War II aggravated the crisis of the colonial system, as expressed in the rise of a powerful movement for national liberation in the colonies and dependencies.   This has placed the rear of the capitalist system in jeopardy.   The peoples of the colonies no longer wish to live in the old way.   The ruling classes of the metropolitan countries can no longer govern the colonies on the old lines.   Attempts to crush the national liberation movement by military force now increasingly encounter armed resistance on the part of the colonial peoples and lead to protracted colonial wars (Holland-Indonesia, France-Viet Nam).[41]

Even this paragraph reveals clearly that Zhdanov's and presumably Moscow's, interest in the colonies was only secondary and arose from the fact that the West could be attacked through them from the rear—a line of Communist thought that goes back to Lenin.

The Zhdanov speech identifies the so-called national liberation, that is, Communist-led, movements in the colonies with the Soviet "camp" and thus promises them at least its moral support.   The speech also envisages, if it does not advocate, the use of armed force in the colonies. Its sharp denunciations of the socialist parties alone are enough to show that it marks a clear shift away from the "right" strategy. It was therefore widely assumed that the speech heralded a return to the "left" strategy. Actually, however, there is in it virtually no class analysis that makes possible a clear distinction between the "left" and the neo-Maoist strategy. The tenor of the speech is merely anti-imperialist and not, at least expressly, anti-bourgeois; and what Zhdanov offers by way of direct guidance to the Communist parties is at least as open to the interpretation that it recommends the neo-Maoist line as to the interpretation that it suggests a return to the "left" strategy. Here we read that:

> Communists must support all the really patriotic elements who do not want their countries to be imposed upon, who want to resist enthrallment of their countries to foreign capital, and to uphold their national sovereignty. The Communists must be the leaders in enlisting all anti-fascist and freedom-loving elements in the struggle against the new American expansionist plans for the enslavement of Europe.

Zhdanov also says that "the Communist parties . . . must rally their ranks and unite their efforts on the basis of a common anti-imperialist and democratic platform, and gather around them all the democratic and patriotic forces of the people," they must "take the lead of all the forces prepared to uphold the national honour and independence."[42] Just what classes are to furnish these "really patriotic elements" is not specified, but the language is so broad that it is not unreasonable to suppose that the anti-imperialist sections of the bourgeoisie might be among them. And, it might be contended, the fact that these directions are given by Zhdanov to Communist parties in Europe would make them not less but even more applicable to Asia, the original home of Maoism. It may be concluded that the Zhdanov speech certainly did not make it entirely clear whether the "right" strategy was to be replaced by the "left" or the neo-Maoist strategy, though perhaps it leaned toward the latter. It thus fits well into the pattern of uncertainty on this question then prevailing in Moscow which we have just described.

The neo-Maoist application to the colonies of Zhdanov's report by Zhukov, December 1947. The task of elaborating and applying the Zhdanov thesis to the colonial areas was undertaken by Zhukov in an important article the title of which, "The Growing Crisis of the Colonial System," is derived from the Zhdanov speech.[43] Considering the views he had already expressed at the Academy of Sciences in June of 1947, it comes as no surprise that Zhukov gave the Zhdanov analysis a thoroughly neo-Maoist interpretation. He diagnoses an upsurge of the national liberation movement as the determining factor in the political development of the colonies, and states, as he had already in June, that the working class is in the vanguard of this movement. But this time he not only is careful to include merely the "big" bourgeoisie, rather than the entire bourgeoisie, among its opponents, but he also clearly defines this "big" bourgeoisie in strictly Maoist terms as the "comprador and industrial" bourgeoisie "connected with foreign capital."[44] He does not leave the inclusion of the "middle" bourgeoisie in the Communist-led movement to implication, but states clearly that the Communist party, in leading the national liberation movement, unites "not only the proletariat and the peasantry but also the remaining strata of the toilers and in many countries also part of the bourgeoisie, mainly the petty and middle bourgeoisie."[45] At the same time, Zhukov declares that the Communist Party of India ". . . fights for the solidarity of all democratic forces of the people, for complete liberation of India from medieval survivals, for broad democratic reforms, which are the guarantee of attainment of genuine independence from foreign imperialism."[46] He thus makes it very clear that the CPI's enemies are to remain, as they were under the "right" strategy, feudalism and imperialism, and not, as under the "left" strategy, capitalism.

Here we have what appears to be the first unambiguous and authoritative statement of the neo-Maoist strategy to emanate from Moscow. The fact that it was pronounced by as important a figure as Zhukov in the leading theoretical journal of the Communist Party of the Soviet Union and as an interpretation of the fundamental Zhdanov speech makes it of the greatest importance. And yet we would be hasty in concluding that Moscow had now settled on this interpretation and that the neo-Maoist strategy was now the sole one enjoying Soviet support. In the very same month as the Zhukov article, and in the following month, there appeared articles by Balabushevich and Dyakov,[47] respectively, in which these writers continue to show their hostility to the bourgeoisie and therefore to the neo-Maoist orientation, although they now occasionally use the term "big" bourgeoisie. The difference of opinion between the advocates of the neo-Maoist strategy and the advocates of the "left" strategy, which had first been revealed at the session of the Academy of Sciences in June 1947, thus persisted half a year later and were apparently still ignored or considered so unimportant as to require no reconciliation. They had not been resolved by the Zhdanov speech, which was open to both a neo-Maoist and a "left" interpretation.

Mao's speech of December 25, 1947, and its report in Moscow. During the same period, on December 25, 1947, Mao Tse-tung delivered a report to the Central Committee of the Chinese Communist Party[48] containing some vigorous statements characteristic of the Maoist and neo-Maoist strategy. These are particularly noteworthy for us since the report became well known both in Moscow and India. In it Mao speaks of both the petty and middle bourgeoisie: "Wherever the state power of the New Democracy reaches, these classes must be firmly and unhesitatingly protected."[49] The difference between the Maoist and neo-Maoist anti-imperialist and anti-feudal strategy with its belief in two revolutions, on the one hand, and the "left" anti-capitalist strategy of a single revolution, on the other, is made strikingly clear in his statement that "all that the New Democratic revolution aims to eliminate are feudalism and monopoly capitalism, the landlord class and the bureaucratic bourgeoisie, not capitalism in general nor the petty or middle bourgeoisie"; capitalism must continue "for a long period."[50] Mao then expressly denounces the "left" strategy and proceeds to condemn excessively high standards in working conditions and income tax rates and to sneer at the "welfare of the toilers," but to speak seriously of bringing benefits to both labor and capital, all in language more reminiscent of that of an employers' association than that of Marx, which illustrates the very real difference between the neo-Maoist and the traditional Communist strategies and also shows why its acceptance may meet with resistance or at least hesitation on the part of men and parties reared in the traditions of the class struggle. Mao says: "We must by no means allow a recurrence of such ultra-left, erroneous policies as were adopted toward the petty and middle bourgeoisie by our party in the period from 1931 to 1934 (the advocation of uneconomically high standards in working conditions; excessively high income-tax rates; . . . the taking of a shortsighted, one-sided view of the so-called 'welfare of the toilers' instead of making our objective the development of production, the prosperity of our economy, the taking into account of both public and private interests and benefits to both labour and capital)."[51] He expresses corresponding views with regard to the agricultural sector of the economy.*

---

* "Our policy is to rely on the poor peasants and maintain a stable alliance with the middle peasants in order to destroy the system of feudal and semi-feudal exploitation by the landlord class and the old type of rich peasants. The land and properties which the landlords and rich peasants receive must not exceed those

Mao concludes his report with a passage that shows clearly that already in 1947, before his final victory in China, his interests went far beyond the confines of that country: "All the anti-imperialist forces of the various Eastern countries should also unite to oppose the oppression of imperialism and the reactionaries in their countries, and set as the goal of their struggle the liberation of the more than one thousand million oppressed people of the East."[52] Since he had earlier in his speech made it clear that he did not consider capitalists in general as among the "reactionaries" but on the contrary as among the anti-imperialist forces who were to unite against imperialism and against these reactionaries, this exhortation may be regarded as among the first Chinese Communist appeals to other Asian Communist parties to follow the neo-Maoist strategy.

Mao's report of December 1947 is thus a document of some importance in international Communist affairs. The Indian Communists seem to have recognized it as such (although, as we shall see, its real significance was ignored by them), for they dealt with it at some length in their weekly newspaper[53] and reprinted it in their theoretical organ.[54] Equally important, Moscow considered Mao's address of sufficient interest to international Communism to report on it in the journal of the newly founded Cominform, although, to be sure, only at the bottom of the last page of an issue otherwise wholly devoted to European Communist parties.[55]

We cannot be sure whether the character of the Cominform report proves merely the Cominform's editors' lack of understanding of the neo-Maoist strategy or their intention of concealing, by means of omission and distortion, the main features of this strategy from their readers among the leadership of the various Communist parties. At any rate, the effect must have been the latter. Nothing is said of Mao's concern for the protection of capitalism and the middle bourgeoisie; only his attacks on monopoly capitalism are reported, leaving the impression that this was an anti-capitalist rather than a pro-capitalist speech. Mao's attack on the "left" strategy is mentioned, but in this form: "Mao Tse-tung warned against pursuing an 'ultra-left' incorrect

---

which the mass of peasants get. But neither should there be a repetition of the ultra-left, erroneous policy carried out between 1931 and 1934, the so-called policy of 'distribute no land to the landlords and poor land to the rich peasants.'" Mao Tse-tung, "On the Present Situation and our Tasks" in Otto B. van der Sprenkel, ed., *New China; Three Views* (London: Turnstile Press, 1950), p. 161. Rich peasants must be given treatment different from that meted out to the landlords (*ibid.*, p. 162) and "it is . . . necessary to heed the opinion of the middle peasants. . . . If they do not agree, concessions should be made to them." (*ibid.*, p. 163).

policy in relation to the middle class and petty-bourgeoisie." Here and in another passage the term "middle class," which in the Communist vocabulary stands for groups like the intelligentsia, white-collar workers, artisans, and small traders, is substituted for Mao's "middle bourgeoisie," which means something very different, namely capitalists, as Mao had made very clear.* The final paragraph of Mao's address appealing to all the anti-imperialist forces of the East to unite is reported in full, but, following upon the changes just noted, it is now devoid of its specifically Maoist content.

Thus this rendition of the Maoist document in the Cominform journal cannot be regarded as constituting an endorsement of the neo-Maoist strategy in Moscow, but on the contrary indicates that that strategy either was not yet understood or was even opposed in some quarters there.   That the neo-Maoist current, though strong, continued to be only one of two running side by side in Moscow is also shown by another article by Balabushevich, which treats the entire Indian bourgeoisie as the enemy of the workers and refers to it as "reactionary" and to the Indian working class as "determined to carry on an active campaign against capitalist exploitation,"[56] two months after Zhukov had spoken of the working class uniting with part of the bourgeoisie and Mao had condemned any excessive activity against capitalist exploitation.

The Calcutta Youth Conference of February 1948.   Finally, we can try to glean an expression of the Soviet view on the strategy to be followed by the CPI from the South East Asia Youth Conference held in Calcutta February 19–26, 1948, by two Moscow-directed international Communist front organizations, the World Federation of Democratic Youth (WFDY) and the International Union of Students (IUS).   Since this meeting was attended by guests from the USSR and also from Europe, America, and Australasia, as well as delegates from India, Pakistan, Ceylon, Burma, Malaya, Vietnam, Indonesia, North and South Korea, and the Philippines, much speculation has centered on it.   It has been widely implied that insurrections breaking out in Burma, Malaya, and Indonesia within the next several months were ordered at this meeting.[57]   This cannot be disproved, but, as one thorough student of the subject states, "there is no tangible evidence for this contention."[58]   At any rate, so far as India is concerned, we have already seen that the Communist-led peasant revolts in Hyderabad began a year and a half before the Calcutta Youth Con-

---

* Similarly, of the passage on the policy to be followed in rural areas, quoted in the footnote above, only the first sentence is reported.

ference. And we cannot accept as literally correct the implication that the CPI received instructions to adopt a new line at this meeting,[59] for, as we shall see in the next section, the CPI had already made the decisive shift two months earlier.

Undoubtedly, however, the Conference presented an opportunity for the Asian delegates to become acquainted or more familiar with the shift away from the "right" strategy in Moscow, which we have been tracing in this section.[60] It would therefore be of great interest to determine whether the Calcutta Conference tended to advocate a turn toward the "left" or the neo-Maoist strategy in India, but unfortunately the published material on the conference[61] furnishes no conclusive answer to this question. It is, of course, quite possible that the Youth Conference, just like the composite voice of Moscow during the preceding half year, which we have now pieced together, was undecided in its choice between the "left" and neo-Maoist strategies and probably not even aware of the choice, but only sounded a vaguely radical, anti-"right" strategy call. This view finds some support in the report of the Conference in the CPI press that, on the one hand, relates that the Conference called on the youth of Southeast Asia to unite with all democratic and progressive forces in their countries, a statement with a rather neo-Maoist flavor, but, on the other hand, makes the decidedly "left" and anti-Maoist assertion that "the national bourgeoisie . . . afraid of the revolutionary mass movement, has compromised with imperialism."[62] This may or may not be a correct report on the decisions of the Conference, but it is significant as an indication that the Indian Communist leadership, which was at any rate, as we shall shortly see, disposed in this direction, could come away from the Conference with the impression that it had supported a "left" line.

Summarizing this section, we can conclude that by February 1948 no clear decision had been reached in Moscow as to whether the neo-Maoist or the "left" strategy was to replace the "right" strategy that had been given up after mid-1947. There is no evidence that there was any conflict or even any keen awareness of important differences between the alternative strategies. It is possible, however, that at least by the end of 1947 the neo-Maoist strategy was more and more appreciated and preferred in Moscow, as is indicated perhaps by the highly important Zhdanov speech of September and certainly by its interpretation by the authoritative Zhukov. That this was not a universal tendency, however, is clear from the continued recognition given in Moscow to the views of Balabushevich and Dyakov, who remained faithful to the "left" strategy in this period.

III. The Shift from the "Right" Strategy in India

We must now return to the Communist Party of India, which we left in the fall of 1947 when it was receiving little useful guidance from Moscow and following a "right" strategy of vigorously advocating a united front from above with Nehru and his wing of the Congress. In view of the inherent "leftist" tendency of the CPI, it is not surprising that there was growing dissatisfaction within the Party with this policy of P. C. Joshi, its General Secretary, of cooperation with part of the Congress leadership. Some Indian Communist leaders found great significance in the Communist-led peasant uprisings in Telengana and were perhaps already impressed by the successes of the Chinese Communists;[63] others seemed to desire better exploitation of the discontent of the urban workers[64] and consequently greater emphasis on attacks on the bourgeoisie. We shall have more to say in the next chapter about this division into a rural and an urban wing among the advocates of the united front from below. In the fall of 1947, in the absence of a decisive lead from Moscow suggesting the abandonment of the strategy of the united front from above, both wings, including B. T. Ranadive, the leader of the "left" faction, were reluctantly following the "right" policy. It is very probable that the proceedings of the Soviet Academy of Sciences of June 1947, which heralded a shift away from the "right" strategy in Moscow, either remained unknown in India or were not recognized as indicating a change of policy, for they would undoubtedly have been seized upon by the dissatisfied elements of the CPI leadership as a welcome excuse for the change of strategy they desired.

The CPI Central Committee meeting of December 1947. It was in this situation of internal discontent and factionalism and of lack of guidance from abroad that the Zhdanov speech to the first meeting of the Cominform found the CPI. The first report of this meeting appeared in the Indian Communist press in the middle of October,[65] and the CPI recognized its importance by reprinting the full text of the *Pravda* editorial on the subject three weeks later.[66] The full text of Zhdanov's speech itself appeared in the first issue of the Cominform journal of November 10, 1947. From December 7 to 16 the Central Committee of the Communist Party of India met and made the necessary adjustments. Ranadive, who shortly before then still supported the policy of cooperation with Nehru,[67] later claimed that the change in policy made at this meeting was the result of the discovery during the preceding months by a majority of Central Committee members from "their own experience" of how far they had "strayed";[68] but, if the sequence of events was not convincing enough, we have Joshi's own word for it that in December 1947 "the old CC revises its postwar policy on the basis of Zhdanov's Report to the Nine Parties Conference."[69]

As we have seen, Zhdanov said virtually nothing about Communist strategy in underdeveloped areas in his speech. That speech did, however, mark a clear and sharp turn away from the "right" strategy, and it also seemed to sanction the use of armed force in the colonies. It is probable that the neo-Maoist interpretation Zhukov made in applying the Zhdanov thesis to the colonial areas was not yet available to the CPI Central Committee, whose meeting adjourned on December 16, for it was printed only in the issue of *Bolshevik* dated December 15 (and Soviet periodicals apparently often do not appear until some time after their date of issue).* With nothing but Zhdanov's vague and largely inapplicable language to guide it, but with the certainty that it was now expected to discard its "right" strategy, the CPI leadership, inclined to be "leftist" as much of it was, especially at this time, and having never known any alternative to the "right" strategy other than the "left" strategy, inevitably executed a sharp turn to the "left." This turn was embodied in an apparently little-known resolution of the Central Committee[70] that is important enough to merit some detailed analysis. It may be noted that, although the Central Committee met under the nominal leadership of Joshi, its General Secretary, Ranadive later noted that Joshi accepted the statement of the new policy but did not vote for it, since he had not yet made a complete turn.[71] Thus, as was to be expected, with the change in policy from "right" to "left," effective leadership passed largely from Joshi, who was associated with the former, to Ranadive, who was identified with the latter.

The "Left" December 1947 resolution. The December 1947 resolution contains all the essential elements of the "left" strategy. Most important, it looks upon the Indian bourgeoisie as an enemy along with imperialism and feudalism; "it shed all illusions about the national bourgeoisie,"[72] as the "left" official Party history says. The bourgeoisie is now regarded as an ally of imperialism: "The Indian bourgeoisie has given up the path of opposition to imperialist domination and has become collaborationist";[73] "the Indian bourgeoisie is afraid of the masses whom it is determined to suppress"; "it is . . . servile and anti-national." The Mountbatten Award gave the people "not real but fake independence. Through this award, British im-

---

* This chronological argument is not essential to our interpretation; see pp. 39–40, below.

perialism . . . gave to the bourgeoisie an important share of state power, subservient to itself . . . in order to drown the national revolution in blood." The Mountbatten Award was thus not really a retreat of imperialism, as the CPI had held during the past half year, "but its cunning counteroffensive against the rising forces of the Indian people."

It is to be noted that throughout the resolution the entire bourgeoisie is being condemned. No distinction whatever is made between anti-imperialist and pro-imperialist sections of the bourgeoisie, as is characteristic of the neo-Maoist strategy, or between its "progressive" Nehru and "reactionary" Patel wings, as was made under the "right" strategy until a few days earlier. The possibility of the first kind of distinction is never even taken into account, indicating that the neo-Maoist strategy was not considered and probably not known as an available alternative to the "right" strategy; but the second distinction is expressly disavowed. The Indian Government and the leadership of the Congress, both of which included the Nehru wing, and the leadership of the Muslim League are all identified with the bourgeoisie and thus with imperialism: "The leadership of these two organizations, who represent the interests of capitalists and landlords, have reconciled themselves to the position of collaboration with Anglo-American imperialism." The "Government of India . . . is trailing behind the imperialist warmongers." It is collaborating with "Anglo-American imperialism in order to satisfy the selfish greed of national Big Business." Thus, what Ranadive had only a few days earlier hailed as Nehru's progressive foreign policy is now Nehru's "so-called neutrality . . . only leading to subservience to the Anglo-American imperialist camp." "To sum up, since August 15, the leadership of the Indian National Congress and the Muslim League, strongly entrenched in the Governments of India and Pakistan respectively, have started making political, economic and military alliances with Anglo-American imperialism. They are strengthening the camp of reaction all along the line."*

Another characteristic of the "left" strategy is the expectation that the coming revolution will lay the foundation of socialism rather than, as in both the "right" and the neo-Maoist strategies, be merely the bourgeois-democratic revolution that is separated from the socialist revolution by a considerable length of time. This feature, too, may be found in the resolution of December 1947 where it says that the aim of the Communist-led movement "shall be such a fundamental

* The references to the Anglo-American imperialist "camp" and the "camp" of reaction are indications of the influence of the Zhdanov speech on this resolution.

reorganization of government both in India and Pakistan as will assure complete independence and progressive democracy as a transition to Socialism." As we shall see, this belief of the Indian Communist leadership in a single revolution became more radical and clearly expressed within the following three months.

As always, the "left" strategy is to be implemented by the united front from below aimed at weakening the major non-Communist parties by winning over some of their members and subsidiary organizations: "A Democratic Front composed of all Left parties, progressive people inside the Congress and the League, sections of the Congress and the League, mass organizations of workers, peasants and progressive intellectuals, can and must be built up for complete independence and real democracy." That it is to be a united front from below is made quite explicit: "Such a front will be built up from below by the solidarity of the toiling people and backed by the joint efforts of all Left parties and progressive sections." The separation of the rank and file of the non-Communist parties from their leaders is a necessary part of this scheme, and a statement that the Congress and League masses must be released from the influence "of the bourgeois leaders" is therefore not lacking in the resolution. Needless to say, this "left" united front from below, unlike the neo-Maoist united front from below, does not include any section of the bourgeoisie—on the contrary, it is to "fight for the programme of democratic revolution . . . against reaction and the bourgeoisie."

While there is no outright appeal for violence, it is made clear that the methods to be relied upon in the execution of the new policy are not entirely peaceful ones: ". . . the upsurge of States people's struggles, the peasant unrest in South India, Bihar, Orissa and Bengal, the strike struggles of the workers, the mass demonstrations against special Emergency Powers in Calcutta, the struggles of middle-class employees, and students, these are the forces that will grow and defeat Anglo-American imperialism and its reactionary allies." Gone, once again, are the days of the slogans "Increase Production" and "Don't foment Strikes."

In fact, all that was left of Joshi's "right" policy in this complete about-face of December 1947 was a certain continuity in the Communist attitude toward the communal riots. These, to be sure, are now no longer blamed solely on the imperialists and the feudal order, but are described as "the direct results of the imperialist conspiracy and bourgeois compromise." The "workers, peasants and progressive intelligentsia" are the most determined forces resisting the riots, but in doing so, it is still said, "they will unhesitatingly support every move of the government and of the national leadership and press upon them to adopt serious measures." But the "left" strategy reasserts itself immediately, for it is added that "until the bourgeois policy of collaboration with imperialism . . . is successfully defeated, riots will take place again and again."

The relation between Ranadive's and Moscow's policies. Shortly after the December 1947 meeting of the Central Committee the Zhukov analysis applying the Zhdanov thesis to the colonial areas must have become known among the CPI leadership. Although its neo-Maoist tendency, expressed in remarks envisaging the cooperation of Communists with certain sections of the bourgeoisie, was clearly in conflict with the "left" wholesale condemnation of the bourgeoisie of the new CPI policy, no change in this policy was made; on the contrary, it subsequently became even more pronounced in its anti-bourgeois tendencies under Ranadive's influence.* To explain this disregard by the Indian Communists of an authoritative Soviet analysis of their situation, it must, first of all, be remembered that the most striking aspect of the Zhukov article, as of the Zhdanov speech, was not its neo-Maoist features but rather its emphatic abandonment of the "right" strategy. Men steeped in the "left" tradition of Communism and eager to return to it could easily overlook its essential neo-Maoist message in the mass of radical language, which distinguishes equally the "left" and the neo-Maoist strategy from the "right" one. That Ranadive was in this frame of mind, there can be no doubt. Joshi relates that during this period Ranadive once told him that "the whole pack of reformists" who got control of the different Communist parties after the dissolution of the Comintern would now get the sack,[74] indicating clearly that he thought that the formation of the Cominform and Zhdanov's report to it signaled a return to the old "left" strategy of Communism and that, the more radically a "left" line he followed, the better his chances of being in tune with Moscow.

That Ranadive should thus have misunderstood Zhukov or perhaps have considered his neo-Maoist passages inapplicable to India is the less surprising when it is recalled that even in Moscow there was no clarity on the issue of whether the "left" or the neo-Maoist strategy should replace the "right" one. As we have seen, V. Balabushevich

* Even Joshi, when he later recognized this policy as "incorrect," did not claim that he had opposed it or had been aware of any Soviet opposition to it, but accepted part of the blame for it: "We came to the conclusion that the bourgeoisie as a whole had gone over to imperialism. This mistaken notion was also the evidence of our theoretical backwardness and subjectivism." P. C. Joshi, "Letter to Comrade Ranadive," dated February 10, 1950, *Views*, May 1950, p. 39.

and A. Dyakov, the recognized Soviet authorities on India, also interpreted the Zhdanov thesis as a return to the "left" strategy. It is conceivable that Ranadive consciously followed these two writers as against Zhukov, but, just as it seemed to us unlikely that Balabushevich and Dyakov on the one hand and Zhukov on the other represented sharply defined and opposed factions in Moscow, so it is much more probable that Ranadive was simply interpreting and following Moscow's line as well as he could—although Balabushevich's and Dyakov's writings must have confirmed him in his course. Considering his inclinations and the novelty of the neo-Maoist strategy, it was only natural that he should be led on the same path as Balabushevich and Dyakov. He undoubtedly felt that he was enjoying support in Moscow, but whether he thought of it in terms of general Soviet backing or relied on the support of a particular faction is impossible to say.*

It is quite possible that Moscow took no direct hand in installing the Ranadive leadership. Rather, having been Joshi's chief "leftist" rival within the CPI Politburo for some time, Ranadive naturally fell heir to his mantle when the policy shift in Moscow became known in India. This does not exclude the possibility that dissatisfaction with Joshi's policy had become so strong in the CPI leadership that Ranadive took advantage of this shift in Moscow to oust Joshi.[75] At any rate, it is doubtful whether anyone in the Indian Party had at that time a better understanding than Ranadive of what the shift in Moscow might mean and, in particular, of the neo-Maoist strategy of including part of the bourgeoisie in the united front from below.

---

* Two former leading German Communists who have closely studied international Communism, but whose personal experience with its workings in the 1920's predisposes them to think in terms of left-right factional divisions in Moscow and their reflections in the various Communist parties, have suggested that the Ranadive leadership, being "leftist," was set up by Zhdanov—Franz Borkenau, "The Chances of a Mao-Stalin Rift," *Commentary*, XIV (August 1952), 117–123, p. 122—or at least relied on his faction for support—Ruth Fischer, "The Indian Communist Party," *Far Eastern Survey*, XXII, No. 7 (June 1953), 82. We know of no evidence for this. It is also implied that Zhdanov was opposed to Mao (see p. 26, above, and pp. 76–77, below), a matter of which we also know nothing, but which must in any case be sharply distinguished from the question of the various Communist strategies with which we are here primarily concerned. Zhdanov did not clearly favor the "left" strategy, as we have seen from his speech and from the fact that it was left to the neo-Maoist Zhukov for interpretation, nor, of course, has Mao championed the "right" strategy since World War II. As will become clear as we progress, any attempt to divide all Communist strategies into "right" and "left" and to ignore the neo-Maoist strategy as a third independent strategy leaves the postwar history of the CPI inexplicable.

The rural wing of the CPI did, indeed, come closer to Maoism in its emphasis on peasant uprisings than did Ranadive with his chief reliance on urban action; but this specifically Chinese aspect of Mao-ism, as we have noted, had remained unappreciated in Moscow by all sides, by the neo-Maoist Zhukov no less than by the "leftists" Dyakov and Balabushevich.

It is thus likely that, in spite of the clear conflict between Ranadive's policy and that advocated by Zhukov, Moscow, itself not too sure of its strategy and chiefly aware only of its abandonment of the "right" strategy, had no strenuous objections to Ranadive's "left" course and certainly did nothing drastic to change it. The publication in the Indian Communist press of Mao's report to the Central Committee of the Chinese Communist Party of December 1947 and especially the manner in which it was reported in the Cominform journal could even have reinforced Ranadive's "leftist" thinking, since its emphasis was chiefly on the military victories of the Chinese Communists. At any rate, Mao did not have enough prestige in the CPI then to cause it to modify in accordance with his ideas a course that it thought was in line with Moscow's demands. The Calcutta Youth Conference, which gave the CPI leadership an opportunity to hold face-to-face dis-cussions with Soviet emissaries, also must—whether he interpreted their words rightly or wrongly—have confirmed Ranadive's conviction that his policy had Moscow's approval, for, if it changed at all after this Conference, it was only to turn somewhat further to the "left."

December 1947—the turning point from "right" to "left." Since the various indications of the Soviet and Chinese Communist attitude that became available to the CPI in the period between the meeting of its Central Committee in December 1947 and its Second Congress at the beginning of March 1948 failed to modify its "left" position, it is clear that the turning point in Indian Communist strategy is to be found at the Central Committee meeting and was a result of the Zhdanov speech. This has often been overlooked because the Con-gress with its formal change of leadership and the bitter denunciation by Ranadive of Joshi and his policy was a spectacular event, while the Central Committee session and its important resolution seem to have gone largely unreported.* The attention of most observers has thus

* Remarkably enough, the CPI's chief organ, *People's Age,* contains no report on either the Central Committee meeting or its December resolution until February 15 and apparently never printed the resolution. It is by no means clear why the Party refrained for two full months from publicizing beyond its own ranks its great policy switch. Possibly Ranadive was not yet in full control of the Party machinery during this period and Joshi could prevent the publication; perhaps, having acted merely

been focused on the Congress, and this in turn has led to the belief that the South East Asia Youth Conference, which closed in Calcutta just two days before the Second Congress of the CPI opened in the same city, played a far greater role in the determination of the new Indian Party line than it actually could have.

The two and a half months following the December meeting of the Central Committee were, then, no longer a period of policy change but rather one in which the new policy already adopted was passed down to the lower levels of the Party's leadership and it was made certain that the delegates to the forthcoming Congress would be in favor of and thoroughly imbued with the new line. As the CPI's official history states, the Central Committee's resolution was issued to the entire Party ranks and on its basis a "self-critical review" was held throughout the Party in January and February, after which provincial conferences met to elect delegates to the Congress.[76] During this same period a drafting commission appointed by the Central Committee in December prepared a Draft Political Thesis for the Congress that was published on February 15[77] and that will be discussed in the next chapter. The Congress itself, as Joshi states quite frankly, merely endorsed the new policy decided upon by the Central Committee three months earlier.[78] Its further discussion therefore does not belong in this chapter, which has dealt with the postwar "right" strategy and the shift away from it, both in Moscow and in India, but in the following chapter, which takes up the development of the "left" strategy in India during the next two years.

NOTES FOR CHAPTER 2

1. See Masani, *The Communist Party of India*, pp. 30–31, 42, and 43, for quotations documenting both Moscow's and the CPI's adherence to the "left" strategy during this period.

2. See *ibid.*, pp. 56–59 and 61–62, on instructions to the CPI to switch from the "left" to the "right" strategy issued at the 7th Comintern Congress and by the Communist Party of Great Britain; and *ibid.*, pp. 59, 66, and 73, for Indian Communist statements showing adherence to the "right" strategy.

3. See *ibid.*, pp. 78–79 and 276, on the CPI's "left" strategy in 1939–1940.

4. See *ibid.*, pp. 80 and 277, on the CPI's initial hesitation to switch to the pro-

---

on the basis of Zhdanov's speech, which gave them so little guidance, the leadership did not want to commit itself to the new policy in all details until Moscow had had an opportunity to react to it, and may then have received a real or imagined sign of Soviet approval or taken the absence of rebuke as its equivalent; or the Central Committee may simply have decided to create the impression that the initiative for the change came not from the top but from the rank and file and culminated at the Party Congress.

British "right" strategy, and pp. 80–85 and 278–279, on its adherence to that strategy.

5. Milton Sacks, "The Strategy of Communism in Southeast Asia," *Pacific Affairs,* XXIII, No. 3 (September 1950), 227–247, on p. 230; Philip E. Mosely, "Soviet Policy and the Revolutions in Asia," *Annals of the American Academy of Political and Social Science,* vol. 276 (July 1951), 91–98, on p. 95.

6. Zhukov, "Porazheniie iaponskogo imperializma i natsional'no-osvoboditel'naia bor'ba narodov Vostochnoi Azii," *Bol'shevik,* No. 23–24, December 1945, pp. 79–87; A. Dyakov, "India after the War," *New Times,* No. 2, January 15, 1946, pp. 10–13. References to these as well as some Soviet statements subsequently referred to in this chapter may be found in Gene D. Overstreet, *The Soviet View of India, 1945– 1948* (Columbia University: unpublished M.A. Thesis in Political Science, February 1953). The aid obtained from this very useful thesis is here gratefully acknowledged.

7. A. Dyakov, "Sovremennaia India," *Bol'shevik,* No. 4, February 1946, pp. 38–53.

8. S. A. Dange, "Industrial India," *World News and Views,* XXV, No. 5 (February 3, 1945), 38; P. C. Joshi, "India—What Now?," *ibid.,* No. 31 (August 11, 1945), 243; "Indian Communists and the Congress," *ibid.,* No. 45 (November 17, 1945), 362.

9. "Review of the Second Congress of Communist Party of India," *People's Age,* March 21, 1948, Supplement, p. 4; Limaye, *Communist Party,* pp. 53–54.

10. "For a Free and Happy India," *World News and Views,* XXV, No. 47 (December 1, 1945), 391.

11. "Review of the Second Congress of Communist Party of India," *op. cit.,* p. 4.

12. *People's Age,* January 13, 1946; also reprinted as "The Final Battle for Indian Freedom," *World News and Views,* XXVI, No. 10 (March 9, 1946), 78.

13. "Election Manifesto of the Communist Party of India," appendix to P. C. Joshi, *For the Final Bid for Power!* (Bombay: People's Publishing House, no date).

14. "For a Free and Happy India," *op. cit.*

15. R. Palme Dutt, "India and Pakistan," *Labour Monthly,* XXVIII, No. 2 (February 1946), 83–93.

16. "A New Plan for India," *New Times,* No. 11, June 1, 1946, pp. 20–21.

17. V. Bushevich, "Bor'ba Indii za nezavisimost'," *Mirovoe Khozia'stvo i Mirovaia Politika,* No. 9, September 1946, pp. 39–52.

18. "Forward to Final Struggle for Power," *People's Age,* August 11, 1946, p. 4.

19. "Review of the Second Congress of Communist Party of India," *op. cit.,* p. 4; see also *ibid.,* p. 1.

20. Ramesh Sanghvi, "Indian Notes: The New Upsurge," *World News and Views,* XXVII, No. 5 (February 1, 1947), 60.

21. Ramesh Sanghvi, "The Rise of the Indian Trade Union Congress," *ibid.,* No. 15 (April 26, 1947), 172: "To fight this unity and militancy of the working class movement, the bureaucracy has launched unprecedented repression."

22. "Review of the Second Congress of Communist Party of India," *op. cit.,* p. 4; see also *ibid.,* p. 1.

23. A. Dyakov, "The New British Plan for India," *New Times,* No. 24, June 13, 1947, pp. 12–15.

24. "Mountbatten Award: British Manoeuvre to Make Transition from Direct to Indirect Rule," *People's Age,* June 29, 1947, pp. 6–7 and 10.

25. B. T. Ranadive, "Three Months of Indian Struggle," *World News and Views,* XXVII, No. 47 (December 6, 1947), 555–557.

26. "Review of the Second Congress of Communist Party of India," *op. cit.,* p. 4;

Dyakov, "Crisis of British Rule in India and the Liberation Struggle of her Peoples," *Crisis of the Colonial System* (Bombay: People's Publishing House, 1951), p. 26.

27. See, for example, B. T. Ranadive, "Working Class Upsurge; Part of Indian People's Struggle against Imperialist Economy—Tasks before the AITUC Session," *People's Age*, February 16, 1947, pp. 6–7, on p. 7, and articles directed against communalism *ibid.*, March 30, 1947, pp. 5–6; *ibid.*, November 9, 1947, p. 4; and *ibid.*, January 11, 1948, pp. 8–9.

28. Limaye, *Communist Party*, p. 56.

29. *People's Age*, October 19, 1947, pp. 1 and 5.

30. P. C. Joshi, "The Punjab Riots," *Labour Monthly*, XXIX, No. 10 (October 1947), 312–316.

31. "Review of the Second Congress of Communist Party of India," *op. cit.*, p. 4.

32. Ranadive, *op. cit.*

33. Limaye, *Communist Party*, p. 57, also quoted in Masani, *The Communist Party of India*, p. 280.

34. E. Zhukov, "K polozheniiu v Indii," *Mirovoe Khoziastvo i Mirovaia Politika*, No. 7, July 1947, pp. 3–14.

35. V. V. Balabushevich, "Rabochii klass i rabochee dvizhenie v sovremennoi Indii," Akademiia nauk SSSR, *Uchenye Zapiski Tikhookeanskogo Instituta* (Moscow, 1949), Tom. II. Indiiskii Sbornik, pp. 5–28. It is noteworthy that only Zhukov's report was published immediately after the Academy's meeting.

36. A. M. Dyakov, "Poslevoennie angliiskie planii gosudarstvennogo ustroistva Indii," *ibid.*, pp. 54–66.

37. S. M. Mel'man, "Ekonomicheskie posledstviia vtoroi mirovoi voinii dlia Indii," *ibid.*, pp. 29–53.

38. See pp. 6–7, above.

39. See pp. 9–10, above.

40. A. Zhdanov, "The International Situation," *For a Lasting Peace, for a People's Democracy!*, November 10, 1947, pp. 2–4.

41. *Ibid.*, p. 2.

42. *Ibid.*, p. 4.

43. E. Zhukov, "Obostrenie krizisa kolonial'noi sistemy," *Bol'shevik*, No. 23, December 15, 1947, pp. 51–64. It is not known whether the assignment of this important job to Zhukov was due to his previously expressed preference for the neo-Maoist strategy—which would be a fact of some significance—or was merely a matter of bureaucratic protocol, since he was the ranking theoretician in this field.

44. *Ibid.*, pp. 55, 57.

45. *Ibid.*, p. 55.

46. *Ibid.*, p. 57.

47. V. Balabushevich, "India posle razdela," *Mirovoe Khoziastvo i Mirovaia Politika*, No. 12, December 1947, pp. 41–62; A. Dyakov, "Partitioned India," *New Times*, No. 3, January 14, 1948, pp. 3–12.

48. Mao Tse-tung, "On the Present Situation and our Tasks," in Otto B. van der Sprenkel, ed., *New China; Three Views* (London: Turnstile Press, 1950), pp. 152–175.

49. *Ibid.*, p. 166.

50. *Ibid.*

51. *Ibid.*, pp. 167–168.

52. *Ibid.*, p. 174.

53. *People's Age,* January 18, 1948, pp. 12–13.

54. *Communist* (Bombay), I, No. 8 (February 1948), 341–356.

55. "Mao Tse-tung's Report to the Central Committee of the Communist Party of China," *For a Lasting Peace, for a People's Democracy!,* January 15, 1948, p. 6.

56. V. Balabushevitch, "What is Happening in India," *Trud,* February 18, 1948; in *Soviet Press Translations,* III, No. 11 (June 1, 1948), 326–329.

57. See, for example, S. R. Mohan Das, *Communist Activity in India (1925–1950)* (Bombay: Democratic Research Service, 1950), pp. 8–9; Masani, *The Communist Party of India,* pp. 89–90, and Masani, "The Communist Party in India," *Pacific Affairs,* XXIV, No. 1 (March 1951), p. 26.

58. Joseph Frankel, "Soviet Policy in South East Asia," Chapter VIII of Max Beloff, *Soviet Policy in the Far East, 1944–1951* (London: Oxford University Press, 1953), p. 209.

59. Mohan Das, *op. cit.,* pp. 8–9, Masani, "The Communist Party in India," *op. cit.,* p. 26. See pp. 41–42, above.

60. Sacks, *op. cit.,* and Frankel, *op. cit.,* pp. 209–210.

61. International Union of Students (Prague), *Hands off South East Asia.* Conference of the Youth and Students of South East Asia Fighting for Freedom and Independence. (No. 1. Special Bulletin of the Colonial Bureau of the I.U.S., Prague, April 1948.)

62. Satyapal Dang, "For Fighting Unity Against Sell-Out to Imperialism," *People's Age,* March 14, 1948, p. 2.

63. Jean A. Curran, Jr., "Dissension Among India's Communists," *Far Eastern Survey,* XIX, No. 13 (July 12, 1950), 133.

64. S. A. Dange, "The Labour Movement in India," *New Times,* No. 41 (October 8, 1947), 9–13; S. A. Dange, "Recent Events in India and the Working Class," *World News and Views,* XXVII, No. 39 (October 11, 1947), 461–462; B. T. Ranadive, "Three Months of Indian Struggle," *ibid.,* No. 47 (December 6, 1947), 555–557.

65. *People's Age,* October 12, 1947, p. 11.

66. *Ibid.,* November 2, 1947, p. 11.

67. See p. 23, above.

68. "Review of the Second Congress of Communist Party of India," *op. cit.,* p. 4.

69. P. C. Joshi, "Letter to Foreign Comrades," *Views* (Calcutta), May 1950, p. 5. As far as is known, this is the only issue of this periodical. It is composed entirely of material written by Joshi after his ouster from the CPI to attack Ranadive and is an extremely revealing document.

70. "For Full Independence and People's Democracy" (Extracts from the Resolution adopted by the Central Committee of the Communist Party of India at its meeting of December 7–16, 1947), *World News and Views,* XXVIII, No. 3 (January 17, 1948), 27–29.

71. "Review of the Second Congress of Communist Party of India," *op. cit.,* p. 4.

72. *Ibid.,* p. 1.

73. "For Full Independence and People's Democracy," *op. cit.* Until otherwise noted, all the following quotations are from this resolution.

74. P. C. Joshi, "Letter to Foreign Comrades," *Views,* p. 27.

75. Limaye, *Communist Party,* pp. 58–59.

76. "Review of the Second Congress of Communist Party of India," *op. cit.,* p. 1.

77. "Draft Political Thesis for the Second Congress of the Communist Party of India," *People's Age,* February 15, 1948, Supplement.

78. Joshi, "Letter to Foreign Comrades," *Views,* p. 5.

CHAPTER

—— 3 ——————————————————

THE "LEFT" STRATEGY IN INDIA (1948–1949)

I. THE LINE OF THE SECOND CONGRESS OF THE CPI

The Second Congress of the Communist Party of India met in Calcutta from February 28 to March 6, 1948. As we have just seen, its main task was to ratify the CPI's new "left" policy that had been initiated by the December 1947 resolution. This policy was successively elaborated in the Draft Political Thesis mentioned at the end of the last chapter, in Ranadive's report to the Congress on this Draft Thesis,[1] and finally in the Political Thesis,[2] a document of 95 pages, largely identical with the Draft Thesis but amended by the Central Committee after the Second Congress "in the light of the discussion"[3] there and thus constituting the most authoritative statement of the new strategy during this period.

The enemy—the entire bourgeoisie. The dominant influence in the documents of the Second Congress, as it was in the December 1947 resolution, is that of the Zhdanov report and its two-camp theory. In its conviction that this doctrine meant a return to the "left" strategy, the CPI leadership gave it an interpretation that is not to be found in Zhdanov's own speech: it identified the entire bourgeoisie all over the world with the camp of imperialism. Thus the Political Thesis states that "the entire world bourgeoisie . . . is attempting to blend itself together to stem the tide of revolution and oppose the working class."[4] Ranadive makes the point even more clearly when he says in his report to the Congress: "In every country, including the colonies, the bourgeoisie and their servitors, the social democrats, menaced by the revolution, are lining up with the Anglo-American imperialists in their fight against the forces of democracy and socialism . . . . This new correlation of forces expresses itself in the formation of two camps, which face each other in irreconcilable

46

conflict . . . ." "In every country the bourgeoisie and its henchmen have gone over to the camp of Anglo-American imperialism."

The "left" strategy thus seemed to flow logically from the two-camp doctrine; and its neo-Maoist alternative, which is at least equally compatible with the Zhdanov thesis, was ignored. It is clear by now that this was not surprising in view of Moscow's own uncertainty on the matter at the time. In the CPI leadership, not only Ranadive, but Joshi, who also knew only the alternatives of "right" and "left," agreed to the "left" interpretation. Only two years later, when Moscow's view had become clear, did Joshi realize and state in a letter to Ranadive that "we" got the wrong idea from the Zhdanov report that the world bourgeoisie as a whole had gone counterrevolutionary and was in a bloc with imperialism.[5]

Like the December resolution, then, the Political Thesis is full of condemnation of the bourgeoisie. It states repeatedly that the bourgeoisie has "gone over to collaboration,"[6] that there is now a "combine of imperialism, feudalism and the bourgeoisie,"[7] and that therefore "every step forward of the popular struggle is to be taken not only in opposition to imperialism but in opposition to the bourgeoisie."[8] Again the bourgeoisie is denounced in its entirety. The Draft Thesis still admits that there could be differences between bourgeois leaders and that the working class "distinguishes between the progressive and the reactionary" bourgeoisie, but it emphasizes that differences between Sardar Patel and Nehru are merely "imaginary."[9] The final version of the Thesis admits of no possible significant differences at all: "All shades of difference within the bourgeois camp . . . are entirely subordinated to the new basic realignment of the class as a whole, namely its role of collaboration with imperialism . . . . That is why today it is anti-Marxist for the working class to base its strategy on 'differences' within the bourgeois camp such as 'Patel-Nehru' differences."[10]

The rejection of any such strategy is thus phrased so broadly as to include not only the former "right" strategy of the CPI, but, most probably unwittingly, also the neo-Maoist strategy. The attack is aimed only at the "right" strategy, however, since the existence of the neo-Maoist strategy is not even acknowledged. Again and again it is emphasized that the entire Congress leadership represents "bourgeois vested interests,"[11] that "Nehru has completely surrendered to Patel's policy."[12] In particular, Nehru's foreign policy is denounced as representing "the interests of Big Business inasmuch as it kept India away from the democratic camp and opened the way to the imperialist camp"[13] and as merely hiding "its subservience to the Anglo-American

bloc in world politics under the cover of 'neutrality' between opposing camps."[14]

While the tenor of the Thesis is undoubtedly at least as anti-
bourgeois as it is anti-imperialist, the Indian bourgeoisie is characterized as dependent on the imperialists for its very existence,[15] as
"playing the role of a junior partner to imperialism."[16] "Imperialism
was basing itself on a new class, the national bourgeoisie,"[17] and it is
the imperialists who "establish a new line-up of imperialism, Princes,
landlords and the bourgeoisie."[18] India's status is described as "not
real but fake independence";[19] and it is concluded that the colonial
order has been retained.[20] Thus, in theory if not in emphasis, imperialism rather than the bourgeoisie continues to be regarded as the
main enemy, as it had been under the "right" strategy. Parallel to
this, and also noteworthy in view of later developments, is the reten-
tion of the anti-feudal rather than anti-capitalist emphasis in agriculture. The "Tasks on the Peasant Front," to which a section of the
Thesis is devoted, are almost wholly anti-feudal,[21] the "middle" peasant being unequivocally included with the poor and landless peasants
in the anti-feudal line-up.[22]

One-stage revolution; united front from below; violence. The resolution of December 1947 had already somewhat vaguely indicated
an expectation, usually associated with the "left" strategy, of a single
revolution accomplishing the goals of the bourgeois-democratic and
the proletarian-socialist revolution. This now becomes more outspoken. The Thesis states that the revolutionary struggles of the
postwar period are so powerful "that the achievement at one stroke
of People's Democracy (as in the countries of Eastern Europe) becomes
an immediately attainable objective."[23] The Draft Thesis had still
somewhat cautiously followed this thought with the statement that
"the achievement of this objective lays the preparatory ground for
the Socialist revolution,"[24] but the final Thesis replaces even this
hint at two revolutions with the statement that "the imperialists and
their bourgeois collaborators are overthrown and power passes into
the hands of the toiling people led by the working class, which assures
not only complete national independence but also the liquidation of
the capitalist social order and the building of Socialism."[25] And the
final Thesis also includes a passage, not contained in the Draft, declar-
ing that the Communist-led front would "create the pre-conditions for
the establishment of a democratic state, which will really be an instrument for implementing the full program of the democratic movement
and for simultaneously passing on to Socialist construction, without
an intermediary stage of capitalism."[26]

The united front from below, of course, remains the instrument of the "left" strategy. The new Democratic Front is to be "an alliance between the working class, the peasantry and the progressive intelligentsia," it is to seek the cooperation of all left parties and elements, but it is to be based on the masses and not to be a top alliance of parties.[27] The masses of the Congress and Muslim League must be brought "in opposition to their leaders"[28] as must the ranks of the Socialist Party.[29] Characteristically, one page of the Thesis is devoted to the Congress and Muslim League while four pages are given over to denunciation of the far smaller Socialist Party. No doubt is left that "the core of the new Front will be the Communist Party," which must be independent and lead the masses.[30]

The Political Thesis, generalizing Zhdanov's remark in his speech at the first Cominform meeting, is more explicit on the subject of violence than the December resolution, stating that "the postwar revolutionary epoch has brought the colonies to the path of armed struggle against the imperialists and their allies."[31] Much more must have been said on the subject in the oral discussions at the Second Congress. Those reported stress the fighting in Telengana, which, as we have seen, was not a result of the recent policy shift but had been going on for well over a year. Thus Ranadive stated that:

> Telengana is another big landmark in the history of struggles led under the leadership of our party. Here we took the struggle to new qualitative heights with exemplary organization. . . . Telengana today means Communists and Communists means Telengana.[32]

Another speaker at the Congress goes even further in charting the CPI's future course:

> The heroic people of Telengana, the great example of their fight against autocracy, not only show what will happen inside the States, but also what will be the real future of India and Pakistan. That is the way the victorious people must march to freedom and real democracy. Therefore we must respect this battle . . . as a struggle of a new type. We must be proud to say that here at least there is the force that will achieve Indian liberation. . . . If we can create this spirit of revolution among the masses, among the toiling people, we shall find reaction collapsing like a house of cards.[33]

On the whole, then, the documents of the Second Congress of the CPI are essentially an elaboration of the December 1947 resolution, going somewhat beyond it only on the questions of the one-stage revolution and violence. It is noteworthy that the last remnant of Joshi's policy in that resolution, the promise of support to the government against the communal riots, is expunged. Of it the Thesis says that "the riot offensive . . . has led many people to believe . . . that it was the business of the people to line up unconditionally behind the government. This is a totally wrong understanding of the situation."[34]

Ranadive's expectation of an imminent revolution. We mentioned in the last chapter that Ranadive was clearly under the impression that Zhdanov's speech and the formation of the Cominform heralded a return to the old radical "left" strategy. Not only was he wrong in foreseeing the development of the Soviet strategy for international Communism; the documents of the Second Congress make it clear that he was also wrong in predicting the social development of the next few years, for he expected an imminent breakdown of capitalism and outbreaks of revolution everywhere. These two expectations were not unrelated; rather, Ranadive deduced his perspective of the imminent world revolution, just like his belief in a sharp turn to the "left" in Moscow, from Zhdanov's speech itself and not from any independent investigation of the world situation. It is only on the basis of these two expectations that the policy followed by the CPI during the next two years can be understood.

The introductory section of the Political Thesis on "The International Situation," which is clearly an effort to follow the Zhdanov speech closely, declares that "Europe for the capitalists is on the brink of disaster,"[35] it refers to "the imminent menace of revolution"[36] and to imperialism "faced with the biggest revolutionary wave menacing its very existence, with the utter collapse of the capitalist order in Europe."[37] At the same time, the "people's victory in the Chinese struggle will change the entire shape of Asia and the world and ensure the doom of the colonial and capitalist order."[38]

Two years later Joshi realized that the Thesis had misinterpreted Zhdanov here and should instead have spoken only of a "deepening crisis."[39] But Ranadive, having formed his picture of the European and world situation through this misinterpretation, went a step further and transferred it to India. "What is happening in our country," he said, "is an integral part of what is happening elsewhere, the crack-up of the world imperialist system . . ., a crack-up of its economic system."[40] He apparently mistook some disillusionment with the Congress and newly won independence, especially in Indian intellectual circles, for a "mounting revolutionary upsurge."[41]

According to Joshi, the Second Congress expected a revolutionary seizure of power within a few months through the conversion of all native states into Telenganas.[42] That this completely unrealistic attitude prevailed among the CPI leadership is also confirmed by a

Communist circular of February 23, 1948, a few days before the Second Congress, which viewed the railway strike set for March 9 as a struggle for the seizure of power, told the Party members that it would be the onset of the Indian October Revolution, and directed them "to organize clashes from beforehand, to engage the police . . . to keep ready plans for seizure of government strong points."[43] Actually, the strike was a major defeat for the Communists and a dismal failure, for hardly any of the workers struck.

Replacement of Joshi by Ranadive; Joshi's attitude. A Communist party congress ratifying a switch to a new party line faces a certain dilemma with regard to its leadership. Formally, the new party leadership is not elected by the congress until its very end, since the adoption of the new policy must logically precede it. However, it would be inconceivable to leave the discredited leadership in control of the congress. Thus we have the spectacle of the entire Second Congress of the CPI being dominated by Ranadive, although he was not yet elected General Secretary, while Joshi, who nominally still held this office, was in disgrace and was not even re-elected to the new Central Committee.[44] There is no doubt that Joshi's power had come to an end before the Congress. As we saw in the last chapter, this probably happened at the meeting of the Central Committee in December 1947, although it may also have been a result of Zhukov's article of December 15 or of the February Youth Conference in Calcutta. Ranadive, on the other hand, not only presented the report on the Draft Thesis but also delivered the other major report to the Congress, a long one on "self-criticism." We have referred to it occasionally throughout the last chapter and can summarize it here as an attack on the policy followed by the CPI from 1945 to 1947, and particularly on Joshi for not recognizing the "collaborationist" role of the bourgeoisie and for "trailing behind" the bourgeoisie.[45] The impression we have gained of Ranadive's frame of mind is confirmed by the fact that he spent, according to the official report, fully four and a half hours delving into this subject and that the new Central Committee was later authorized to draft a complete analysis of "the reformist deviation" in the Party during the past.[46]

During his "self-critical" speech, Ranadive, to drive home his victory, stated: "Today, Comrade Joshi unreservedly accepts the political thesis, though he will certainly have to struggle very much to make a complete turn."[47] He was followed to the rostrum by Joshi himself, who, according to the report of the Congress,

> . . . fully supported Comrade Ranadive's report. He said that he himself was the leader and organizer of the right-reformist devi-

ations inside the party and he was the last among the Central Committee members to accept the political line of the thesis. He mercilessly criticized his own mistakes and traced its ideological roots to the repudiation of Marxism and Leninism. He was overwhelmed with emotion as he made these points in the course of his one-hour speech.[48]

A week after the Congress there appeared a statement by Joshi in the CPI's newspaper "contradicting the canard published in a section of the press" that he disagreed with the policy of the Congress. In it he said that:

> The main thesis . . . was unanimously adopted. . . . It is utterly wrong to say that I differ with it or opposed it. The Communist Party is united to a man behind its policy. . . . Our party has no factions inside it.[49]

Hypocritical as these statements may appear, there is reason to believe that they were sincere in the sense that Joshi recognized the need for a change. He had himself led the CPI along Moscow's zigzag course too long not to realize that Zhdanov's speech signaled a sharp turn away from the "right" policy he had followed. Two years later, when he was sharply critical of Ranadive, he still wrote that his acceptance of his "mistakes" at the Second Congress had been sincere and that the direction of change at that Congress had been correct,[50] that the Political Thesis had merely contained "sectarian oversimplifications" that were not noticed by the delegates,[51] and that he had not been critical of the Thesis for nearly a year.[52]

II. THE SOVIET VIEW IN 1948

That the Indian Communists' radical turn of December 1947–March 1948 away from the "right" strategy of cooperation with the Congress government had Moscow's approval goes without saying, for, as we have seen, it had been carried out in response to the advocacy of such a shift by Moscow itself, noticeable as early as June 1947 and made clear and urgent by Zhdanov's speech in September. Throughout 1948 the Soviet press and radio carried on a vigorous campaign of denunciation, which reached its peak in early 1949, of India, denying her independence, referring to the Congress as a party of reaction, and calling Nehru a hireling of Anglo-American imperialism. The only question to be answered here is whether the shift as it was accomplished by the CPI, that is, from "right" to "left," was the one desired by Moscow or whether a shift from the "right" to the neo-Maoist strategy would have been preferred there.

Lack of comment on the Second Congress. In seeking to ascertain the Soviet reaction to the Second CPI Congress one is, above all, struck by the paucity of expressions on the subject. The Cominform journal printed only one belated and brief report on the Congress, which, while mentioning Ranadive's selection as General Secretary, gives no indication that the old leadership had been replaced or that any new policy had been adopted.[53] The British Communist periodical *World News and Views*, which had hitherto covered CPI affairs rather fully, followed a similarly brief article[54] with the promise that "a fuller report of the Indian Party Congress will be published shortly," but no such report ever appeared. In view of the wide publicity in the world Communist press given to later, Moscow-approved CPI programs, there is little question that this silence is of significance. However, we cannot be sure whether it was due merely to uncertainty and a wait-and-see attitude on the part of Moscow toward the new CPI leadership and policy or expressed outright disapproval and, if the latter, just what it was that Moscow disapproved of.*

Continued advocacy of the "left" strategy. Some support for the CPI was implied in occasional Communist press statements describing the Indian government's countermeasures against Communist violence as attacks on the CPI as the most militant and advanced organizer of all democratic forces,[55] but that much might be expected even if Moscow disapproved of CPI policy. However, more significantly, the "left" view condemning the entire bourgeoisie also continued to have its advocates in Moscow. Outstanding among these remains Balabushevich, who, late in 1948, still speaks of "the Indian bourgeoisie's

---

* In June 1948 there appeared an article in *Bolshevik* containing some non-critical passages on the Second Congress, but also mentioning the Indian "big" bourgeoisie as collaborationist. M. Alekseev, "Indiiskii Soiuz i Pakistan posle raschleneniia Indii," *Bol'shevik*, No. 11 (June 15, 1948), pp. 54–66. In his attack on Ranadive a year and a half later, Joshi uses this as ammunition and refers to it as an article virtually reviewing the Second Congress and positively correcting its mistake of condemning the entire bourgeoisie by making alternative formulations. "Letter to Foreign Comrades," *Views*, p. 9, and "Letter to Comrade Ranadive," *ibid.*, p. 41. As we have seen, the distinction between the "big" and the "middle" bourgeoisie had also been made earlier by some Soviet experts on colonial affairs, notably by Zhukov, and its occurrence (in less clear fashion than in Zhukov's article of December 1947) in an article also dealing with the Second Congress can hardly be construed as an outright criticism of that Congress. However, even if Joshi's far-fetched interpretation could be accepted, it would still have to be proved that the *Bolshevik* article of June 1948 represented the sole view prevailing in Moscow at the time before it could be safely assumed that Moscow was critical of the specifically "leftist," as distinguished from neo-Maoist, formulations of the Ranadive leadership. This, it appears, cannot be demonstrated.

outright betrayal of the cause of national liberation."[56] This view is
echoed in East Berlin by a professor who declares that "the colonial
bourgeoisie sinks ever deeper into betrayal, turns into a force inimical
to the people, into an immediate agency of imperialism."[57] Another
Soviet writer defines the national liberation movement as consisting
of the industrial workers, the poor and landless peasants, the poor
population of the cities, and the intelligentsia,[58] thus excluding all
of the bourgeoisie. It may be noted that these writers now sometimes
refer to the "big" or "top" bourgeoisie, rather than simply the "bourgeoisie," in their denunciatory statements and thus make a slight
approach to Zhukov's neo-Maoist line; but they do not yet, like
Zhukov, include any section of the bourgeoisie among the forces led
by the Communist party. The difference between their "left" strategy
and the neo-Maoist strategy is brought out strikingly by a comparison
of this range of forces with that envisaged by Mao in a speech given
during the same year. There he states:

> The united front . . . is very broad. It comprises workers, peas-
> ants, artisans, professional people, intelligentsia, the liberal bour-
> geoisie and the enlightened gentry who have split off from the
> landlord class. This is what we call "the broad masses of the peo-
> ple" . . . . The enemies . . . are only, and must be only, imperial-
> ism, feudalism and bureaucratic capitalism.[59]

Palme Dutt on CPI strategy. Palme Dutt, the leading Western
Communist specialist on India, also seemed to approve of the line
of the Second CPI Congress throughout 1948. In an article dated
May 15 he calls "the Indian bourgeoisie . . . the weak junior partner
of Anglo-American imperialism" and says that

> the aim of the Democratic Front, proclaimed by the Indian Com-
> munists in their Congress in the beginning of March, corresponds
> to the new stage of the Indian fight for freedom. This fight links
> up with the advance of the popular democratic fight in all countries
> of hitherto subject Asia . . . .[60]

While this article, with its express approval of Ranadive's united front
and its attack on the entire bourgeoisie, is wholly in sympathy with
the CPI's "left" strategy, a report given by Dutt on October 2, 1948,
to a Conference on the Crisis of British Imperialism, published in the
form of two articles in the journal of the Cominform, contains distinct traces of neo-Maoism. It hails the "advance to armed struggle
of the national liberation movements in Malaya and Burma, and the
local peasants' uprisings and states peoples' revolts in India,"[61] carefully limits its attacks to the "big" bourgeoisie, and speaks of the

hegemony of the working class expressed in Communist party leadership uniting the widest sections of the people in a broad democratic anti-imperialist front.[62]   But, far from opposing this line to that of Ranadive, Dutt claims that it found expression at the Second Congress and thus again seems to put his seal of approval on the policy shift made there.   More consistently than Balabushevich and his school in Moscow, Dutt now refrains from attacking the entire bourgeoisie, but like them he refuses to take the crucial neo-Maoist step advanced by Zhukov of including some sections of that class in the Communist-led united front.

Continued indecision between the "left" and neo-Maoist strategies. Whether Balabushevich and his group and Dutt were deliberately sitting on the fence between the "left" and the neo-Maoist strategy or were merely engaged in the slow process of climbing that fence from its "left" to its neo-Maoist side is, of course, debatable.   But in either case it is clear that no firm position on this issue had as yet emerged in Moscow in 1948.*

In trying to assess Moscow's attitude toward the CPI's line in 1948 we can only conclude that there was no wholehearted approval of this policy, for we find no direct praise or even clear exposition of it and no publication of the CPI's documents setting it forth in the press of international Communism.   Clearly, however, there was no sharp disapproval either.   If there had been, it is inconceivable that the

---

* The report of Palme Dutt just cited, as summarized in Britain—R. Palme Dutt, "The Crisis of British Imperialism," *World News and Views,* XXVIII, No. 43 (October 30, 1948) , 480–483, and No. 44 (November 6, 1948) , 489–494—begins with an enumeration of five features of the post-World War II national liberation movement not present after World War I, including the "advance to armed struggle" and the leadership of the working class and the Communists.   Point No. 2 reads: "The advance of democratic China represents a powerful force in the world situation which exercises a profound influence on the development of the liberation struggle of the colonial peoples throughout Asia."   In the version of this report published by the Cominform journal only four features are listed and this point No. 2, which is the only one dealing with China, is completely omitted.   It is, of course, quite impossible to determine the reason for this excision, but, whether made by Dutt in submitting his article or by the Cominform editors, it could hardly have been accidental and one cannot help speculating that it might have been due to a certain reluctance on the part of at least some Soviet authorities as late as the end of 1948 to recognize the Chinese Communists as an example for other Asian Communist parties.   This hypothesis might find support in the fact that an important statement by Liu Shao-chi, made in China during the same period, which vigorously asserted that the neo-Maoist strategy must be used by other Asian Communist parties, was not published in Moscow until the middle of 1949 (see pp. 87–88, below).   This, too, suggests that the neo-Maoist strategy was not yet established as the sole approved one in Moscow in 1948.

Indian Communists could have carried out their "left" strategy for
two full years without being stopped or even rebuked by Moscow.
Furthermore, the comments made in Moscow, cited above, are themselves more "left" than neo-Maoist in tone.   It appears, then, that
the uncertainty between the "left" and neo-Maoist strategies, which
emerged in Moscow when the "right" strategy was abandoned in 1947,
continued on throughout 1948.   Opposition on the part of the CPI
to the Congress and its government and also to the Socialists, and,
therefore, its resort to a strategy of the united front from below, were
clearly desired by Moscow since its shift in 1947, and the use of violence was probably also approved in 1948.   However, whether its aims
were to be accomplished within the framework of a "left" or a neo-
Maoist strategy, that is, whether the entire bourgeoisie was to be
regarded as the main enemy or part of it could be included in the
united front from below directed against imperialism as the main
enemy, simply did not seem to be important to Moscow in 1948, for
the question was left unresolved and perhaps was still largely unrec-
ognized.*

III. THE CPI's "LEFT" ATTACK ON THE NEO-MAOIST STRATEGY

Undoubtedly in the belief that he enjoyed the support of Moscow
and, in fact, at least not discouraged by Moscow, Ranadive emerged
from the Second Congress at the beginning of March 1948 as the
CPI's recognized new leader ready to put his new "left" strategy into
action.   According to Joshi, no tactics were worked out after the Congress, and confusion prevailed;[63] but it soon became clear that the
Party's main reliance would be on force, and there it remained
throughout 1948 and 1949.

The policy of violence and its disastrous results for the Party.   The
CPI now embarked on a policy of violent strikes, riots, looting, arson,
sabotage, and murder.   A Party booklet entitled "Course for the
Cadres of the Shock Brigade," excerpts from which appear in an

* Attention may be drawn here to the implications of this discussion for the
question of Soviet expectations of a Chinese Communist victory.   Obviously no
examination of the Soviet attitude on CPI strategy alone can yield conclusive
answers to this question, and there need in any case be no perfect correlation
between Moscow's understanding and championship of the neo-Maoist strategy and
its expectation of a Maoist victory in China.   It is, nevertheless, of interest that our
analysis tends to support the cautious conclusion of Max Beloff, one of the foremost
students of Soviet foreign policy, that until the end of 1948 and possibly even early
1949 the Soviet government did not seem to expect a complete Communist victory
in China.   Max Beloff, *Soviet Policy in the Far East, 1944–1951* (London: Oxford
University Press, 1953), pp. 59–64 and also p. 248.

Indian government publication, states that this policy's "main political objective is to help the mass movement developing all over the country and raise it to the higher level when the people in general will take up arms."[64] Other pamphlets typical of the CPI's efforts to incite violence during this period were entitled: "Take revenge for the murder of mothers and sisters, give a fitting reply for the murder of the laborers. Attack the murderous Congress Government and tear to pieces the satanic Ministers";[65] and "Organize mass upsurge in defence of hunger-striking political prisoners. Storm the jail gates to snatch the prisoners away."[66] The last-mentioned declares that:

> This new and higher form of resistance inside jails and in factories, streets and fields outside is the sounding of the death knell of the Congress ruling class . . . . The task before our comrades is to lead this mass upsurge to still higher and higher forms.*

Although Ranadive, in accordance with his "left" ideology, was primarily interested in the "proletarian," that is, urban, struggle, banditry, terrorism, and attempts at guerrilla warfare were also carried on in rural areas, notably in Telengana, the area in Hyderabad where, as we have seen, Communists seized the leadership of peasant uprisings as early as 1946.

The results of the CPI's violent tactics were almost uniformly disastrous for the Party. Not only did the Communists fail to seize power in any urban area, but also several provincial governments now took such strong measures against them that thousands of Communist agitators were arrested, and by May 1948 most Communist leaders were either in detention or underground.[67] Far from developing a mass movement or "upsurge," the new tactics led to widespread loss of support for Communism. They alienated fellow travelers, an important factor of strength for a party that claimed less than 90,000 members[68] out of a population of 350,000,000. In particular, the Communists lost much of what power they had maintained since the war years in the organized peasant and labor movements. According to Joshi, the peasant movement was virtually liquidated through the Party's efforts to establish liberated areas,[69] practically all of which failed. There was much resentment on the part of labor against political strikes, and the Communist-dominated All-India Trade Union Congress lost heavily to the labor organizations led by the

---

* Ministry of Home Affairs, Government of India, *Communist Violence in India* (September 1949) , p. 28. Numerous similar pamphlets are quoted in this government publication. One of them contains exhortations such as "Hang those murderers . . . . Citizens should cut them to pieces . . . . Assault the reactionary Congress leaders severely, set fire to Congress offices . . . . Attack the houses of the Ministers and create chaos there . . . . Proceed in defiance of death." *Ibid.,* p. 30.

Congress and the Socialists.[70]   The Communists lost control over many of the unions they had previously captured.[71]   Joshi reports that, even in the Party's old strongholds, every strike call proved a "complete fiasco,"[72] and that the "Party has become detached from our own class."[73] This rapidly increasing isolation only drove the CPI into further adventures that brought further repression and further isolation.   Its failure, as Joshi says, "only whipped it into such blind fury as to go in for terrorist acts."[74]   Not only did the Party become separated from its former sympathizers, and its front groups crumbled, but many doubts and protests arose in its own rank and file.   According to a "self-critical" report of the CPI's Bengal Provincial Committee, many asked:

> Is it correct to attack railway stations? . . . to throw bombs in trams and buses? . . . to set fire to Congress offices? Why are the workers not participating in these actions?[75]

Toward the end of the two-year period of Ranadive's rule Joshi could state that only "a tiny percentage" of the Party's membership was active, and that "passivity, frustration, demoralization constitute inner party morale."[76]   Summing up the state of affairs in the CPI, he exclaims: "Victory of Chinese Communists is the glory of world Communism; the collapse of Indian Communists its shame."[77]

With the CPI's non-Party following decimated and the morale of its rank and file shattered, opposition to Ranadive's policies grew also in the Party's leadership, and there were more and more open accusations against him of "left sectarianism," "adventurism," and "terrorism."   By the end of 1948 there was criticism from Communist labor leaders who were dissatisfied with the use of trade unions exclusively for political strikes and the fact that efforts to strengthen Communist control of labor by emphasizing the workers' immediate interests, which had been demanded by the documents of the Second Congress, were now being virtually abandoned.[78]   Many of the intellectuals, always the most important segment of the CPI's leadership, were increasingly alienated by Ranadive's dictatorial tendencies.   Ranadive met criticism of his policies within the Party with suppression, which naturally only increased the opposition to him.   More and more members were expelled, and entire provincial committees were reshuffled and dissolved by the central Party leadership.*   As long

---

* Joshi, "Letter to Foreign Comrades," *Views*, p. 24. Joshi, the CPI's General Secretary until March 1948, himself was more and more isolated from the Party, formally suspended in December 1948, and finally expelled early in January 1950. See his "Letter to Comrade Ranadive," *ibid.*, pp. 31 and 33.

as he was convinced that his policy was "correct," that is, Moscow-approved, Ranadive undoubtedly felt that these purges merely strengthened the Party. In fact, however, the result was chaos; the CPI was shaken to its foundation in a few months, and within two years Joshi could claim that it had "ceased to function as an organization."[79]

The Andhra committee and the Telengana uprising. In this dismal picture of failure and disorganization there stands out as a striking exception the Communist organization in the Telegu-speaking areas of North Madras and South Hyderabad known as Andhra and since organized as a separate state by that name. The Andhra Provincial Committee of the CPI has apparently been able to maintain considerable strength and a peculiar internal cohesion and individual character of its own, perhaps ever since the Communists captured the Socialists' organization in this area during the period of the united front from above of the CPI and the Congress Socialist Party in the late 1930's. As a result, while other regional CPI organizations were at Ranadive's mercy, the Andhra Committee seems to have remained relatively immune from his interference. Joshi describes its Secretariat as a united team with which the Politburo did not dare "do any monkey tricks."[80]

It was this organization that was in charge of the Telengana districts of Hyderabad, where peasant unrest and fighting had been going on since 1946. While the violent activities in large cities favored by Ranadive and attempts at armed outbreaks in other rural areas failed utterly in producing any results favorable to the Communists, the Telengana uprising was a relatively successful enterprise. Armed groups of Communists moved into the area with a radical program of land reform, succeeded in gaining a considerable following among the peasantry, and "liberated" a significant number of villages—according to Communist claims, 2,500 by July 1948[81]—that is, they killed or drove out the landlords, their agents, and government officials and established some local governments.

This measure of success is to be explained in terms of the peculiarities of the area and the period. Telengana is a backward region where, under the Nizam's rule, land ownership was, even by Indian standards, incredibly unjust and the condition of the peasantry shockingly inhuman.[82] Though the Communists' methods of terrorism, directed against non-cooperating peasants as well as their exploiters, must have alienated some of the peasants, there is little doubt that the stoppage of rent payments, the cancellation of debts, and the distribution of land among the landless won for them much popularity, as was later shown by election results. Moreover, this was the period when the Muslim Nizam of Hyderabad, opposed by most of his Hindu people, was still trying to establish the independence of his state from the new Indian Republic, and when the local administration—always much weaker in the princely states than in British India —was particularly ineffective.[83]   In September 1948 India took over the state of Hyderabad, and Indian troops moved against the Communists in Telengana.   The Communists were on the defensive from then on, but sporadic guerrilla fighting continued for several years.

Although, then, the Andhra Provincial Committee maintained its independence against Ranadive and enjoyed some of its greatest successes during the early part of his Party leadership, it did not support him.   On the contrary, because of its very strength and cohesion, it was by far the most dangerous of Ranadive's many opponents inside the CPI.   It is impossible to know all the reasons underlying such intra-Party factionalism and rivalry, but it is clear that the Andhra Committee's long-established independence and Ranadive's dictatorial tendencies were almost bound to lead to a clash.   Furthermore, it appears that the Ranadive leadership, which had at the Second Congress early in 1948 heavily emphasized Telengana in order to point to a successful example of the violent tactics it was then proposing, lent no effective support to the local leadership in Telengana.   After the Indian invasion of Hyderabad it exhorted the Communists to fight on more defiantly, but in 1949, when they were gradually being crushed, it ignored them altogether.[84]

One reason for this failure to support the local leadership in Telengana—though it may have resulted from a rationalization of some deeper causes—was of an ideological nature.   Ranadive was either so dogmatic and inflexible as really to believe that the Communist movement must be based on the urban proletariat, or he thought that Moscow's then current policy as expressed in the Zhdanov speech demanded the position he took.   He strongly objected to the Andhra Communists' reliance on the peasantry as the base of Communist operations.   The fact that their efforts were more successful than his own at urban violence must, given his state of mind, only have infuriated him further.   Since both Ranadive and the Andhra Committee were too strong for either to attack the other by the means used by Ranadive against his other opponents—suppression of criticism and effective expulsion from the Party—they were forced to move to the level of theoretical discussions in their efforts to discredit each other.   There ensued an exchange that was of the greatest significance in the CPI's history of the next two or three

years.   It is of great interest to us because the positions taken by the
two sides reflected in an extreme fashion the uncertainty between
the "left" and the neo-Maoist views then prevailing in Moscow, and
because the eventual resolution of this uncertainty in Moscow, to
which the Andhra-Ranadive exchange itself may have contributed,
was followed by the resolution, in a very interesting and complex
process, of the conflict in India.

The neo-Maoist Andhra document of June 1948.   In June 1948,
less than four months after the Second Congress, the Secretariat of
the Andhra Provincial Committee submitted an important document
to the central leadership of the CPI.*   It is apparent that it was
meant both to be an attack on Ranadive's policy and to lay the theoretical basis for tactics to be adopted in pursuance of the program of the
Second Congress.   It seems that the Andhra Communists had wholeheartedly agreed with that program, for they had been as eager as
was Ranadive to turn from Joshi's "right" strategy of attempts at a
united front from above *with* the Congress government to a violent
one of the united front from below *against* the Congress; and they
had not yet become aware of the differences between the "left" and
neo-Maoist strategies, which were now, in their exchange with
Ranadive, to become crystal clear.

Being engaged in armed clashes in a backward area and leaning
on peasant support mobilized through a program of agrarian reform,
the Andhra Committee, searching for a theoretical basis for its
activities, naturally turned to the Chinese example.   In doing so
it had to rely directly on Mao rather than on Zhukov, the foremost
Soviet advocate of the neo-Maoist strategy, since the latter tended
to emphasize the Maoist appeal to the national bourgeoisie but not
its reliance on the peasantry, which was the Andhra Committee's
chief concern.   There is no evidence, however, that the Andhra
Communists regarded themselves as championing Mao in opposition
to Moscow† or considered Ranadive as representing Moscow's views—
although their approach did give Ranadive the opportunity of putting
the matter exactly in this light.

* Unfortunately, the full text of this document has not been available to us, but
its main features can be reconstructed from Ranadive's attack on it and a later
defense of it by the Andhra Committee. We shall at this point confine ourselves to
these definitely known features and let a fuller picture of its contents emerge from
a more detailed discussion of Ranadive's reply.

† To avoid such an implication, we shall refer to the Andhra Committee's strategy
as "neo-Maoist" though it came considerably closer to the Maoist original than the
neo-Maoist strategy eventually recommended by Moscow and adopted by most
Communist parties.

The Andhra document proposed that the program of the Second Congress be realized through a strategy based on Mao's *New Democracy*,[85] "that the path followed by the Chinese Communist Party . . . is the path which Indian Communists must adopt in the present phase."[86] Arguing that Russia had been industrially developed in 1917, it states:

> Our revolution in many respects differs from the classical Russian Revolution; and is to a great extent similar to that of the Chinese Revolution. The perspective is likely not that of general strikes and general rising leading to the liberation of the rural side; but the dogged resistance and prolonged civil war in the form of an agrarian revolution culminating in the capture of political power by democratic front.[87]

The Party, therefore, was to "concentrate on the task of unleashing the militant struggles of the peasants for urgently needed agrarian reforms."[88] At the same time, the Andhra document conceived of the CPI's fight as part of the so-called rising national liberation movement in Southeast Asia and claimed that since March 1948 the imperialists had launched an armed offensive against this movement and that the "Nehru-Patel Government's terror" was part of this offensive.[89]

Thus, just as in Mao's *New Democracy*, the main enemies emerging from the Andhra Committee's analysis are feudalism and imperialism, but not the bourgeoisie. The stage of the revolution now beginning is therefore not the proletarian but the "new democratic" stage, which the document defines, with many quotations from Mao, as a "dictatorship of many classes."[90] The document explains that:

> Mao, the leader of the historic Chinese liberation struggle, from his unique and rich experience and study, has formulated a theory of new democracy. This is a new form of revolutionary struggle to advance toward socialism in colonies and semi-colonies. Mao advanced new democracy as distinct from the dictatorship of the proletariat.[91]

In this new democratic revolution the forces led by the Communist party include not only the proletariat, the petty bourgeoisie, and the poor peasantry, as under the "left" strategy. According to the Andhra document, the middle peasant, too, is a firm ally, the rich peasant can be neutralized, that is, at least not antagonized, and, where feudalism is very strong, a section of the rich peasantry can be drawn into the anti-feudal struggle.[92] While this justification for its collaboration with all strata of the peasantry was undoubtedly uppermost in the Andhra Committee's mind, once having adopted the Maoist strategy as its own, it also advocated its most characteristic feature, the inclusion of a section of the bourgeoisie in the united front from below.   With imperialism and feudalism the main enemies, it is contended that only the big Indian bourgeoisie was collaborationist and that the middle bourgeoisie continued to be oppressed by imperialism and Indian monopoly capitalism.[93]   The CPI, therefore, "will have to adopt a correct attitude toward the middle bourgeoisie."[94]   And the Andhra Committee approvingly quotes the following characteristic statement made by Mao to the Seventh Congress of the Chinese Communist Party on April 24, 1945:

> Some people cannot understand why the Communist Party of China, far from being unsympathetic to capitalism, actually promotes its development.   What China does not want is foreign imperialism and native feudalism and not native capitalism which is too weak.[95]

Even from the fragments known to us, it is quite clear that the document of the Andhra Committee contains all the basic elements of the neo-Maoist strategy—imperialism and feudalism as the main enemy, a revolution in at least two stages, the united front from below against the non-Communist parties, and the inclusion of a section of the bourgeoisie in that front—and its characteristically Chinese elements—chief reliance on the peasantry and armed struggle.

Ranadive's "left" reply: "On People's Democracy," January 1949. Ranadive's immediate reaction to this document is not known, but soon after its submission a full session of his Politburo took place, lasting from September to December 1948.   It was there that four important articles were approved which were published in the CPI's theoretical organ, *Communist,* in the period from January to July 1949 as statements "by the Editorial Board."[96]   Although they are repetitious, these statements form a definite sequence, and we shall therefore consider them individually.

The first two articles, "On People's Democracy" and "On the Agrarian Question in India,"[97] which appeared together in January 1949, constitute a theoretical defense of those features of the "left" strategy that distinguish it from the neo-Maoist strategy and, thus, implicitly and explicitly, are an attack upon the latter.   However, the Andhra Committee, Mao Tse-tung, and the Chinese Communist Party are never mentioned by name in them.   Relying characteristically, in part, on documents of the extreme "leftist" Sixth Congress of the Comintern of 1928, "On People's Democracy" sets forth what amounts to a theory of a single revolution leading to socialism.   The democratic revolution is described as a short stage leading directly and without interruption to the proletarian revolution.[98] The present revolution is a "People's Democratic Revolution—which emphasizes its extreme nearness to the Socialist Revolution and, at the same time, sharply demarcates it from the bourgeois democratic revolution."[99]

> So far as we can see, in our country the immediate State form will be a bloc of the proletariat with non-proletarian elements, a Democratic Dictatorship of the Workers and Peasants. But this State, arising in the context of world Socialist Revolution, and in the course of direct struggle against the rule of capital, will quickly pass into the Dictatorship of the Proletariat.*

Only the proletariat will lead the delayed democratic revolution ripening into the Socialist revolution. Its firm allies will be only the rural proletarians and poor peasants; the middle peasants, the petty bourgeoisie, and the intellectuals vacillate, but some may be won over.[100]

The revolution envisaged by Ranadive being an anti-capitalist rather than a "new democratic" revolution like that of the neo-Maoist Andhra document, clearly no section of the bourgeoisie could have a part in it. On the contrary, the delayed democratic revolutions in the backward countries "are breaking out in the midst of the most intense and sharpened conflict in each country between the bourgeoisie and the proletariat";[101] "the immediate aim of the revolution is to dethrone the bourgeoisie from power";[102] and the people's democratic revolution "begins by throwing the bourgeoisie out of power."[103] Imperialism is to be overthrown not to put the bourgeoisie in power but to exclude it from power;[104] and (this is unmistakably aimed at Mao) it is therefore "impermissible to talk about building capitalism, giving a long period of development for capitalism, as certain Communist leaders have done."[105] Looking for authority to support his thesis, Ranadive claims to find it in Zhdanov's Cominform speech of September 1947: "Zhdanov, in his Report on the International Situation at the Warsaw Nine Parties' Conference, describes the People's Democratic Government as a bloc headed by the working class—a bloc of peasants, people, etc., i.e., one in which the bourgeoisie has no place."†

---

* "On People's Democracy," *Communist*, II, No. 1 (January 1949), p. 10. We are not here concerned with the preposterousness of Ranadive's expectation of an early dictatorship of the proletariat, i.e., a dictatorship of the Communist Party, held at a time when he was ruining whatever little strength the CPI had ever had.

† *Ibid.*, p. 11. While Ranadive very probably believed that he was but giving a correct interpretation to the Zhdanov speech, that speech actually lends little support to his thesis. Not only were the remarks referred to concerned with the

Taking a different position from that of the Andhra Communists, who looked upon their fight as anti-colonial and "national liberationist," and from that of the *Political Thesis* of the Second Congress, which still spoke of the "colonial" order in India, Ranadive now regards India, since she became independent, as primarily a capitalist rather than a colonial country. A crucial point that had still been somewhat obscure in the documents of the Second Congress therefore now emerges quite clearly: the main enemy is no longer foreign imperialism but the Indian bourgeoisie. Referring to the anti-bourgeois character of the revolution, "On People's Democracy" says:

> This . . . totally new feature of the situation . . . is missed by those who take an opportunist line by saying that nothing has changed, argue as if it is imperialism that is to be overthrown. . . . What place does fight against imperialism occupy in the struggle? . . . the bourgeoisie has secured a National State, linked with world capitalism—and, therefore, a satellite State. Freedom and independence now mean freedom from the world capitalist order—not from this or that imperialism only. Thus, again, the task of fighting for real freedom is linked with the defeat of capital at home. . . .[106]

Here we are face to face with a fascinating situation: The Andhra Communists, relying solely on Mao and, so far as we know, never referring to Zhdanov or any other Soviet authority, concentrate their fire on Anglo-American imperialism. This being also Moscow's chief enemy, they are firmly within the framework of Zhdanov's two-camp theory, which had mentioned the national liberation movement in the colonies as in the Communist-led camp. Ranadive, on the other hand, has now carried the "left" strategy to its logical extreme and to a point that its Soviet champions, Dyakov and Balabushevich, never reached. These latter, to be sure, condemned the entire bourgeoisie, but they never went so far as to imply that it superseded Anglo-American imperialism as the main enemy. Though constantly citing Zhdanov's two-camp theory and speaking in "internationalist" terms—"world capitalism," "world Socialist Revolution"—Ranadive is now actually more and more ignoring the fight against the American-

---

eastern European Soviet satellites and therefore probably irrelevant to colonial countries, but, vague as Zhdanov is in his class analysis, he is nowhere guilty of a formulation as absurdly imprecise as "a bloc of peasants, people, etc."—which would, in any case, not necessarily exclude all or part of the bourgeoisie. In fact, Zhdanov speaks of the "big" capitalists and the "removal from power of the top bourgeoisie and landlords. . . . In these countries, representatives of the workers, the peasants and the progressive intellectuals took over power." A. Zhdanov, "The International Situation," *For a Lasting Peace, for a People's Democracy!*, November 10, 1947, p. 2.

led camp and concentrating on the Indian bourgeoisie, a group of decidedly inferior importance to Moscow and not even necessarily its enemy.

"On the Agrarian Question in India," January 1949. The second Politburo statement, "On the Agrarian Question in India," though more than three times as long as "On People's Democracy," is essentially a supplement on one specific problem to that more general statement. Its greater length is due to the fact that, whereas "On People's Democracy" pretended to be no more than a restatement of the principles of the Second Congress, "On the Agrarian Question" frankly sets out to make a new analysis of class relations in rural areas in order to frame a new strategy and new slogans—with the excuse that the Second Congress was too busy "rescuing the Party from collaboration with the national bourgeoisie" to tackle this task.[107]

Fortified with many figures and long quotations from Lenin on Russian agriculture, this new analysis is designed to show that, while feudalism is not yet dead, capitalism is developing rapidly and with increasing speed in the countryside through the great increase in the number of landless laborers and the emergence of the rich peasant.* Devoting seventeen pages to capitalism and less than three to feudalism, the article gives the distinct impression that the former rather than the latter already dominates Indian agriculture. It therefore attacks the formula that the agrarian struggle is directed only against feudalism, which it calls a counterpart to the formula that the national struggle is directed only against imperialism.[108]   Even in the countryside, capitalism and the bourgeoisie, rather than feudalism and imperialism as Mao and the Andhra Communists declare, are the main enemy.

> The task of liquidating the feudal order is linked with the task of overthrowing the political rule of the bourgeoisie. . . . The task of national independence is linked with the task of breaking away from the capitalist orbit.[109]

---

* We have mentioned Communist classifications of the rural population before, and it is now time that we distinguish clearly among them. There are five such classifications, and they may, according to the article under discussion, be defined as follows: (1) the rural proletarian is a landless agricultural laborer; (2) the poor peasant has some land, but not enough to support himself, and is therefore forced to work for others; (3) the middle peasant has enough land to support himself—he neither works for others nor hires the labor of others; (4) the rich peasant hires others to work for him—living on profit, he is a capitalist exploiter; (5) the landlord rents out his land—living on rent, he is a feudal exploiter.

The revolution must not only abolish feudalism but also squeeze out capitalism in rural areas; the slogan "Nationalization of Land" must be added to that of "Abolition of Landlordism."[110]

If "the struggle against feudal landlordism cannot be carried on without simultaneously carrying on the struggle against capitalist exploitation,"[111] the class forces to be led by the Communists must necessarily differ from those relied upon by the Andhra Committee and the Chinese Communists.* While "On People's Democracy" sought to demonstrate that the entire bourgeoisie must be fought, "On the Agrarian Question in India" is intent upon narrowing the Party's base in rural areas. The middle peasant, a firm ally according to the Andhra Communists, is but a vacillating ally according to the Politburo. He can be won over, but Communists cannot wait for his doubts to be dissolved; he cannot be the base of the anti-feudal, anti-capitalist struggle.[112] The rich peasant, whom the Andhra Committee wanted to neutralize, does not vacillate; he cannot be neutralized; he is "the spearhead of bourgeois feudal reaction in rural areas . . . he is a capitalist."[113]

There thus emerges the following class analysis of the revolutionary forces: the driving forces of the People's Democratic Revolution are the urban proletariat and, closest to it in rural areas, the rural proletariat. The latter leads the poor peasants, another firm ally. These three groups are followed by vacillating allies: the middle peasants in the country and certain sections of the petty bourgeoisie—employees, school teachers, students, clerks—in towns and cities. Other parts of the petty bourgeoisie—intellectuals, bureaucracy, army, managers—are listed as ranging themselves against the proletariat. The bourgeoisie (no distinction between middle and big bourgeoisie is drawn) and the rich peasants constitute the capitalist enemy who is even more important than the feudal and foreign imperialist enemies.[114]

"Struggle Against Revisionism Today," February 1949. Having apparently to his satisfaction destroyed the theories of his chief intra-Party enemy, the Andhra Committee, Ranadive devoted the third Politburo statement, "Struggle Against Revisionism Today, in the Light of Lenin's Teachings,"[115] to an attack on his various enemies within the CPI without naming any of them specifically.

Perhaps to prove his "internationalism" and his faithfulness to Moscow and to show that he represented a trend in Communist policy

* The Andhra view, set forth above, corresponds to the Chinese Communist one: ". . . to rely on the poor peasants and farm laborers, unite with the middle peasants, neutralize the rich peasants. . . ." Liu Shao-chi, "On the Agrarian Reform Law," *People's China*, II, No. 2 (July 16, 1950), 30.

that was needed in other Communist parties as well, Ranadive introduces this article with a long and sharp assault on "revisionism" in many Communist parties. At the end of World War II, he says, "in a number of Parties some leaders took up an openly revisionist attitude";[116] "these revisionist tendencies . . . made their appearance in some of the most advanced Parties also, and also among leaders who were the most loyal and unflinching fighters in the cause of Marxism-Leninism."[117] He goes on to say that not all Communist parties in capitalist countries were equally affected: "in some there were revisionist mistakes; in others revisionism had become a policy."[118] Among the manifestations of revisionism he lists are statements by some parties in Europe that the dictatorship of the proletariat was not necessary, failure to expose the treachery of the Social Democrats, refusal to be self-critical, and repudiation of the vanguard role of the party. The charges are vague, and the accused are not named. With the exception of the Yugoslav and United States Communist Parties and of Tito and Browder, who could be safely attacked, there are references only to "certain" and "some" Communist parties.

It was indeed an amazing performance for Ranadive, the leader of a tiny Communist party who had been in power just long enough to lead it from failure to failure, to set himself up as critic of most of the international Communist movement, including apparently some of its most powerful parties and leaders who were still in Moscow's graces. That he did so demonstrates once again that Ranadive must, rightly or wrongly, have felt very sure that he enjoyed support in Moscow. He must have been equally certain that the Zhdanov speech heralded a sharp turn to the "left" strategy that would be accompanied by a general shake-up of the international Communist leadership which had adhered to the "right" strategy during the postwar years.[119]

The CPI, according to the statement, manifested some of the worst revisionist trends. Among them are listed a rejection of the dictatorship of the proletariat, liquidation of the Leninist principles of organization, bourgeois nationalism, "failure to correctly assess the international role of the Soviet Union as the fortress of world Socialism,"[120] and the fact that the struggle for proletarian hegemony was made to recede in the name of fighting sectarianism and of a united national front, which led to a non-class conception of peasant unity, to control of the peasant movement by the vacillating middle peasant, and frequent compromises with the rich peasant.[121] Examples furnished for these deviations range from 1936 to 1947, and it is darkly hinted that while some were sharply nailed down at the Second Congress, "others, perhaps, were not mended."[122] Since the Second Congress, "revisionism has donned the robe of a fight against reformism";[123] fighting is done only in words, and the actual mass struggle is abjured. Revisionism in the CPI is the result of "the petty-bourgeois composition of the Party."[124]

It is not entirely clear against whom all these attacks were directed, but it appears that both the "right" followers of Joshi and the neo-Maoist followers of the Andhra Committee and, indeed, perhaps even some of the "leftists" who were not active enough, were to be discredited as revisionists. The solution advocated was the purge, to justify which may have been the chief purpose of this Politburo statement. There was to be waged "a serious inner-Party struggle against such tendencies, by giving them no quarter . . . by quickly taking steps to change the social composition of the Party and its leading committees."[125]

"Struggle for People's Democracy and Socialism," July 1949. After the appearance of the third Politburo statement in February 1949 there was a pause, probably dictated by tactical considerations not known to us, but in July there appeared the fourth statement, "Struggle for People's Democracy and Socialism—Some Questions of Strategy and Tactics,"[126] the last and longest of the series and the most important and most startling. It re-emphasizes some of the points made in the two documents published in January, describing the situation in even more extreme terms. Just as he had a year and a half earlier at the Second CPI Congress, Ranadive still speaks of "the growing collapse of capitalist production," "the looming shadows of the world crisis in the near future,"[127] and being "on the eve of revolutionary battles."[128] Thus, in spite of their repeated failure, he continues to advocate his tactics of violence:

The partial struggles of the present period, therefore, become wide mass battles, miniature civil wars, which, when they are organized on a sufficiently big scale, easily develop into political battles and throw up embryonic State forms (Telengana) —such is the situation.[129]

More specifically, "strikes, agrarian struggles, general strikes, political strikes, rising to higher forms of struggle and to a general rising— such are the forms of struggle."[130]

This article also contains an even more outspoken statement and longer elaborations than the first one on the point that the Indian bourgeoisie rather than foreign imperialism is the main enemy and that Communists must concentrate their fire on the former. That such action might run counter to Soviet interests seems to have escaped Ranadive, who wanted above all to be a faithful follower of Moscow.

> The Indian bourgeoisie is the most fighting, active partner in the bourgeois-feudal-imperialist combine. In relation to the people it is the strongest of the three and today, when the main immediate task of the combine is to stem the tide of revolution, the Indian bourgeoisie comes forward as the leading member of the combine.
>
> The fight for revolution, therefore, breaks out directly against the rule of the Congress Government—and no amount of curses and abuses against imperialism can alter the fact. . . . It is so because the Congress Government and the bourgeoisie are not mere puppets but because in reality they are active partners and leading forces in the combine.[131]

However, this fourth Politburo statement is primarily distinguished from its predecessors by the fact that it directly and explicitly attacks Ranadive's opponents within the CPI and, in doing so, goes to such lengths that it marks the high point but also the beginning of the end of Ranadive's "left" strategy. His opening attack is on various unstable elements in the Party who were becoming demoralized and were beginning to waver and raise doubts about the Party line under conditions of government suppression. This weakness in the Party is blamed on its overwhelmingly petty-bourgeois composition, said to be a result of the reformist policy of basing the Party on the wrong classes.[132] Thus, says Ranadive, in Calcutta the CPI was "almost exclusively . . . non-proletarian,"[133] and in Andhra the sons of rich peasants and middle peasants preponderated in important positions and the Party politically based itself on the vacillating policies of the middle peasants and was even influenced by rich peasant ideology.[134] It is demanded that the social composition of the Party be "quickly changed."[135]

Various vacillations regarding the Party line are then described and that of the Andhra Secretariat is characterized as a "reformist conception of class relations" dressed by "Left phraseology . . . about Telengana, etc."[136] Here Ranadive catches a glimpse of the real nature of the neo-Maoist strategy, which unites elements of the "right" and "left" strategies. He obviously has no understanding of it, however, and thinks only in terms of "right" and "left." Since the Andhra Communists do not agree with him, that is, are not "left," they must obviously be "right"; and the "left" elements in their program, the united front from below and opposition to the Congress, which they actually took very seriously, must, in order to fit into his old-fashioned picture of Communist strategy, be discarded as mere phraseology and window dressing.*

Fully half of this last article is devoted to a detailed critique of the Andhra Provincial Committee's document, submitted a year earlier, which, it is said, "reveals reformism in its most naked and gross form."[137] Ranadive's analysis comes to this withering conclusion: "These views expressed in the entire outlook represented by the Andhra document must be rejected as anti-Party, anti-Leninist and being in utter repudiation of the Political Thesis of the Second Congress of the Party and of the accepted Marxist outlook on world situation, People's Democracy, stage of revolution, as given in Zhdanov's statement."[138] Thus taking strong issue with the assertion in the Andhra document that the Russian example was not wholly applicable to India and less so than the Chinese one, the article states that "it should be understood . . . that the entire experience of the Russian Revolution is fully valid in the case of India also,"[139] and that it is wrong to regard China as the only example of a long civil war and an agrarian revolution. These factors were present in the Russian Revolution, too, while, on the other hand, strikes in Shanghai and Canton played a great revolutionary role in China.[140]

Ranadive attacks the Andhra Communists (and, through them, neo-Maoism) for making a distinction between the hegemony of the proletariat and the dictatorship of the proletariat. Through a discussion of the Russian Revolution, supported by long quotations from Stalin, he seeks to prove that proletarian hegemony in the struggle for power ripens into hegemony in the state, which is identical with the dictatorship of the proletariat.[141] More fundamental and more telling from a Marxist point of view is Ranadive's assertion that, in the name of the anti-feudal and agrarian revolution, Maoism and neo-Maoism have, in fact, abandoned the notion of proletarian hegemony.

> Some of those who advocate what they call the Chinese way, formally stand for the hegemony of the proletariat. But they suggest that the Chinese experience shows that it is exercised through the Communist Party—politically and ideologically and organizationally—which in reality reduces itself to the assertion that a Communist Party, basing itself on the ideological and political platform of the proletariat, can successfully lead the revolution

---

* This manifest lack of comprehension of the essentials of neo-Maoism on the part of Ranadive in 1949 supports our interpretation on pp. 39–40, above, that the crucial neo-Maoist passages in Zhukov's important article of December 1947 were simply not understood and therefore were ignored by Ranadive when he embarked on his "left" policy at that time.

without setting the working class itself, the mass of workers, in motion, the hegemony to be secured through the leadership of the Communist Party and not through the direct participation and lead of the working class in struggle.[142]

Ranadive declares that this conception is wrong, and, to explain the victory of the Chinese Communists, he claims that it does not hold in China. He says that the Chinese Communist Party arose out of the struggle of the Chinese proletariat in the great urban centers such as Shanghai and Canton and that it was the proletarian fighters "who carried the flame of revolution to agrarian China."[143] "It is thus clear that hegemony cannot mean hegemony of the Party without the working class being in action, but directly the hegemony of the working class led by the Party, the entire working class in action."[144]

Here for once Ranadive escapes the utter unreality in which Communist "theoretical" discussion usually moves when, in an underdeveloped country, it employs Marxian, that is, essentially Western European, concepts like proletarian revolution and dictatorship. He brushes aside the Maoist verbiage of proletarian hegemony and shows that in reality the proletariat, as distinguished from the Communist party, plays little part in Maoist theory (though he must, of course, claim that in practice it played the decisive role in the Chinese Revolution). Here Ranadive has put his finger on a real weak spot —from the point of view of Marxian theory—of Maoism and neo-Maoism. We see at once, however, why it is very dangerous for Communists to face reality and why they do it so rarely. Although the abandonment of reliance on the real working class is most obvious in the case of Chinese Communists, who clearly based themselves primarily on the peasantry, it is actually inherent in all of Leninism. It was Lenin, not Mao, who took the decisive step in cutting himself off from the Marxism of Marx and Engels by doing what Ranadive here implicitly attacks. Lenin drew a sharp distinction between the party and the working class, asserting that the former—a "shock troop" of professional revolutionaries, that is, largely of intellectuals—rather than the working class itself embodied true proletarian class consciousness, and assigning to the party, rather than to the class, the active and creative role in history. This step was a fundamental one, indeed, for it marked the abandonment both of the materialist conception of history as Marx had understood it and of democracy in the labor movement, in the party, and, where the party captures power, in the state.

Manifestly, Ranadive cannot and does not understand that what he is attacking is not a Maoist innovation but a basic aspect of the Leninist—and therefore also of his own—creed. In fact, his very attack on it shows that he never really frees himself of the Leninist conception. Thus, he takes for granted that the Communist party truly represents the working class politically and ideologically. He goes so far as to speak at one point in Marxian terms of the "lead of the working class," but he is really thinking of the "working class led by the Party" and, in typically Blanquist-Bakuninist-Leninist terms, of the party "setting the working class in motion." Since Ranadive's purpose obviously is not to attack Leninism, he cannot attack the bases of Maoism, which is but Leninism in a more developed form. His point is merely the very modest one that the working class should at least participate in what is supposed to be its own struggle. His objection is to the fact that the Andhra Communists in effect developed a theory of peasant leadership[145] and, more accurately, that, by belittling the general strike as a weapon, they really took the position that the fighting center is the peasantry and not the proletariat.[146]

What makes the Andhra document's reliance on the peasantry particularly galling to Ranadive is the fact that it regards the middle peasant as a firm member of the united front and justifies the neutralization of or even collaboration with the rich peasant. To Ranadive "this constitutes the real practical gist of the document, a program of class collaboration in rural areas."[147] Similarly, Ranadive denounces the Andhra Communists' theory that only the big bourgeoisie is collaborating with imperialism while other sections of the bourgeoisie are its victims and can therefore be included in the united front as "open advocacy of class collaboration."[148] Quite rightly, Ranadive accuses the Andhra Committee of forgetting the dominant contradiction between the exploiters and the exploited,[149] which is asserted by Marxism, and the obliteration of which is, indeed, a Maoist contribution to "Marxism"-Leninism.

Ranadive's attack on Mao, July 1949. The Ranadive Politburo had, in its first two statements, assailed the bases of the neo-Maoist strategy. It had, in its third one, attacked "revisionism" in the CPI and other Communist parties. It had now, in the fourth statement, come to grips with the Andhra document itself and thus again with Maoist theory. If, as is likely, its chief purpose was to launch a counterattack against its Andhra rivals, it could have stopped at this point. However, for reasons on which we can only speculate, Ranadive chose to go further and attack directly the Maoist and neo-Maoist theory and strategy and, indeed, Mao Tse-tung himself. So important is this event in the historical sequence we are discussing, so astounding is the attack by the unsuccessful leader of a party of a few thousand members on the head of the powerful Chinese Communist Party and

architect of the greatest Communist success since the Bolshevik Revolution on the eve of his victory, that it is well worth our while to
reproduce the most important passages in full—especially since the
original document is difficult to obtain and only fragmentary quotations or brief references may be found in the secondary literature.[150]

Quoting the passage of the Andhra document that credited Mao
with having formulated a new theory and strategy,[151] the Ranadive
Politburo statement replies:

> Firstly, we must state emphatically that the Communist Party of
> India has accepted Marx, Engels, Lenin and Stalin as the authori-
> tative sources of Marxism. It has not discovered new sources of
> Marxism beyond these. Nor for that matter is there any Commu-
> nist Party which declares adherence to the so-called theory of new
> democracy alleged to be propounded by Mao and declares it to be
> a new addition to Marxism.[152]

This tends to confirm our impression that Ranadive could never
have completely understood Zhukov's neo-Maoist application of the
Zhdanov thesis to the colonial areas, and was relying on Zhdanov's
1947 speech itself, which gave him little practical guidance but which,
it seems, he had no doubt he was interpreting correctly. He leans
heavily on it as he proceeds:

> . . . . Singularly enough there was no reference to this new addition
> to Marxism in the conference of Nine Parties in Europe. Under
> these circumstances it is very wrong for a section of the leadership
> of the Central Committee to take upon itself the task of recom-
> mending new discoveries which one of the most authoritative con-
> ferences of Marxists has not thought fit to recommend. . . . It is
> impermissible for Communists to talk lightly about new discoveries,
> enrichment, because such claims have proved too often to be a thin
> cloak for revisionism (Tito, Browder, etc.).
>   Secondly, the documents of the Andhra Secretariat . . . do not
> even mention by a word that a Conference of leading Communist
> Parties including the CPSU(B) took place, that at that Confer-
> ence, Zhdanov submitted a report explaining the nature of People's
> Democracies . . . . A very precise class character of People's Democ-
> racy is given there—a characterization which excludes the bourgeoisie
> from power . . . .*

Having now affirmed his own orthodoxy and condemned and ridi-

---

* "Struggle for People's Democracy and Socialism," *Communist, II* No. 4 (June–
July 1949) , 77–78. We already noted that not only did Zhdanov's report deal with
the Eastern European satellites after the Communist seizure of power rather than
colonial countries before Communist assumption of power but that its class analysis
was anything but precise and that it by no means clearly excluded the bourgeoisie.
See p. 29 and the footnote on pp. 64–65, above.

culed Mao's additions to Marxism by mentioning him in one breath with Tito and Browder rather than with Marx, Engels, Lenin, and Stalin, Ranadive is finally ready to switch his attack from the Andhra Committee directly to Mao:

> This is not the place to sit in judgment over the formulations of Comrade Mao in his *New Democracy*. At the same time since the Andhra Secretariat quotes Mao against the understanding of world situation and People's Democracies as given by Zhdanov and CPSU(B), it is necessary to examine some of the formulations.
> It must be admitted that some of Mao's formulations are such that no Communist Party can accept them; they are in contradiction to the world understanding of the Communist Parties.[153]

He then quotes from the Andhra document the passage from Mao saying that the Chinese Communist Party promotes the development of capitalism.[154] He calls it a "horrifying formulation" and says that "no Marxist can ever agree with this reactionary formulation." He asks: "Are we to understand that while Communists in Europe, USSR, India fight world capitalism, the CCP proposes to rebuild it in China?"[155] Is this a return to the theory that capitalism must run its full course before socialism can be established, and a revision of Lenin's theory of the colonies going to socialism without passing through capitalism? It is, according to Ranadive, elementary Marxism that the class dominating economically dominates politically; thus, by promoting capitalism, one promotes the rule of capitalism in the state, a rule that can exist only in the form of fascism in China at the present time. It almost seems as if Mao is being unmasked as a fascist by Ranadive, who goes on to declare that "it is obvious that this idea of promoting capitalism is reactionary and counterrevolutionary."[156] The best Ranadive can say about Mao is that he is right in stressing that socialism cannot be introduced immediately but that he confuses toleration of commodity production under people's rule with promoting capitalism.[157]

Ranadive centers his attack on Mao on the latter's attitude toward the bourgeoisie and capitalism, thus apparently recognizing that this is the most characteristic aspect of Maoism and neo-Maoism. But, as we have already seen when he sought to equate Joshi's "right" and the Andhra Committee's neo-Maoist strategy under the label of revisionism or reformism, he does not seem to understand that a friendly attitude toward capitalism in conjunction with a united front from below against the bourgeois parties (the neo-Maoist strategy) differs radically from its combination with a united front from above with bourgeois parties (the old "right" strategy).

Ranadive also assails the Chinese Communists when he accuses the Andhra Committee of basing its strategy on the peasantry and not taking proletarian hegemony seriously:

> Why had the Chinese to go through the protracted civil war? Just because the leadership of the Chinese Communist Party at times failed to fight for the hegemony of the proletariat, for bringing the majority of the masses in alliance and under the leadership of the proletariat, because it followed tactical policies which led to a disaster.[158]

Again he shows that he does not distinguish between the old "right" and the neo-Maoist strategy, for he is here attacking Mao, and the Andhra Communists who are following Mao, with what appears to be a reference primarily to the "right" period of the Chinese Communist Party.   Characteristically, he supports this with long quotations of the criticism of the Chinese Communist Party's "opportunism" in not being sufficiently independent of the Kuomintang and the bourgeoisie from the Thesis on the Colonial Movement of the ("left") Sixth Congress of the Communist International of 1928.[159]

Possible reasons for Ranadive's attack on Mao. The question inevitably arises as to why Ranadive seemed to go deliberately out of his way to attack Mao.   Naturally, no definite answer can be given; but the most obvious explanation should not be completely excluded, at least as a partial one.   Ranadive was engaged in a serious conflict with the Andhra Provincial Committee of the CPI.   Once this conflict reached the level of theory and strategy, it was almost impossible to avoid the issue of Maoism, since the Andhra Communists openly proclaimed their adherence to Maoism and defended their strategy by reliance on the Chinese example.   Yet it seems that Ranadive went beyond what was necessary when he attacked Mao himself.   We can hardly credit him with enough intellectual honesty to justify us in assuming that he did so merely because he felt that he ought to go to the very source of the theories he was opposing.   Ranadive's repeated references to the first meeting of the Cominform, to Zhdanov's report given there, and to the Communist Party of the Soviet Union, all of which he seeks to line up, with himself behind them, against Mao, make it fairly clear that he felt he enjoyed Moscow's support.

Beyond this point one can only speculate.   It is quite possible that, although Ranadive received no support or encouragement from Moscow, he was sure that his own "left" interpretation of the Zhdanov speech was the sole correct and possible one, and that, seeing the differences between it and Maoism (and neo-Maoism), he felt quite safe in attacking Maoism and neo-Maoism. Ruth Fischer states flatly that Ranadive, "in the belief that a discussion on the character of the Chinese Communist Party and the state regime it was setting up was going on between Moscow and Peking, hoped to curry Moscow's favor by taking sides against the Mao Party."[160] This, too, is a possible explanation of Ranadive's action, but it does not answer the question whether Ranadive was right or wrong in believing that such a discussion was in progress. On the other hand, it is possible that Ranadive was actually receiving support from Moscow. Again, various possibilities are open. It may have been a case of tacit approval or active encouragement, or even, as Franz Borkenau asserts, of Ranadive's having been left in power by Moscow precisely because of his bitter enmity toward Mao.[161]

There is also the question whether Ranadive had full Soviet support or only that of an anti-Mao faction in Moscow. Ruth Fischer believes that Ranadive acted with the encouragement of a particular Moscow group, hoping that he could gain favor by attacking the Chinese Communists, who were then, she states, the subject of secret Moscow discussions.[162] She couples this with the rather questionable explanation that at the time of Ranadive's attack on Mao (July 1949) the Chinese Communists were executing a retreat and there was no indication of their ultimate triumph. Both Borkenau and Fischer clearly imply that Ranadive was Zhdanov's man and that Zhdanov headed the "left," anti-Mao faction in Moscow. That Ranadive may well have conceived of himself as playing this role does not necessarily prove the correctness of the theory—though its falsity cannot be proved either. We have already noted in the preceding chapter that Zhdanov's report to the Cominform was by no means clearly "leftist," as distinguished from neo-Maoist, in character, and that it was applied to the colonial areas in an essentially neo-Maoist manner by Zhukov. But even if Zhdanov (who, incidentally, had died almost a year before Ranadive's attack on Mao) was not anti-Maoist, he may possibly have been anti-Mao; his attitude toward the neo-Maoist strategy need not necessarily reflect his attitude toward the Chinese Communists and their leader, a subject of which we know nothing. It is clear that so many unknown factors enter into a consideration of the relationships between Zhdanov and Mao and between Ranadive and Zhdanov that it is best to admit ignorance on them, important as it would be to have some answers to the questions raised.

Some anti-Maoist but pro-Chinese Communist documents. The four Politburo statements of 1949 were the most characteristic documents of the CPI's "left" period. Before we leave that period, we may briefly examine some documents that, at first glance, seem to constitute a retreat from the extreme position of July 1949.

In the September-October 1949 issue of *Communist* there appeared a short article by G. Voitinsky, presumably reprinted from a Soviet publication, as much of the contents of *Communist* was, entitled "Chinese Communist Party in the Vanguard of Fight for Peace and Democracy."[163]   The inclusion of this piece praising the Chinese Communists in the issue of the CPI's monthly following the one denouncing Mao could hardly have been a coincidence, and at first it would almost seem to repudiate the latter.   Upon closer inspection of the article it appears more likely, however, that its appearance in *Communist* was designed to prove both that Ranadive was not opposed to Chinese Communism but only to some of its doctrines and that his own doctrines were "correct," that is, approved in Moscow.   It may well have been carefully selected for the support it seems to lend to some of Ranadive's main points in his preceding debate with the Andhra Committee.

Thus, Ranadive's belief in a one-step revolution with socialism as its goal, as opposed to any New Democracy preserving capitalism, is echoed in statements that the Chinese Communist victories are "leading China toward Socialism,"[164] and that "under the leadership of the Communist Party the entire economic system in town and countryside is being turned away from capitalism in the direction of Socialist development."[165]   Like Ranadive, Voitinsky gives some appearance of viewing the bourgeoisie as an enemy when he speaks of the fight "by China's democratic forces against the camp of feudal-bourgeois reaction and American imperialism."[166]   He does not mention the national bourgeoisie as a member of the united front, but speaks only of "an alliance between the working class and peasantry, with the workers leading the entire liberation movement (through the Communist Party) ";[167] and he even states that the history of the Chinese Communist Party is "the history of the struggle of the Chinese working class for hegemony."[168]   Finally, the article gives strong support to Ranadive's insistence that the Soviet Union rather than China must furnish the leading example to Indian Communists.   It emphasizes the point that the Chinese themselves followed the Russian example, and quotes Mao as saying that the Communist Party of the Soviet Union "is our finest teacher from whom we must learn"[169] and that "we must take the path of the Russians."[170]

Actually, the Voitinsky article is not wholly opposed to the neo-Maoist strategy.   It speaks of "the anti-imperialist, anti-feudal revolution, for the establishment of a people's democratic power and complete national sovereignty,"[171] and of the Chinese Communists enjoying "the wide support of all the democratic and anti-imperialist groups and organizations."[172]   But its omission of any more direct mention of the four-class appeal is striking, and, by and large, it seems to serve Ranadive's purposes admirably.

The article's praise for Mao's violent tactics is also to Ranadive's liking.   It should be noted that, although he attacks every essential element of the Maoist and neo-Maoist strategy in his four Politburo statements, Ranadive never takes issue with the use of armed struggle. As will become clear in subsequent chapters, armed struggle is not an essential aspect of the neo-Maoist strategy, and on it Ranadive wholly agreed with the Andhra Communists and with Mao.   Throughout 1948 and 1949 there appeared frequent reports in the CPI's weekly *People's Age* hailing the advances of the Chinese Communists and also the armed Communist uprisings in Burma, Malaya, and Indonesia; but these articles combine no appreciation of the pro-bourgeois essentials of the neo-Maoist strategy with that of its armed tactics. Thus, an editorial written when the four Politburo statements were drawn up and entitled "March of China's Liberation Army Heralds Doom of Colonial Rule in Asia and the World"[173] speaks of the "imperialists relying upon the treacherous national bourgeoisie who in return for petty concessions had everywhere struck a deal with the imperialists in order to crush the revolutionary forces of their own peoples" and asserts that "the final victory of the Chinese revolution . . . will decisively shift the balance of forces in favor of the fighting peoples of Asia and against the imperialist-bourgeois axis."

A final example of Ranadive's stand favoring the Chinese Communists which does not contradict his opposition to the Maoist strategy is a message of greetings he sent to Mao Tse-tung on October 12, 1949, on the occasion of the formation of the Communist People's Government of China.[174]   It does not in any real sense mark a retreat from Ranadive's anti-Mao position, but seems to be merely a routine affair. The issue of whether the bourgeoisie is on the side of imperialism is sidestepped by a reference to "the doom of foreign imperialism and its national agents on the continent of Asia"; and the remark that "the victory scored by the Communist Party of China is the victory of Marxism-Leninism, of the Stalinist Line," can, given Ranadive's interpretation of what constitutes the Stalinist line and Marxism-Leninism, even be understood as a hint that the Communist victory in China was achieved in spite of rather than as a result of the Maoist strategy. Ranadive could not have been very popular in Peking in this period, and Mao's reply to him, dated October 19, 1949, is very brief.[175]   It does, however, in one sentence, which starts with a somewhat less than profound statement, manage to reassert that China can serve as an example to the Indian Communists: "The Indian people is one of the great Asian people with a long history and a vast population; her fate in the past and her path to the future are similar to those of China in many points."*

In this chapter we have seen how the "left" strategy adopted by the CPI in December 1947 as a result of an earlier Soviet policy shift grew, largely as a consequence of intra-Party developments, more and more extreme under the leadership of Ranadive in 1948 and 1949. We have noted that in 1948, before it had become quite so clear as it did in 1949 how sharply opposed to the neo-Maoist strategy this "left" strategy was, the latter was neither wholeheartedly approved nor disapproved of in Moscow. In the next chater we shall turn to the gradual crystallization of the Soviet attitude toward the neo-Maoist strategy during 1949, the events marking the completion of that process at the end of 1949, and their spectacular results within the CPI at the beginning of 1950.

NOTES FOR CHAPTER 3

1. "Review of the Second Congress of Communist Party of India," *People's Age,* March 21, 1948, Supplement, pp. 2–3.

2. Communist Party of India, *Political Thesis,* adopted at the Second Congress, Calcutta, February 28–March 6, 1948 (Bombay, 1949). For a summary of the Political Thesis, see a Statement of Policy issued by the newly elected Central Committee after the Congress, "Communist Party Calls on People to Renew Fight for Real Independence and Freedom," *People's Age,* March 21, 1948, pp. 1, 11. Another "left" document of this period is the pamphlet by B. T. Ranadive, *Nehru Gov't. declares War against Toilers* (Bombay: M. B. Rao, April 1948).

3. "Review of the Second Congress of Communist Party of India," *op. cit.,* p. 4.

4. *Political Thesis,* p. 4.

5. Joshi, "Letter to Comrade Ranadive" (February 10, 1950), *Views,* pp. 34–35.

6. *Political Thesis,* p. 40.

7. *Ibid.,* p. 60.

8. *Ibid.*

9. "Draft Political Thesis for the Second Congress of the Communist Party of India," *People's Age,* February 15, 1948, Supplement, p. 7.

* Mao continues with a prediction which, coming from the head of a government, is startlingly undiplomatic toward the Nehru government, but of less significance for the question of Communist strategy: "I firmly believe that relying on the brave Communist Party of India and the unity and struggle of all Indian patriots, India will certainly not remain long under the yoke of imperialism and its collaborators. Like free China, a free India will one day emerge in the Socialist and People's Democratic family; that day will end the imperialist reactionary era in the history of mankind."

10. *Political Thesis*, p. 44.
11. *Ibid.*, p. 29; also pp. 39 and 59.
12. *Ibid.*, p. 43.
13. *Ibid.*, p. 37.
14. *Ibid.*, p. 92.
15. *Ibid.*, p. 21.
16. *Ibid.*, p. 24.
17. *Ibid.*, p. 13.
18. *Ibid.*, p. 32.
19. *Ibid.*
20. *Ibid.*, p. 13.
21. *Ibid.*, pp. 78–80.
22. *Ibid.*, p. 48.
23. *Ibid.*, p. 8.
24. "Draft Political Thesis," *op. cit.*, p. 2.
25. *Political Thesis,* p. 8.
26. *Ibid.*, p. 94; see also similar remarks in Ranadive's report, "Review of the Second Congress of Communist Party of India," *op. cit.*, p. 2.
27. *Political Thesis*, p. 61.
28. *Ibid.*, p. 63.
29. *Ibid.*, p. 65.
30. *Ibid.*, p. 62.
31. *Ibid.*, p. 8.
32. "Review of the Second Congress of Communist Party of India," *op. cit.*, p. 3.
33. Bhovani Sen's report on Pakistan, *ibid.*
34. *Political Thesis,* p. 40.
35. *Ibid.*, p. 2.
36. *Ibid.*, p. 4.
37. *Ibid.*, p. 6.
38. *Ibid.*, p. 8.
39. Joshi, "Letter to Foreign Comrades," *Views*, p. 6.
40. "Review of the Second Congress of Communist Party of India," *op. cit.*, p. 2.
41. Joshi, "Letter to Foreign Comrades," *Views*, p. 3.
42. *Ibid.*, p. 19.
43. Quoted in Limaye, *Communist Party*, p. 61; see also *ibid.*, p. 68, and Masani, *The Communist Party of India*, pp. 94–95.
44. "Review of the Second Congress of Communist Party of India," *op. cit.*, p. 4.
45. *Ibid.*, pp. 3–4.
46. *Ibid.*, p. 4.
47. *Ibid.*
48. *Ibid.*
49. "Slanderous Report of Differences in Party, P. C. Joshi's Statement," *People's Age*, March 14, 1948, p. 1.
50. Joshi, "Letter to Foreign Comrades," *Views*, p. 2.
51. *Ibid.*, p. 5.
52. Joshi, "Letter to Comrade Ranadive," *ibid.*, p. 31.
53. "Congress of the Communist Party of India," *For a Lasting Peace, for a People's Democracy!*, April 15, 1948, p. 3.
54. "Second Congress of the Communist Party of India," *World News and Views*, XXVIII, No. 13 (April 3, 1948), 135.

55. D. Cambey, "Repressions against the Communist Party of India," *For a Lasting Peace, for a People's Democracy!*, May 15, 1948, p. 4; see also "Banning of Communist Press in India," *ibid.*, August 15, 1948, p. 6; "Zaiavlenie Tsentral'nogo komiteta Indiiskoi Kompartii," *Pravda*, September 19, 1948, p. 4; "What's Happening in Hyderabad?," *World News and Views*, XXVIII, No. 38 (September 25, 1948), 423.

56. V. Balabushevich, "The Anti-Labor Campaign in India and Pakistan," *Trud*, November 21, 1948, in *Soviet Press Translations*, IV, No. 4 (February 15, 1949), 108–110.

57. E. Steinberg, "Lenin und Stalin über den nationalen Freiheitskampf der Völker des Ostens," *Neue Welt* (Berlin), IV, No. 1 (January 1949), 28–31.

58. I. Alexandrow, "Die Volksbefreiungskräfte Asiens im Kampf für Unabhängigkeit und Demokratie," *ibid.*, III, No. 24 (December 1948), 15–21.

59. Mao Tse-tung, "China's New Democratic Revolution" (Speech to a meeting of cadres of the Shansi-Suiyuan Liberated Area), *World News and Views*, XXVII, No. 33 (August 21, 1948), 355–356.

60. R. Palme Dutt, "Whither India?," *Labour Monthly*, XXX, No. 6 (June 1948), 161–170.

61. R. Palme Dutt, "Struggle of Colonial Peoples Against Imperialism," *For a Lasting Peace, for a People's Democracy!*, October 15, 1948, p. 5.

62. R. Palme Dutt, "Right-Wing Social Democracy in the Service of Imperialism," *ibid.*, November 1, 1948, pp. 6–7.

63. Joshi, "Letter to Foreign Comrades," *Views*, p. 15.

64. Ministry of Home Affairs, Government of India, *Communist Violence in India* (September 1949), p. 10.

65. *Ibid.*, p. 26.

66. *Ibid.*, p. 28. Other CPI circulars of this period are quoted in Limaye, *Communist Party*, pp. 61–62. See also Masani, *The Communist Party of India*, pp. 90–94.

67. *Ibid.*, p. 91; Jean A. Curran, Jr., "Dissension Among India's Communists," *Far Eastern Survey*, XIX, No. 13 (July 12, 1950), p. 133; Bowles, *Ambassador's Report*, p. 125.

68. A membership of 89,260 was claimed at the Second CPI Congress. "Congress of the Communist Party of India," *For a Lasting Peace, for a People's Democracy!*, April 15, 1948, p. 3.

69. Joshi, "Letter to Foreign Comrades," *Views*, p. 18.

70. Curran, *op. cit.*, p. 133.

71. Bowles, *Ambassador's Report*, p. 125.

72. Joshi, "Letter to Foreign Comrades," *Views*, p. 3.

73. *Ibid.*, p. 4.

74. *Ibid.*

75. Quoted in Limaye, *Communist Party*, p. 62.

76. Joshi, "Letter to Foreign Comrades," *Views*, p. 28.

77. *Ibid.*, p. 29.

78. *Ibid.*, p. 17.

79. *Ibid.*, p. 22.

80. *Ibid.*, p. 24.

81. J. M., "The People Fight Back," *World News and Views*, XXIX, No. 35 (August 27, 1949), 416–417.

82. Clare and Harris Wofford, Jr., *India Afire* (New York: John Day Co., 1951), pp. 105–124; Bowles, *Ambassador's Report*, pp. 126–127.

83. *Ibid.;* Curran, *op. cit.,* p. 133; Chanakya, *Indian Revolution* (Bombay: National Information and Publications, 1951), p. 217.

84. Joshi, "Letter to Foreign Comrades," *Views,* pp. 20–22.

85. "Statement of Editorial Board of *Communist* on Anti-Leninist Criticism of Comrade Mao Tse-tung," *Communist,* III, No. 3 (July–August 1950), 7.

86. Description of the Andhra document, *ibid.;* see also *ibid.,* p. 9.

87. Quoted from the Andhra document in "Struggle for People's Democracy and Socialism—Some Questions of Strategy and Tactics," *Communist,* II, No. 4 (June–July 1949), 83; see also *ibid.,* p. 60, and "Statement of Editorial Board," *op. cit.,* p. 10.

88. Description of Andhra document, *ibid.*

89. *Ibid.,* p. 9.

90. "Struggle for People's Democracy and Socialism," *op. cit.,* pp. 61–62.

91. Quoted from Andhra document, *ibid.,* p. 77.

92. *Ibid.,* pp. 71–72; see also *ibid.,* pp. 37 and 61–62.

93. *Ibid.,* pp. 37, 61–66; "Statement of Editorial Board," *op. cit.,* pp. 8–9.

94. *Ibid.,* p. 9.

95. Quoted from the Andhra document in "Struggle for People's Democracy and Socialism," *op. cit.,* p. 78. The passage may also be found in Mao Tse-tung, *The Fight for a New China* (New York: New Century Publishers, 1945), p. 38.

96. Joshi, "Letter to Foreign Comrades," *Views,* p. 2.

97. "On People's Democracy," *Communist,* II, No. 1 (January 1949), 1–12. "On the Agrarian Question in India," *ibid.,* pp. 13–53.

98. "On People's Democracy," *ibid.,* pp. 1 and 4–6.

99. *Ibid.,* pp. 7–8.

100. *Ibid.,* p. 11.

101. *Ibid.,* p. 7.

102. *Ibid.,* p. 8.

103. *Ibid.,* p. 10.

104. *Ibid.,* p. 1.

105. *Ibid.,* p. 7.

106. *Ibid.,* p. 9.

107. "On the Agrarian Question in India," *ibid.,* p. 17; see also *ibid.,* p. 13.

108. *Ibid.,* p. 16.

109. *Ibid.,* p. 51.

110. *Ibid.,* pp. 44–45.

111. *Ibid.,* p. 33.

112. *Ibid.,* pp. 36–37 and 49; see also *ibid.,* p. 15.

113. *Ibid.,* p. 62; see also *ibid.,* p. 15.

114. *Ibid.,* pp. 47–48 and 51–53.

115. "Struggle Against Revisionism Today, in the Light of Lenin's Teachings," *ibid.,* No. 2 (February 1949), 53–66.

116. *Ibid.,* p. 54.

117. *Ibid.,* p. 58.

118. *Ibid.*

119. See p. 39, above.

120. "Struggle Against Revisionism Today," *op. cit.,* p. 59.

121. *Ibid.,* p. 63.

122. *Ibid.,* p. 59.

123. *Ibid.,* p. 65.

124. *Ibid.*, p. 62.

125. *Ibid.*, p. 65.

126. "Struggle for People's Democracy and Socialism—Some Questions of Strategy and Tactics," *ibid.*, No. 4 (June–July 1949) , 21–89.

127. *Ibid.*, p. 24.

128. *Ibid.*, p. 25.

129. *Ibid.*

130. *Ibid.*, p. 49.

131. *Ibid.*, p. 30; see also *ibid.*, pp. 30–33, 39, 68–69.

132. *Ibid.*, p. 34.

133. *Ibid.*, p. 35.

134. *Ibid.*

135. *Ibid.*

136. *Ibid.*, pp. 36–38.

137. *Ibid.*, p. 54.

138. *Ibid.*, p. 89.

139. *Ibid.*, p. 61.

140. *Ibid.*, pp. 83–84.

141. *Ibid.*, pp. 57–58.

142. *Ibid.*, p. 88; see also *ibid.*, pp. 54–56. Most of the above quotation may also be found in Robert C. North, *Moscow and Chinese Communists* (Stanford: Stanford University Press, 1953) , p. 242.

143. "Struggle for People's Democracy and Socialism," *op. cit.*, p. 89.

144. *Ibid.*

145. *Ibid.*, p. 88.

146. *Ibid.*, p. 84.

147. *Ibid.*, p. 72.

148. *Ibid.*, p. 37; see also *ibid.*, pp. 61–66.

149. *Ibid.*, p. 70.

150. E.g. Curran, *op. cit.*, p. 135; Limaye, *Communist Party*, p. 67; Masani, *The Communist Party of India*, p. 101; Masani, "The Communist Party in India," *Pacific Affairs*, XXIV, No. 1 (March 1951) , footnote on p. 29; Franz Borkenau, "The Chances of a Mao-Stalin Rift," *Commentary*, XIV (August 1952) , 122; Fischer, "The Indian Communist Party," *Far Eastern Survey*, XXII, No. 7 (June 1953) , 82, and "The Indian Communist Party," Russian Research Center, Harvard University, Minutes of the Seminar Meeting, July 11, 1952; Frank Moraes, "Can Communism Conquer India?," *United Nations World*, VII, No. 7 (July 1953) , 27; North, *op. cit.*, p. 243; Bowles, *Ambassador's Report*, p. 128.

151. Quoted on p. 62, above.

152. "Struggle for People's Democracy and Socialism," *op. cit.*, p. 77.

153. *Ibid.*, p. 78.

154. Quoted on p. 63, above.

155. "Struggle for People's Democracy and Socialism," *op. cit.*, p. 78.

156. *Ibid.*, p. 79.

157. *Ibid.*, pp. 80–81.

158. *Ibid.*, p. 84.

159. *Ibid.*, pp. 84–87.

160. Fischer, "The Indian Communist Party," Harvard Russian Research Center Seminar, p. 16.

161. Borkenau, *op. cit.*, p. 122.

162. Fischer, "The Indian Communist Party," *Far Eastern Survey,* XXII, No. 7 (June 1953), 79–84, on p. 82.

163. *Communist,* II, No. 5 (September–October 1949), 78–81.

164. *Ibid.,* p. 78.

165. *Ibid.,* p. 80.

166. *Ibid.,* p. 78.

167. *Ibid.,* p. 79.

168. *Ibid.*

169. *Ibid.,* p. 78.

170. *Ibid.,* p. 79.

171. *Ibid.*

172. *Ibid.,* p. 80.

173. *People's Age,* December 5, 1948, p. 3.

174. "Message of Greetings from Comrade B. T. Ranadive to Comrade Mao Tse-tung," *Communist,* III, No. 1 (January 1950), 108–109, reprinted in Masani, *The Communist Party of India,* pp. 96–97.

175. "Comrade Mao Tse-tung's Reply to Comrade B. T. Ranadive," *Communist,* III, No. 1 (January 1950), 110.

— 4 ————————————————

THE SHIFT TO THE NEO-MAOIST

STRATEGY (1949–1950)

I. THE SOVIET VIEW IN 1949

We have seen that, beginning in the middle of 1947, when the "right" strategy of the united front from above was being abandoned and throughout 1948 both the neo-Maoist strategy of including sections of the bourgeoisie in the united front from below and the "left" strategy of excluding the entire bourgeoisie from that front were being advanced by different Soviet writers. We have also noted that, beginning in 1948, there were indications of neo-Maoist influence on the advocates of the "left" strategy to the extent that they now tended to confine their condemnations to the "big" bourgeoisie. In such a gradual process, it is impossible to set a particular date by which the "left" strategy had completely yielded to the neo-Maoist one, but it is clear that the process had continued in the early part of 1949 and, as we shall now show, was substantially completed by the middle of that year when the neo-Maoist strategy emerged as the sole one approved by Moscow for the colonial areas.

Reasons for the adoption of the neo-Maoist strategy. Among the factors responsible for the adoption of the neo-Maoist strategy in Moscow in 1949 the growing victories of the Chinese Communists must have been an important one, especially since more and more attention was now being paid in Moscow to Chinese Communist statements, and the Maoist strategy thus became more widely known and better understood. This alone would not have led to the adoption of neo-Maoism, however, had Moscow not realized that the "left" strategy, with its concentration on the local bourgeoisie in each country, which is not even necessarily anti-Soviet, could divert Communist parties from the important battle against the United States to relatively unimportant and possibly even harmful engagements—fighting (to borrow General Omar Bradley's phrase) "the wrong war, . . . at the wrong time, and

86

with the wrong enemy." Neo-Maoism, with its concentration on foreign imperialism as the main enemy and its reliance on virtually everyone, regardless of class, who is anti-imperialist, was recognized as the strategy best suited to the needs of the Soviet Union's anti-American foreign policy. It is conceivable that Ranadive's Politburo statements of early 1949 coupled with the practical failure of his policy may have helped Moscow understand the disadvantages of the "left" strategy as compared to the neo-Maoist one.[1]

Liu Shao-chi's "Internationalism and Nationalism" in Pravda, June 1949. Two concurrent events in June 1949 herald the complete acceptance by Moscow of the neo-Maoist strategy—at least a full month, be it noted, before Ranadive published his most vigorous attack on it and its originator. One June 7, 8, and 9 *Pravda* published Liu Shao-chi's "Internationalism and Nationalism."[2] This pamphlet by the foremost theoretician of the Chinese Communist Party, devoted to a discussion of bourgeois nationalism and proletarian patriotism and internationalism, was occasioned by Tito's expulsion from the Cominform and had been written as early as November 1948. Since it fully supports the Soviet position against Tito, there would have been ample reason for its earlier publication in the Soviet press at a time when all Communist parties protested their loyalty to Moscow against the Titoist heresy. It is most likely that the delay in publication was caused by Moscow's unwillingness at an earlier date to give its official approval to a few lines at the end of the pamphlet. Concentrating entirely on the inclusion of sections of the bourgeoisie in the united front from below, the most characteristic feature of the Maoist and neo-Maoist strategy, and worded in the unequivocal terms of a directive, these lines are indeed far more outspoken and clearer than anything hitherto published on the subject in Moscow. The fact that they now received official Soviet sanction by being reprinted in *Pravda* is, therefore, of all the more importance. These lines read:

> Of course, the Communists in other colonial and semi-colonial countries such as India, Burma, Siam, the Philippines, Indonesia, Indo-China, South Korea, etc., must for the sake of their national interests similarly adopt a firm and irreconcilable policy against national betrayal by the reactionary section of the bourgeoisie, especially the big bourgeoisie, which has already surrendered to imperialism. If this were not done, it would be a grave mistake.
>
> On the other hand, the Communists in these countries should enter into an anti-imperialist alliance with that section of the national bourgeoisie which is still opposing imperialism and which does not oppose the anti-imperialist struggle of the masses of the people. Should the Communists fail to do so in earnest, should

they, to the contrary, oppose or reject such an alliance, it would also constitute a grave mistake.   Such an alliance must be established in all sincerity even if it should be of an unreliable, temporary and unstable nature.[3]

The meeting of the USSR Academy of Sciences of June 1949.   The day before these paragraphs appeared in *Pravda* there opened a joint meeting of the learned councils of the Institute of Economics and the Pacific Institute of the USSR Academy of Sciences devoted to problems of the national and colonial movement since World War II.   A similar meeting of the Academy exactly two years earlier had provided the first indication of both the shift away from the "right" strategy and the divisions between the advocates of the new neo-Maoist strategy, notably Zhukov, and those of the old "left" strategy, notably Bala- bushevich and Dyakov.   The present meeting demonstrated the sub- stantial end of this division.   It was opened by Zhukov, the director of the Pacific Institute, with a general report on "Problems of the National-Colonial Struggle since the Second World War."[4]   We are not surprised to find him expressing the neo-Maoist point of view. He speaks of the deepening crisis of the colonial system and the fact that the national liberation movement has "entered a new and higher stage of its development" as indicated by the use of armed struggle in "a number of colonial and dependent countries."[5]   Then Zhukov assigns only one section of the bourgeoisie to the side of the enemy: "the big bourgeoisie has finally gone over into the camp of imperi- alist reaction."[6]   He makes his neo-Maoist position even clearer when he explicitly includes another section in the united front: "In the struggle for People's Democracy in the colonies and semi-colonies are united not only the workers, the peasantry, the urban petty-bour- geoisie, the intelligentsia, but even certain sections of the middle bourgeoisie which is interested in saving itself from cut-throat foreign competition and from imperialist oppression."[7]   The differences be- tween this neo-Maoist view and Ranadive's "left" view are also striking where Zhukov states that the people's democratic revolution in the colonies and semi-colonies is first and foremost an anti-imperialist and anti-feudal one, and that it may therefore take longer to pass to the solution of socialist tasks than in central and southeastern Europe, though the general pattern of social development is said to be the same in both areas.[8]

Zhukov's report was followed by another general one by Maslen- nikov "On the Leading Role of the Working Class in the National Liberation Movement of the Colonial Peoples,"[9] while all the other numerous reports at the Academy meeting dealt with individual underdeveloped countries. Maslennikov illustrates his advocacy of the neo-Maoist strategy primarily by references to the experience of the Chinese Communists—but preceded by an assertion of the primacy of the Soviet example: "The experience of the revolutionary struggle in Russia was and still is of tremendous significance for the national liberation movement of the colonies, semi-colonies and the dependent countries." Their successes and "above all the historic victory of the Chinese people . . . are the most striking demonstrations of the triumph of the Leninist-Stalinist teachings on the national-colonial revolution. . . ."[10] This report contains a number of references to the four-class strategy of the Chinese Communists, one of which is worth quoting:

A single united front, unprecedented in breadth and depth and unifying the workers, the peasants, the urban petty bourgeoisie, the national minorities and certain sections of the middle industrial and trading bourgeoisie was created inside the country. The petty and the middle bourgeoisie in China suffered oppression and persecution at the hands of the reactionary big bourgeoisie, the landlord class and the Kuomintang power (which was in the hands of monopoly capital). The petty and middle bourgeoisie is not or very little connected with imperialism. That is why this bourgeoisie, according to the definition of Mao Tse-tung "a real national bourgeoisie," enters into a united front of struggle against internal reaction and foreign imperialism.[11]

That this characteristic of Maoism is applicable not in China alone is made clear by Maslennikov when he points out that "in all the countries of the colonial world, the peasantry, the intelligentsia, the urban petty bourgeoisie, and that section of the national bourgeoisie which is coming forth against imperialism are rallying around the proletariat."[12]

Of great significance as marking the completion of the turn to the neo-Maoist strategy in Moscow is the report to the Academy on India, entitled "A New Stage in the National Liberation Struggle of the Peoples of India,"[13] for it was delivered by Balabushevich, who throughout the preceding period was the outstanding advocate of the "left" strategy in Moscow. Balabushevich has no difficulty in accepting the neo-Maoist postulate that the Communists' fight is directed against foreign imperialism and feudalism,[14] since he had never gone as far as Ranadive in regarding the Indian bourgeoisie as the main enemy. Interestingly enough, however, his main concern seems to be with feudalism rather than imperialism, and the main lesson he has learned from Mao is the emphasis on the agrarian revolution and armed struggle in the countryside, those elements of Maoism which, as we shall see, turned out in the long run not to be the essential ones of the neo-Maoist strategy but which were the very ones which were also most important to the Andhra Communists. "The peasantry is the most important driving force in the colonial revolution . . ."[15] Balabushevich proclaims, and he goes all out in his stress on the Telengana revolt. There, he says, the peasant movement "attained its highest peak"[16] and "assumed the character of an armed revolt and an agrarian revolution."[17] It was "the first attempt at creating People's Democracy in India and, although this attempt is limited in its scale and in its character, it has indisputably tremendous importance for the further development and intensification of the general democratic movement in India and Pakistan. The struggle in Telengana is the harbinger of the agrarian revolution and constitutes the most important content of the present stage of the national liberation struggle in India."[18]

When we turn to the essential element of the neo-Maoist strategy, the inclusion of a section of the bourgeoisie among the anti-imperialist forces, we get the impression that Balabushevich has not yet accepted neo-Maoism wholeheartedly. While generally referring to the "big" or "upper" bourgeoisie as the ally of imperialism, he repeatedly relapses into the use of "left" terminology, mentioning simply "the bourgeoisie" or "the capitalists" in this connection.[19] He goes so far as to call the "left" Second Congress of the CPI "an important step in the life of the Communist Party of India" which "demonstrated a big increase in the influence of the Communist Party"; and he even speaks approvingly of the non-Maoist united front it had demanded, an "alliance of the working class, the peasantry and the urban petty-bourgeoisie."[20]

However, at the end of his long report Balabushevich finally and, to be sure, very grudgingly takes the crucial step from the "left" to the neo-Maoist strategy of admitting a section of the bourgeoisie to the united front:

> The final going over of the Indian big bourgeoisie into the camp of reaction and imperialism does not exclude the fact that individual groupings in the national bourgeoisie can still at one time or another, during one or another period, become fellow-travellers with the democratic forces in their struggle against imperialism and its allies. . . . In the first instance, they comprise those elements of the bourgeoisie whose interests in particular run counter to those of foreign capital that is flowing increasingly into the country. It also comprises the rising bourgeoisie of those national regions of India which are more backward in their development. This bourgeoisie is dissatisfied with the predominance of the already

constituted monopolist groups. . . . These oppositional strata of
the Indian bourgeoisie ought not to be regarded in any way as reliable or stable members of the anti-imperialist camp.[21]

Especially when compared with Zhukov's and Maslennikov's passages
on the same subject, quoted above, it is strikingly evident that Balabushevich is reluctant to take this step and that he seeks to minimize
its importance by implying the relative insignificance and stressing
the unreliability of the sections of the bourgeoisie who might join the
proletariat, that is, the Communists. However, the test of adherence
to the neo-Maoist strategy is not necessarily belief in large and stable
bourgeois membership in the united front from below. The contention that any capitalists at all can join the proletariat, peasantry, and
petty-bourgeoisie, and that their interests, too, are represented by the
Communist party, radically distinguishes the neo-Maoist from the
"left" strategy. We are therefore justified in stating that with his
report to the Academy of Sciences in June 1949 Balabushevich has,
however reluctantly, become an advocate of neo-Maoism, and that the
differences between him and Zhukov, between the "left" and the neo-
Maoist strategy that had existed in Moscow for the past two years,
have now been resolved in favor of the latter.

Summing up the results of the session of the Academy, Zhukov
stated that the "controversy as to at what stage the colonial bourgeoisie begins to play a reactionary role can be solved only when an
answer is given to this main question" of "its attitude towards the
Soviet Union."[22] This, he states, is the determinant of the progressive
character of any social movement since the main enemy everywhere
is American imperialism. Here we have a remarkably frank answer,
devoid of the usual complicated social and economic analysis, to the
question of which parts of the bourgeoisie constitute the "national"
or "middle" bourgeoisie and which the "comprador" or "big" bourgeoisie. Pro-Soviet, anti-American capitalists make up the former;
anti-Soviet, pro-American ones the latter—it is as simple as that.
Zhukov's remark thus provides us with the most fundamental characterization of the neo-Maoist strategy as a grouping of all anti-
American forces regardless of class membership.*

The Cominform journal in favor of the neo-Maoist strategy. During
the months following June 1949 the pages of the Cominform journal
and *Pravda* show clearly, by featuring pronouncements of Chinese

* Liu Shao-chi, in his pamphlet mentioned above, even includes feudal elements
in this grouping, which is only logical if its prime purpose is anti-Americanism,
though less so if the revolution is regarded as anti-feudal. See footnote on p. 12,
above.

Communist leaders advancing it, that the neo-Maoist strategy now had Moscow's approval. Thus Mao's statement that "with the exception of the imperialists—feudal lords, bureaucratic bourgeoisie, Kuomintang reactionaries and their accomplices—all the rest of the people are our friends. We have a broad and strong revolutionary united front—so broad that it includes the working class, the peasantry, the petty-bourgeoisie and national bourgeoisie,"[23] made in a speech delivered on June 15, was reprinted. Two weeks later there appeared in full Mao's famous "The Dictatorship of People's Democracy," which states: "Who are 'the people'? At the present stage in China the people are the working class, the class of the peasantry, the petty-bourgeoisie and national bourgeoisie,"[24] and defines the internal enemy as "the lackeys of imperialism—the class of landlords and bureaucratic capital." A few weeks later General Chu-Teh told the readers of the Cominform journal, after speaking of the proletariat's alliance with the peasantry and petty bourgeoisie, that "under certain conditions, it is furthermore necessary, in the struggle against imperialism, to win over the national bourgeoisie or to neutralize it."[25] He expressly warned against "leftist adventurism" and "closed door" tendencies. Finally, an editorial on the Communist victory in China in the journal of the Cominform declared that the Chinese Communist Party, equipped with the teaching of Lenin and Stalin and basing itself on the experience of the USSR and the CPSU(B), had "rallied all sections of the Chinese people." Its victory "will inspire the peoples of the colonial and dependent countries to intensify the national liberation struggle. . . . The People's Republic of China will be their loyal friend and reliable bulwark in the struggle against imperialism."[26] It was thus made fairly clear to the Asian Communist parties that, while the Soviet Union remained paramount, they could also look to China for support.

Reports to the Academy on the "Crisis of the Colonial System." In the latter half of 1949 a number of reports were presented to the Pacific Institute of the Soviet Academy of Sciences on the "Crisis of the Colonial System"[27] that are strikingly similar to those given at the Academy's June session. Again the head of the Institute, Zhukov, submitted a general paper on the subject, entitled "Sharpening Crisis of the Colonial System after World War II."[28] Whereas in June he had merely spoken of armed struggle in "a number of colonial countries," he now draws a distinction between Southeast Asia and India, a matter that was, as we shall see, destined to be of considerable importance during the next period of the CPI's history. Zhukov states that armed struggle in the colonial countries has assumed the broadest sweep in Burma, Vietnam, Malaya, Indonesia, and the Philippines, but of India he merely says that the toiling masses are organizing themselves to defend their rights.[29]

The usual statement including part of the bourgeoisie in the united front again makes its appearance:

> It goes without saying that in the East, in the colonial and semi-colonial countries, it is possible to have a broader national front against imperialist forces than in the West. It can certainly include those strata of the bourgeoisie which have suffered from the ruin of local industry as a result of the flooding of the market by goods from the metropolitan country.*

Zhukov is far less hesitant in this matter than Balabushevich, although even he is never as outspoken as Mao and other Chinese spokesmen and is still often careless in referring to the "bourgeoisie" instead of the "big bourgeoisie" as an ally of imperialism. As in June, he makes the distinction between the European and the colonial people's democracies, with the latter farther removed from socialism and more concerned with bourgeois democratic, that is, anti-feudal and anti-imperialist, tasks;[30] and he again asserts unequivocally that "the main enemy of the national liberation movement in the colonies and semi-colonies is aggressive American imperialism."[31] Lastly, as is almost obligatory in Soviet pronouncements on the subject, Zhukov ascribes all Communist successes in the colonies to the "ideological and political support from the USSR. . . . This determines the entire development of the national-colonial struggles after the Second World War."[32] China, on the other hand, is mentioned only as bearing out this statement, not as influencing the rest of Asia.

The report on China in this collection, "China from a Semi-Colony to a People's Democracy" by G. Astafyev,[33] makes the membership of the national bourgeoisie in the united front fairly clear[34] and contains this important passage: "The Chinese people's liberation movement, which, in the conditions of a semi-colonial country, creatively applied the teachings of Lenin and Stalin . . . and which has profited from the tremendous experience of the CPSU(B) and on the basis of this achieved its present successes, is itself a vast treasury of revolutionary experience, which helps all the oppressed peoples of the East in their struggle against imperialism to choose the correct path, to avoid many mistakes, and to achieve their aims with less losses and in shorter

---

* *Crisis of the Colonial System* (Bombay: People's Publishing House, 1951), p. 73. In the long run, Zhukov, a Far-Eastern expert, has turned out to be wrong in drawing this distinction between the East and the West, for the neo-Maoist strategy has come to be applied in both areas.

time."[35] Preceded by a reference to "the peoples of Indo-China, Burma, Malaya and even Philippines, Indonesia and India"; this is so far one of the strongest exhortations to emanate from Moscow to the Asian Communist parties to follow what will soon be widely referred to as the "Chinese path," that is, the neo-Maoist strategy, an exhortation reinforced by the warning of the "mistakes" and "losses" involved in doing otherwise—for example, as Ranadive was still doing at the very time when this statement was made.

The report on India in this collection of the Pacific Institute was submitted by A. M. Dyakov,[36] who, like his colleague Balabushevich, as we have had occasion to note, had been an adherent of the "left" strategy. The similarity of approach of these two former "leftist" Soviet experts on India, now that they have to follow the neo-Maoist line, is striking. After a long review of the CPI's history notable chiefly for its various distortions and its criticism of the Party's "opportunism" during its prewar and postwar "right" periods, Dyakov turns to the present and, like Balabushevich, places his chief emphasis on the agrarian revolution and rural armed struggle aspects of Maoism: "The most characteristic and distinctive feature of postwar India is the tremendous growth and intensification of the peasant movement."[37] In "Telengana . . . a people's power was created for the first time in the history of India. . . . In Telengana, it was the Communists who stood at the head of the peasant and the national movement. Thus, the alliance of the working class with the peasantry has been established here with the leading role of the working class."* "The active struggle of the peasantry, passing over to an uprising in places and headed by the working class . . . is the most characteristic feature of the new stage and as a result of this it can be termed as an agrarian stage with complete justification."[38]

Dyakov may, except in his historical section, be somewhat more consistent than Balabushevich in the use of the term "big" bourgeoisie, but, like the latter, he still approvingly refers to the Second CPI Congress[39] and alleges that the influence of the CPI is growing

---

* *Ibid.*, p. 40. The usual Communist identification of the "working class" with the Communist party and the assumption, condemned, as we saw in the last chapter, by Ranadive in his attack on the Andhra Committee, that Communist leadership of the peasantry *ipso facto* represents proletarian hegemony, are particularly striking in this passage. We may also note that Dyakov states that the Telengana uprising was not liquidated "even till the middle of 1949" (*ibid.*). Actually, it had not been liquidated at all by the time he wrote, but Ranadive, by not publicizing it in 1949, had apparently succeeded in misleading Moscow and, to that extent, injuring his Andhra rivals—though Dyakov's and Balabushevich's writings were designed to give much more comfort to the Andhra leaders than to Ranadive.

rapidly and that its organization is being strengthened in spite of the government's "terror"[40] at a time when the very opposite was true. However, he too has to take the decisive neo-Maoist step—even though, by seemingly confining the bourgeois sections to be admitted to the united front to those of national minority groups and by dwelling heavily on their weakness and unreliability, he appears to be, if anything, even more intent than Balabushevich on stressing the insignificance of this feature of neo-Maoism:

> The national question has not been solved. . . . It is therefore that the middle and petty-bourgeoisie of those nationalities of India which are suffering most from the feudal survivals and the domination of monopoly capital, which exists in the main in Gujerati and Marwari hands, can be a wavering ally of the democratic camp. The progressive role of these national bourgeois strata is extremely relative and shortlived and on no account must it be overestimated.[41]

"The national bourgeoisie of the peoples mentioned above is very weak and is an extremely unreliable ally in the struggle of the peoples of India for the liquidation of the survivals of its feudal divisions and for national self-determination."*

No matter how hesitantly and reluctantly, Dyakov, like Balabushevich, has now fallen in line with the neo-Maoist strategy, making its victory in Moscow, after two years of uncertainty and division, complete.

II. The Imposition of the Neo-Maoist Strategy on the CPI

Although it was clear from the writings discussed in the preceding section that since the middle of 1949 the neo-Maoist strategy was now the only strategy approved by Moscow for the Asian Communist parties, Moscow took far more obvious steps to call this fact to the attention of these parties and, as we shall see later in this section, of the Indian Party in particular.

The Peking WFTU Conference, November 1949. Just as in February 1948, when the Asian Communist parties were familiarized with the abandonment of the "right" strategy at the Calcutta Youth Conference, a meeting of an international Communist front organization

---

* *Ibid.*, p. 35. In an article on India in November 1949, Dyakov again gives great emphasis to the peasant movement, calls only the "big" bourgeoisie an ally of imperialism and feudalism, but again mentions sections of the bourgeoisie only of minority nationalities as supporting "the workers." A. Dyakov, "Anglo-American Plans in India," *Pravda*, November 25, 1949, p. 3; translated in full in *Soviet Press Translations*, V, No. 3 (February 1, 1950), 80–83; slightly condensed and translated in *Current Digest of the Soviet Press*, I, No. 48 (December 27, 1949), 33–34.

was chosen for the purpose of broadcasting the line now agreed on in Moscow. From November 16 to December 3, 1949, there met in Peking the Trade Union Conference of Asian and Australasian Countries of the World Federation of Trade Unions (WFTU).[42] Though some of its main addresses were delivered by leading Chinese Communists and its locale was the capital of Communist China, the mere facts that its chief pronouncements were promptly published in the Moscow press and the Cominform journal and, above all, that it was a conference of the WFTU, a Moscow-directed organization, leave no doubt whatever that it represented the voice of Moscow as much as that of Peking. The significance of this meeting lies precisely in the fact that the two voices now coincide on the subject of Communist strategy in the colonial areas and that Moscow, quite as much as Peking, wanted to capitalize on the recent Communist victory in China by holding the conference in Peking.

The most important speech of the Peking WFTU Conference was the opening address of Liu Shao-chi,[43] who sounded the keynote of the meeting and, indeed, of the subsequent period in Asian Communist strategy, with the following statement: "The path taken by the Chinese people to defeat imperialism and its lackeys and to establish the People's Republic of China is the path that should be taken by the peoples of the various colonial and semi-colonial countries in their fight for national independence and people's democracy." Liu then proceeded to define to the assembled delegates from the Asian Communist movements this Chinese path as a four-point "formula." Points two and three, dealing with the importance, respectively, of working class and Communist party leadership and of Marxist-Leninist theory, party discipline, and self-criticism, are not peculiar to the Chinese strategy and therefore are of less interest to us, but the first and last of the four points are worth quoting:

1. The working class must unite with all other classes, parties, groups, organizations and individuals who are willing to oppose the oppression of imperialism and its lackeys, to form a broad nationwide united front and ready to wage a resolute struggle against imperialism and its lackeys.

4. It is necessary to set up wherever and whenever possible a people's liberation army led by the Communist Party, an army which is powerful and skillful in fighting enemies, as well as strong points for the operation of these armies and also to coordinate the mass struggles in the enemy controlled areas with the armed struggle. Moreover, armed struggle is the main form of struggle in the national liberation struggle in many colonies and semi-colonies.

That this formula is in the nature of a directive to the Asian Communist parties is then driven home by Liu:

> This is the main path followed in China by the Chinese people in winning their victory. This path is the path of Mao Tse-tung. It can also become the main path of the peoples of other colonial and semi-colonial countries for winning emancipation where similar conditions prevail.

To emphasize this formula even more strongly, and possibly with Ranadive in mind, he warns any recalcitrants that they would be making a "mistake," that is, be deviationists, if they followed any other "path":

> . . . . It is impossible in these countries . . . to overthow the yoke of imperialism and its lackeys and to establish a people's democratic state by taking any easier path other than that indicated above. Anyone attempting to do so would be committing a mistake.

Moscow had finally settled on the neo-Maoist strategy in mid-1949, and the Chinese Communists had completed their conquest of mainland China in the same year and turned their eyes beyond its confines. Now the two are here combining to proclaim in the most unequivocal language that the neo-Maoist strategy is now obligatory for all Communist parties in colonial areas. Among the elements constituting this strategy the one mentioned first and foremost is what we have called the "four-class" approach, stated here in such broad and all-inclusive form ("all other classes, parties and groups, organizations and individuals") that we would be justified in referring to it as the "all-class" or, indeed, the classless approach. Corresponding to this, and equally characteristic of the essence of neo-Maoism, is the definition of the enemy as, for all practical purposes, only imperialism. "Its lackeys," which is regularly added, refers simply to all those native elements opposed to the Communists, but not necessarily even to the entire feudal element. Interestingly enough—especially since this speech was made at a "labor" meeting—the inclusion of the national bourgeoisie and the petty bourgeoisie in this broad united front are so much taken for granted by Liu that subsequent references to it in his speech are devoted not to its defense or explanation at all, but, on the contrary, merely to a demonstration of why these classes cannot be the leaders of the united front, a role naturally reserved to the working class and the Communist party. The peasantry, so often regarded as the main element of the Maoist strategy, is not even considered worthy of explicit mention in Liu's four-point formula, nor is a warning against possible peasant leadership of the united front deemed necessary; but a firm worker-peasant alliance is considered the basis of the united front.

Liu devoted a large part of his speech to the importance of Communist-led armed forces and armed struggle. Superficially this is its most striking aspect, and it can thus easily give the impression of being a general call to arms to the Asian Communists. Not only outside observers but, as we shall see in the next chapter, the CPI, too, seem to have regarded it as such. In the light of subsequent events, however, it is important to note at this point not only that Liu lists armed struggle as only the last of his four points but also that, while the first three dealing with the united front and the Communist party are treated as unconditionally applicable to all colonial areas, this last one is not. An army is to be set up, not everywhere, but only "wherever and whenever possible"; and armed struggle is the main form of struggle, not in all, but only "in many colonies and semi-colonies." Nor can this phrasing be accidental, for in every single instance when armed struggle is mentioned in subsequent paragraphs such cautious limiting words are used in conjunction with it.

Of interest, too, is the report to the Peking WFTU Conference of Li Li-san,[44] who was known as the chief exponent of the "left" strategy in an earlier period of Chinese Communism. Like Liu, Li lists the lessons of the Chinese Communist victory. The first one, again, is "to unite with all the classes, political parties and groups, organizations and individuals who suffer from the oppression of imperialism and its lackeys, in forming a mighty national united front against them." The Chinese workers had won the support of the broad peasant masses, the petty bourgeoisie, and the intelligentsia,* and they had dealt "correctly" with the national bourgeoisie, adopting the "policy of both uniting and struggling, but mainly uniting, with them." The second reason for the Communist victory and the second lesson, according to Li, was resorting to armed struggle in the countryside "in a semi-colonial and semi-feudal country like China." In the cities, on the other hand, the "policy of lying low" was adopted. It is difficult to believe that Li was not speaking for the benefit of Ranadive when he added that for a long time the Chinese Communists had adventurously organized offensives, strikes, and even armed struggles in the cities and had suffered severe losses as a result. "I myself have committed serious mistakes on this question and therefore feel deeply

---

* The intellectuals, Li states with remarkable frankness, are frequently "not only the initiators and propagandists of an anti-imperialist, anti-feudal ideology, but are also frequently vanguards of the revolutionary movement"; that is, Communist parties are based on them rather than on the proletariat.

about this historical lesson." The third reason, finally, for victory, was, of course, the leadership of the Communist Party. Li, like Liu, insists that these lessons be learned:

A study of these reasons, a study of the experiences and lessons of the Chinese revolution, is of great practical significance not only to the Chinese workers, but also to every worker abroad, particularly to the workers of the Asiatic countries still under imperialist oppression—this is a fact which needs no explanation.

The Manifesto issued by the Conference[45] also devoted particular attention to the united front, including the national bourgeoisie, and listed the countries where "armed resistance" was resorted to as "Viet-Nam, Malaya, Indonesia, Burma, Philippines and Southern Korea," but not India. Actually, as much Communist-incited and led violence was then going on in India as in some of the countries mentioned, but it must be recognized that in Communist literature objectively worded descriptive statements seemingly diagnosing some fact are often really meant to express not what is but what ought to be. One of the resolutions of the WFTU Conference also makes it clear that no one method of struggle, including presumably violence, is universally applicable throughout Asia:

The Conference urges the National Trade Union Centres and all trade union members: . . . In the colonial and semi-colonial countries of Asia to take into account local conditions and national character-istics and use the appropriate methods to achieve people's unity in the fight for genuine national independence, for democracy and peace, and against the imperialists and their agents.
For the correct assessment of these methods, valuable lessons may be drawn from the experience of the Chinese people. . . .[46]

To summarize, then, the Peking WFTU Conference of November 1949 made the adoption of the Chinese path, that is, of the neo-Maoist strategy, mandatory for the Asian Communist parties and defined this strategy as the formation everywhere of a broad anti-imperialist united front, including parts of the bourgeoisie, but as the employment of armed violence only in countries where appropriate, India apparently not being among these countries.*

* One concrete achievement of the Peking WFTU Conference was the organiza-tion of a WFTU Liaison Bureau for the Asian and Australasian countries with its seat in Peking. The secondary literature is full of assertions that this Bureau is actually a coordinating center for the Asian or Southeast Asian or Far Eastern Communist movements. However, even the most scholarly works making this claim provide no supporting evidence for it, e.g., Frankel, *op. cit.,* p. 210; Werner Levi, *Modern China's Foreign Policy* (Minneapolis: University of Minnesota Press, 1953), pp. 326–327. Indeed, there is no known evidence that the Liaison Bureau even

The CPI's and Joshi's reactions to the Peking WFTU Conference. We must now turn to India to see how the Communist Party there reacted to the various clear indications of Moscow's turn to the neo-Maoist strategy that we have just reviewed. We find, amazingly enough, that the CPI under Ranadive's leadership did not react at all. The publication of Liu Shao-chi's "Internationalism and Nationalism" in *Pravda* and the meeting of the Soviet Academy of Sciences, both in June 1949, were followed by the appearance in July of Ranadive's strongest attacks on Mao and neo-Maoism. Even the clear exhortations and warnings of the Peking WFTU Conference were ignored by Ranadive, and none of them was published in the January issue of *Communist*, where one might ordinarily have expected to find them. Ranadive seemed blindly convinced of the correctness of his "left" strategy, and was apparently incapable of understanding any but the most direct orders from Moscow to abandon it. Even if he had understood the various strong hints made in 1949, however, he was by now too deeply committed to the "left" strategy to be able to give it up without proving many of his rivals within the CPI correct and losing power to them. Thus he continued to respond to the growing weakness of his position with increased ruthlessness toward his intra-Party foes.

Not all Indian Communists were as blind as Ranadive and his Party leadership, however. On January 13, 1950, P. C. Joshi, sus-

fulfills its avowed purpose of maintaining liaison among the Communist-dominated trade unions in Asian and Australasian countries (which are in each case much more likely to be run by the local Communist party than by one coordinating center), much less that it directs the entire Communist movements of this area. Its only known function is the distribution of WFTU and probably other Communist propaganda in the area.

The Bureau is often likened to a "Far Eastern Cominform" to emphasize its character of an agency coordinating and directing Communist movements, but the comparison is an apt one only because in the case of the Cominform, too, there is no evidence of its playing such a role and, indeed, except for its weekly newspaper, of its very existence. See Bernard S. Morris, "The Cominform: A Five Year Perspective," *World Politics*, V, No. 3 (April 1953) , 369–376.

Nor can the existence of the WFTU Liaison Bureau in Peking be regarded as proof of Chinese, as distinguished from Soviet, predominance over Asian Communism. Not only does the area supposedly served by the Bureau include countries definitely outside the Chinese orbit, such as Australia and New Zealand, but the Bureau has a Soviet as well as a Chinese member, and it may receive its orders from Moscow as well as from Peking or possibly even from WFTU headquarters in Vienna, which is itself, of course, directed by Moscow, rather than Peking. In any case, in view of the minor and non-policy-forming functions of the Bureau, no conflict is likely to arise between Moscow and Peking over its direction. See also footnote on p. 159, below.

pended from the CPI for over a year and just then being expelled, wrote his "Letter to Foreign Comrades," which he published the following May and which shows that he had a clear grasp of the new line called for by Moscow. We have referred to and quoted this interesting document quite frequently in the preceding chapters and here merely want to call attention to those of its passages that demonstrate that it was quite possible for an Indian Communist at this time to understand not only the neo-Maoist strategy but also which of its elements Moscow considered essential.

Joshi senses that the neo-Maoist strategy is neither "right" nor "left." He acknowledges that the direction of the change made by the CPI in December 1947 and at the Second Congress away from his own "right" strategy was correct, but says that, while his own "mistakes" were like those of the Chinese Communist Party during its first united front with the Kuomintang, Ranadive's were like Li Li-san's during the following period.[47] He says that the Second Congress was wrong in condemning the entire bourgeoisie as collaborationist.[48] In other words, it was correct to give up the "right" strategy of the united front from above with bourgeois groups but wrong to substitute for it the "left" strategy of a united front from below excluding the entire bourgeoisie.

Joshi clearly sees what constitutes the greatest weakness of the "left" policy in Moscow's eyes. Referring to this policy of the CPI, he says that "the relative growth of the Indian bourgeoisie consumes up all our class hatred" so that the Party has failed to expose the Marshall Plan[49]—which, indeed, could not have been of as much importance to the Indian Communist Party as was the Indian bourgeoisie, but (and this is the crucial point) was far more important to Moscow. Along the same lines, he also charges that the Party press had failed to emphasize imperialist pressures and influences,[50] and that the Party did not see the democratic-national character of the revolution and thus did not exploit the appeal to national sentiment.[51]

Joshi is also shrewd enough to understand Moscow's attitude on the use of armed violence in India. In general he blames the CPI for its failure to popularize and learn from the Chinese Communist Party and program and for distorting and misrepresenting the latter.[52] However, when it comes to the question of armed struggle, he quickly turns around and blames the Party for its "demagogy" of referring to the Chinese example, calling this a "mechanical transplantation of the tactics of a different set-up, ignoring the 'specific' situation facing our country."[53] He charges that the Party considers the victories of the Chinese "People's Liberation Army" as "welcome heroism by the

Chinese toilers, but Mao's New Democracy was reeking with reformism."[54] Joshi thus displays a good grasp of which aspects of the neo-Maoist strategy were held applicable in India and which were not, and he points out how Ranadive played up exactly the wrong ones.

Finally, Joshi directly accuses the CPI leadership of deviating from the international Communist line, saying that in the past two years international Communist developments, including the Chinese Communist victory, show nothing in common with the policy and practice of the CPI.[55] He attacks the Party for ignoring Liu's "Internationalism and Nationalism," pointing out that it was printed in *Pravda*,[56] and for being the only Communist party in the world which had not published the Chinese Communists' "Common Program."[57] Having devoted thirty pages to a discussion of Ranadive's mistakes and deviations and their disastrous results for the Party, Joshi turns directly to the foreign comrades to whom his letter is addressed, some, if not all, of whom, we may be sure, were in the Soviet orbit. He tells them that no serious self-criticism can be expected from inside the Party, and

... therefore, brothers, it is you from abroad who have to act and act quick . . . . International Communism must intervene . . . . We will accept our mistakes when they are authoritatively pointed out to us . . . .[58]

Here is an open appeal by a deposed Communist leader directed against the present leadership of his party and to what he clearly regards as a higher authority, an episode that casts a revealing light on the nature of international communism.

The Cominform editorial of January 27, 1950. The authoritative intervention Joshi asked for came within two weeks of the date of his letter. Yet we cannot conclude that it was simply the result of his letter. During the same period Mao Tse-tung was in Moscow to negotiate the Sino-Soviet treaty; it is entirely possible that during his visit he, too, called attention to the CPI leadership's anti-Maoism and asked or insisted that something be done about it. But we cannot ascribe the coming intervention by Moscow simply to Mao either. Joshi's and—if one was made—Mao's appeals may merely have precipitated this intervention. As we have shown, ever since 1947, when both abandoned the "right" strategy, Moscow and the CPI had steadily moved apart so that at the very time, in 1949, when Moscow arrived at the adoption of the neo-Maoist strategy the CPI leadership reached an extreme "left," anti-Maoist position. Once Moscow had become aware of this situation, probably some time in the latter half of 1949, some drastic resolution of the difference between the two, naturally in favor of Moscow's position, had become inevitable.

Moscow's intervention took the form of an editorial in the Cominform journal[59] camouflaged as a positive statement hailing Communist successes in all colonial areas. Necessitated by Ranadive's stubborn refusal to be impressed with the message of the Peking WFTU Conference, the editorial is substantially no more than a restatement of the main points Liu had made there two months earlier, applying them in one brief paragraph specifically to India, and, more significantly, an endorsement making it clear beyond any doubt that Liu had spoken for Moscow as well as Peking.

The important part of the editorial begins by quoting Liu's pronouncement that "the path taken by the Chinese people . . . is the path that should be taken by the people of many colonial and dependent countries in their struggle for national independence and people's democracy."* Like Liu's speech, it then proceeds to explain that "the experience of the victorious national liberation struggle of the Chinese people teaches that the working class must unite with all classes, parties, groups, and organizations willing to fight the imperialists and their hirelings to form a broad nation-wide united front, headed by the working class and its vanguard—the Communist Party . . . ." Having thus set forth the generally applicable element of the neo-Maoist strategy, it turns to armed struggle, again in full agreement with Liu, making it clear by the use of cautious limiting phrases that the use of this element of the strategy is not appropriate everywhere. "A decisive condition for the victorious outcome of the national liberation struggle is the formation, when the necessary internal conditions allow for it, of people's liberation armies under the leadership of the Communist Party." "As the examples of China, Viet-Nam, Malaya and other countries show, armed struggle is now becoming the main form of struggle of the national liberation movement in many colonies and dependent countries." To make quite clear which countries are—and which are not—included among these "many" colonies where "the necessary internal conditions allow for it," the editorial briefly lists Vietnam, South Korea, Malaya, the Philippines, Indonesia, and Burma as

---

* It may be noted that the Cominform journal's version of Liu's speech printed four weeks earlier and quoted on page 96, above, had rendered this passage as referring to "the peoples of the various colonial and semi-colonial countries . . . ." The alteration made in the present editorial might conceivably be intentional, to limit the applicability of neo-Maoism to "many" such countries; but it may also

engaging in armed struggle, while in another paragraph India is merely mentioned as having been given sham independence.

There then followed the paragraph of a few lines, quoted here in its entirety, which was designed to and did change the course of the Indian Communist Party:

> In these conditions, the task of the Indian Communists, drawing on the experience of the national liberation movement in China and other countries, is, naturally, to strengthen the alliance of the working class with all the peasantry, to fight for the introduction of the urgently needed agrarian reform and—on the basis of the common struggle for freedom and national independence of their country, against the Anglo-American imperialists oppressing it and against the reactionary big bourgeoisie and feudal princes collaborating with them—to unite all classes, parties, groups and organizations willing to defend the national independence and freedom of India.

Brief and ostensibly uncritical as this passage is, it manages to destroy the very bases of Ranadive's "left" policy. Beginning with a reference to the Chinese example, but not the Soviet example, it defines the objectives of the Communists' fight as Indian freedom and national independence and agrarian reform, but not socialism. The enemies, therefore, are foreign imperialism, the feudal princes (apparently not even necessarily the feudal landlords), and the "big" bourgeoisie, but not capitalism or the entire bourgeoisie. Correspondingly, the potential allies of the Communists are "all" classes and elements opposed to imperialism and, specifically, "all" the peasantry, not just, as Ranadive had held, the urban and rural proletariat, the poor peasantry, and some of the petty bourgeoisie.

III. THE SHIFT OF THE CPI TO THE NEO-MAOIST STRATEGY

The organ of the Cominform, the very organization on whose first meeting Ranadive had placed his main reliance in his defiance of Mao and neo-Maoism, had now told him to follow the Chinese example and the neo-Maoist strategy. His leadership, already weakened by his unrealistic and extreme policies, by government suppression, and by repeated purges of the Party, was now also publicly deprived of the support from Moscow of which he had always felt so sure that he could carry out his suicidal policies with persistence and assurance.

---

be due to the use of a different translation of Liu's speech by the writer or of a careless translation of the editorial from the Russian into English, as is also indicated by the substitution of the word "struggle" for "fight."

Ranadive's and Joshi's initial reactions to the Cominform blast. In the face of the devastating Cominform editorial, it appears that for a few more weeks Ranadive desperately sought to cling to his authority. No statement of self-criticism was forthcoming from him immediately upon its receipt. On February 10, two weeks after its appearance, Joshi still found it necessary to call the editorial to Ranadive's attention.[60] However, many in the CPI who were dissatisfied with Ranadive's leadership and policies were not slow to recognize the weakness of his position. Feeling vindicated by the Cominform editorial, they began to give vent to their opposition more openly. But Ranadive, as in the past, replied with further dictatorial measures, which resulted in a new wave of expulsions and resignations from the Party.[61]

If Ranadive still had any hopes of being able to ride out the storm, the shrewder Joshi no longer had any doubt that Ranadive's star was waning. On February 10, 1950, he forwarded his "Letter to Foreign Comrades" to Ranadive, thus letting him know that a month earlier he had appealed to Moscow against the Party's leadership and over its head. His covering letter repeats the same charges, but in sharper language and concentrating particularly on Ranadive's "mistaken notion" "that the bourgeoisie as a whole had gone over to imperialism."[62] Thus he tells Ranadive that "to state as you do, as a general principle, that you base your tactics on the contradiction between capital and labour, capital and people, and not on contradictions within the bourgeoisie . . . is anti-Leninist,"[63] a statement that may well have surprised Ranadive, who was a sufficiently old-fashioned Leninist to believe that the class struggle was a pretty good general basis for Communist tactics. Since Joshi was right and Ranadive wrong in interpreting the current Moscow line, this remark throws much light on the nature of present-day Communist "theory" in general and on that of neo-Maoism in particular. In his letter Joshi also blames Ranadive for having ignored various articles appearing in the Cominform journal in 1949 and written by leaders of colonial and Latin American Communist parties noting and utilizing the role of different sections of the bourgeoisie.*

* Joshi, "Letter to Comrade Ranadive," *Views,* p. 39. This is a fascinating indication of how a good Communist conceives of Communist strategy as necessarily uniform throughout the world in any one period. If, for example, a West African or a Guatemalan Communist writes that his party has been cooperating with sections of the native bourgeoisie in his country, this is considered tantamount to a directive to the Indian Communist Party to cooperate with sections of the Indian bourgeoisie, although conditions in the various countries may be utterly different.

On February 11, 1950, in a letter to the Central Committee of the Communist Party of Pakistan, Joshi goes so far as to accuse Ranadive of Titoism, then a cardinal sin among Communists, because through his policies he had isolated the CPI in the interest of the Indian government, he had run the Party dictatorially, and he had ignored and withheld international party documents. "I have no doubt in my mind that our leadership is Titoite. It is no question of honest mistakes."[64] And a week later, on February 18, in a strongly worded demand to Ranadive for permission to appeal against his expulsion from the Party, Joshi leaves no doubt of his certainty that Ranadive is on the way out. Referring to "the break of dawn that is broken for our Party with the FLPPD Editorial of 27 January," he contemptuously tells Ranadive: "You can at worst become a dirty and small cloud, and that too only for a while, trying to hold back the light of the rising sun."[65]

The Politburo statement of February 22, 1950. Ranadive must, indeed, in these weeks have found that his position was becoming untenable and that he could not continue in his old way. It is characteristic of the different roles of Peking and Moscow in CPI affairs that it was one thing for him to ignore Liu's speech of November, but would be quite another to ignore a restatement of that speech in the Cominform journal of January. On February 22, 1950, Ranadive's Politburo issued a statement hailing the Cominform editorial and admitting some of the CPI's former errors. But, far from being tantamount to his resignation or even a complete surrender of his position, it was but another attempt on Ranadive's part to save himself, "to hold back the light of the rising sun," that is, to prevent what seems, indeed, to have been as inevitable as the rising of the sun.

Like its cockier predecessors of 1949, the Politburo pronouncement appeared as a statement of the editorial board of *Communist*[66] in the February-March issue of that journal, which reprinted also the Cominform editorial, the Manifesto of the Peking WFTU Conference, and the speech made there by Liu Shao-chi. The document is a remarkable one, demonstrating either that Ranadive was so blinded by his

---

Implicit, of course, is the recognition that the West African and Guatemalan Communists have not adopted their policies as an adjustment to conditions prevailing in their countries either but as a response to the Moscow line and, second, that no article is likely to appear in the Cominform journal that is not setting forth a correct application of the current line. Thus any article in that journal, even those dealing with far-off countries, is to be studied thoroughly by a good Communist leader not only for its general interest but for specific directives applicable to his own party.

fanaticism as still to be unable to understand fully the import of the Cominform editorial or that he was engaging in a desperate gamble trying, by subtly reinterpreting the editorial, to gain time and a basis for his continuance in power.

The statement begins with the obligatory acknowledgement of the Cominform editorial as "a brilliant contribution," "a correct lead," and "a timely reminder"[67] to the CPI that it is lagging behind the immense possibilities of the revolutionary struggle. But far more striking are its efforts throughout at self-justification and its outright self-praise on an occasion when self-criticism would obviously have been in accordance with Communist etiquette. The statement speaks of the "resolute struggles" under CPI leadership that were "assuming new and higher forms in many cities and districts"[68] and that indicated that the Party was rising to the leadership of the national liberation movement; and it still hails the Second Congress as a great step in the Party's life.[69] Seeking to minimize his "mistakes," Ranadive claims that during the past year the CPI had considerable success in mobilizing tens of thousands, but that "certain errors in a dogmatist and sectarian direction" had prevented the mobilization of tens of millions.[70] At the end of his statement, he goes so far as to conclude that the Cominform editorial is really supporting him against his opponents: he claims that, since the Second Congress, that is, since his assumption of power, the "stubborn fight against reformism" had unified the ranks of the Party and that the editorial strengthened that fight while at the same time correcting sectarian deviations.[71]

Practically every paragraph of the statement confessing an "error" begins, in an obvious effort to justify Ranadive's actions, with a passage saying that "in combating the reformists" some correct action was taken. In this fashion it is admitted that the Politburo had been wrong in not laying its main emphasis on the continuing colonial character of India and the consequent anti-imperialist, anti-feudal character of the Communists' fight[72] and in calling the bourgeoisie rather than the imperialists the leader of the "imperialist-bourgeois-feudal combine."[73] This is a fundamental theoretical concession, but it is not at all clear that Ranadive has wholeheartedly drawn the practical consequences, notably on the matter of the inclusion of a section of the bourgeoisie in the anti-imperialist front. He speaks of the struggles of the "working class, peasantry, and other progressive forces, such as the students, democratic youth, women."[74] He calls the most important task advanced in the Political Thesis of the Second Congress the formation of the People's Democratic Front, which he himself defines as an alliance of the working class, the peasantry, and the urban petty bourgeoisie.[75]   Then, after quoting the Cominform editorial's order "to unite all classes . . . ," he proclaims that this People's Democratic Front of the Second Congress, which was the expression of his "left" policy and specifically excluded the entire bourgeoisie, would be the basis for the united front demanded by Moscow.[76]   However, like Balabushevich and Dyakov in the preceding year, Ranadive is forced to take the decisive neo-Maoist step, and he does so just as grudgingly as they had done.   He admits that the Party had failed to distinguish between the big bourgeoisie and other sections of the bourgeoisie and to see that some of these "can still at one time or other play the role of fellow travellers in the national liberation struggle," although they cannot be regarded as reliable.[77] The wording is so strikingly similar to that used by Balabushevich when he had to fall in line with the neo-Maoist strategy[78] that one might suspect that Ranadive had chosen the Balabushevich passage to lean on as the least unpalatable Soviet statement on the subject. It is also conceivable, however, that the similarity is the coincidental result of similar circumstances.

Striking a theme that will become very important during subsequent years, Ranadive states that, in order to draw the broadest masses into the front, the peace movement "must become the pivot of the entire activity of the Party and mass organizations."[79]   Given the broad character of the Communist "peace" movement, which seeks to appeal to all classes, this is clearly not the kind of idea Ranadive would develop himself.   Although it was not derived from the Cominform editorial to which Ranadive here reacted, its source was the Cominform.   Its very language shows that he is here following a directive that had been adopted by the Cominform at its meeting in the second half of November in Hungary, which stated: "The struggle for a stable and lasting peace, for the organization and consolidation of the forces of peace against the forces of war should now become the pivot of the entire activity of the Communist Parties and democratic organizations."[80]

Ranadive's response to the Cominform editorial's order to ally "with all the peasantry," that is, to engage in the "class collaboration" for which he had condemned the Andhra Committee, is also a rather hesitant and reluctant one.   In combating the reformists, his statement says, the Party had correctly stressed reliance on the agricultural workers and the masses of peasants, but it had wrongly lumped the rich peasants with the landlords instead of pointing out that the Party's slogans represent the interests of the entire peasantry.   No doubt, he continues, the political influence of the rich peasants must be fought, but, in the interest of the alliance, nationalization of all land and expropriation of the rich peasants must not be demanded. The reformists would carry this to the point of hindering the "militant struggles of the peasant masses" since these might alienate the rich peasants, but "it is by fighting such deviations that peasant struggles have advanced and will advance."[81] It appears, then, that Ranadive is willing to modify only his slogans but not his methods in order to attract rich peasant support.

Quoting Liu's pronouncement on the Chinese path, Ranadive's statement acknowledges that the Cominform editorial had "drawn the pointed attention" of the CPI to the experience of China led by the Chinese Communist Party and Mao Tse-tung. He then quotes as the two main lessons from this experience the editorial's passages on the broad nationwide united front and on the formation of people's liberation armies, failing to note that one is stated absolutely and the other conditionally, and promises that the Party leadership would re-examine, in the light of these lessons, all its resolutions, including the Report on Strategy and Tactics, that is, the document in which Mao had been attacked by name.[82] Perhaps in a belated attempt to appease his Andhra rivals or in order to head off their rise to power by being equally willing to learn the Chinese lessons, Ranadive shifts his emphasis from urban to rural armed struggle, but there is no recognition on his part that both the Peking WFTU Conference and the Cominform editorial had considered both urban and rural armed struggle as inappropriate for India. Self-satisfied, he states that "the resolutions of the Party Centre, correctly repudiating both reformist restriction of mass struggles into the confines of peaceful constitutionalism as well as petty-bourgeois revolutionism advocating so-called 'militant' actions without the participation of the masses, have rightly laid stress on the supreme importance of combining all forms of struggle. . . ."[83] He again quotes the Cominform editorial's passage on the formation of people's liberation armies, making no further comment on it and its condition—"when the necessary internal conditions allow for it." He thus creates and is probably himself under the impression that Moscow had endorsed armed struggle in India, despite the fact that, as we have seen, it had clearly avoided doing so by speaking of armed struggle in one series of paragraphs mentioning a number of other countries and dealing with India in separate paragraphs not in connection with armed struggle.

In his statement of February 22, 1950, then, Ranadive tried to maintain himself in power by combining the necessary minimum of self-criticism with the permissible maximum of self-justification. In effect, he minimized the importance of the Cominform editorial by implying that he had substantially been following its policies all along and that only relatively minor changes were now required. He therefore put his main emphasis on opposition to reformism, that is, to the "right" strategy, which he, representing the "left" strategy, and the editorial, standing for the neo-Maoist strategy, held in common; and he thus sought to create the impression that the editorial was really supporting him against his intra-Party opponents. But his most dangerous rivals were not the followers of the "right" strategy, which had been discredited ever since the end of 1947. They were the Andhra Committee, whom Ranadive had, indeed, also stigmatized as "reformists," but who were actually neo-Maoists and thus adherents of the very strategy the Cominform editorial was propounding. Ranadive may thus have intended to turn the neo-Maoist editorial against the actual neo-Maoists in his Party.

In any case, his maneuver failed. Moscow apparently did not accept his slight self-criticism as sufficient. It did not reprint his statement but remained silent, thus permitting what must have been a bitter struggle for the CPI leadership to proceed. Encouraged by Moscow's reaction, the Andhra faction, which felt that the Cominform editorial meant that its own opportunity to take over the CPI and to take revenge on the hated Ranadive was at hand, no doubt pressed forward.

The Politburo statement of April 6, 1950, and Joshi's comments. On April 6 Ranadive's Politbureau produced another statement. Unfortunately, its text is not available to us, and for its contents we must rely on a brief and by no means objective report by Joshi.[84] It appears that it was another attempt by Ranadive to stay in power by going somewhat further in confessing his sins than he had in his February statement. The document admits a Trotskyite deviation in the Party's analysis of the nature of Indian society, the revolution, and its strategy. It admits that the CPI had ignored the anti-imperialist and anti-feudal nature of the revolution and had attempted to skip over the present stage of the revolution and resorted to the strategy of a socialist instead of a democratic revolution.[85] But this second Politbureau statement still speaks of "a period of revolutionary advance"[86] and proclaims as its chief tactical slogan making the Telengana way, that is, peasant-based armed struggle on the Chinese pattern, India's "principal way."[87] It thus clearly demonstrates the growing Andhra influence on the Politbureau, but we do not know whether this emphasis in the statement was forced on Ranadive by the Andhra faction against his will or was, on the contrary, adopted by him to take the wind out of the Andhra faction's sails. In either case, it is also clear that Ranadive still did not understand that armed struggle, even in "the Telengana way," was not what Moscow had called for when it told the CPI to follow the Chinese path.

Interestingly, as Joshi says, "Comrade Balabushevich's report is copiously quoted to buttress the arguments of the PB."[88] This, no doubt, refers to the report Balabushevich delivered in June 1949 to the session of the Soviet Academy of Sciences, in which, as we have seen, he placed the greatest emphasis on the Telengana fighting as the most important and typical development of the Communists' fight in India.[89] It seems as if Ranadive, when he is forced to give up his "left" strategy for the neo-Maoist one, almost instinctively turns for support to Balabushevich, who had faced the same problem in 1949, and that, if he must accept neo-Maoism, he clings to the armed-struggle element of the Chinese example, which, while not wholly to his liking because of its reliance on the peasantry, is far more acceptable to him than the detested four-class strategy with its appeal to the hated bourgeoisie. Unfortunately for Ranadive, Balabushevich, though a Soviet expert on India, was not a firm support to lean on in this matter. It is likely that even in the middle of 1949, when Balabushevich expressed his approval of the "Telengana way," Zhukov was more representative of Soviet policy when he mentioned armed struggle as applicable only in some Asian countries, not including India.[90] At any rate, it is clear that this was the Soviet-approved strategy by the end of 1949 and that Balabushevich's emphasis was at best out of date by the time Ranadive came to rely on it.

As we have already noted, Joshi was much more intelligent than Ranadive and, as the next chapter will show, than the Andhra Communists in grasping Moscow's wishes on the matter of armed violence. In his comments on the April Politburo statement he proves that, although the directives of the Peking WFTU Conference and the Cominform editorial on this subject were, no doubt intentionally, somewhat obscure to the outsider, Moscow was justified in expecting a Communist leader, as long as he had some experience in reading "international documents" and was not burdened by any strong ideas of his own (as no good Communist leader should be), to be able to interpret them correctly.

Joshi, somewhat overstating his case, refers to the Politburo's shift of emphasis to Telengana as merely old wine in new bottles,[91] meaning that the wine of violence was now being sold in the neo-Maoist instead of the old "left" bottle. He blames the statement for giving the impression that the Cominform editorial considered India ripe for armed struggle.

The Editorial mentions the name of the countries where the movement has advanced to that stage and India is not among them, and even a cursory reading will show that our country is mentioned in a separate series of paras. . . . It of course speaks of the formation of liberation army 'when the internal necessary conditions allow for it.' The PB has not cared to *objectively* prove that such internal conditions exist.[92]

In his critique of the Politburo statement, Joshi continues: "the Peking Manifesto is invoked to make Telengana way mandatory in every rural area"; and again he gives a lesson to his former colleagues and present rivals on how to read Moscow directives, telling them that paragraph 11 of this Manifesto lists the countries where armed resistance is going on and that India is not among them.

Joshi can easily enough accuse Ranadive, who had been attacked by Moscow, for not understanding Moscow directives, but what is he to do about Balabushevich, whose voice comes from Moscow and on whom Ranadive relied? He solves this delicate problem by saying that Balabushevich had merely made simple generalizations about India from facts he had obtained from reports in the CPI's press, and that these reports were lies.[93] Thus the Soviet expert is very neatly absolved of all guilt, but Ranadive, who said the same thing, is doubly guilty.

Joshi's comments are also interesting because, seeing Ranadive's strength crumbling after the blast of the Cominform editorial, he mercilessly pursues him, undoubtedly both to enjoy his revenge and to try to get back into Moscow's graces himself. Having denounced the Politburo statement of February as a shamefaced self-defense,[94] he finds that the April self-criticism goes farther but not far enough. It only admits that the CPI had not sufficiently emphasized anti-imperialism. It does not confess, as Joshi thinks it should, that the Party had objectively worked for imperialism and had strengthened the pro-imperialist, pro-feudal forces by hiding the main enemy, Anglo-American imperialism.[95] It is typical of Communist thinking that any deviation from the "correct" line is, at least "objectively," tantamount to joining the enemy camp. Joshi was not going to be satisfied with any self-criticism by Ranadive except one confessing such monstrous sins as to make it quite impossible for him to remain in power.

The replacement of Ranadive by the Andhra leadership, May–July 1950. Ranadive's April statement had no more success than his earlier one in regaining Moscow's support for him. Thus encouraged, his enemies now closed in on him, and this phase of the intra-CPI conflict drew to its inevitable conclusion. However, if Joshi had had any hopes that, by virtue of the various anti-Ranadive letters he had written and the other activities he had no doubt engaged in ever since he realized after the Peking WFTU Conference which way the wind from Moscow was blowing, he would be reinstated as the Party's leader, they were doomed to disappointment. He had indeed displayed a remarkable ability to understand Moscow's new neo-Maoist line and no doubt would have been quite willing to carry it out. But Joshi was, above all, the symbol of the "right" strategy which the CPI, like all other Communist parties, had followed in the postwar period under his leadership. It was of the utmost importance to make clear that the abandonment of Ranadive's "left" strategy did not mean a return to the "right" strategy, that the united front from below was not to be replaced by the united front from above with the Congress and Socialist Parties, but was to be broadened by the inclusion of sections of the bourgeoisie. Ranadive and Joshi, "left" and "right," were both to be out of power, and neo-Maoism, a new strategy different from both, was to succeed theirs.

For the past two years the Andhra Provincial Committee of the CPI had been the foremost champion of neo-Maoism among the Indian Communists. It had also been Ranadive's chief rival and the only well-organized opposition to him within the Party. It was therefore only natural that power should pass into its hands at this juncture, even though it understood the new Moscow line far less perfectly than Joshi. During May and June 1950, the Party's Central Committee met, "reconstituted" both itself and the Politburo, and replaced Ranadive as General Secretary with Rajeshwar Rao, the leader of the Andhra faction. The bitterness of the proceedings can be gathered from a résumé of them by the new Politburo,[96] which denounces Ranadive as "the initiator, executor and dogged defender of the Trotsky-Tito type of left-sectarian political line" and accuses him of repudiating the Lenin-Stalin teachings on imperialism and the colonial revolution, sabotage of the agrarian revolution and armed struggle, suppression of inner-Party democracy and poisoning of inner-Party life (this being referred to as Titoist organizational methods), rejection of creative Marxism (meaning neo-Maoism) under the slogan "we recognize nobody except Marx-Engels-Lenin-Stalin," and deliberate suppression of international documents.

The neo-Maoist views of the Andhra leaders emerged triumphant in this document of the newly constituted Politburo. India remained a colonial country after three years of formal independence; the main enemy therefore was foreign imperialism and native feudalism—not, as Ranadive had insisted, the native bourgeoisie. In fact, the "middle" bourgeoisie and its demands for the protection of small industry were to be supported, and it was to be included in the united front against the Congress. The principal form of struggle would be armed struggle, not taking the form of general strikes and armed uprisings based on the urban proletariat, which had been favored by Ranadive, but that of rural peasant-based guerrilla warfare, which had been proved so successful by Mao in China.

Revealing the acute embarrassment of a party that is forced to follow a shifting line imposed on it from the outside, the Politburo résumé states quite frankly: "The tradition of our party specially since the 'People's War' period has been to swing like a pendulum from one extreme to the other."

> It is not necessary to write in detail how during the long period of 1942 to 1948 every time the Central Committee met it used to come out with a resolution beating its breast and saying: "We have underestimated this point," "overestimated that point," but this time "we have correctly estimated all points" and come to a correct conclusion—only to repeat the same sorrowful tale once again. Comrades: In this background of our party history you are perfectly justified in feeling sceptical this time also asking, "What is the guarantee that this time the Central Committee has chalked out a correct path?"

Party morale and discipline must have been in a sorry state for the new leadership to feel that it should bring this question out in the open; and what, indeed, was the guarantee that it was correct this time? Apparently it could merely promise the comrades that it would ensure the functioning of inner-Party democracy and, above all, that it would carefully study the international documents, thus in effect admitting that changes in line are the result of outside direction. As the next chapter will show, this was not a sufficient guarantee, and, in the new Politburo's own words, it had "to repeat the same sorrowful tale once again."

A statement of the CPI Central Committee issued on July 19, a full half-year after the Cominform editorial had initiated the shake-up, officially announced the change in leadership and policy. It was published in the Soviet press,[97] thus being given the stamp of approval that had been denied to Ranadive's attempts to remain at the helm. The statement, as reported in Moscow, announces the reorganization of the Central Committee and the Politburo, the release of Ranadive from his duties as General Secretary, and the election of Rajeshwar Rao, the leader of the Communist organization of Andhra Province, to his post. Although the Moscow version does not show what policy was being given up, it makes the direction of change toward neo-Maoism very clear by stating that the CPI would alter its policy to develop the movement for agrarian reform and for the national liberation of the country.

> The new policy will be based on the experience of the national liberation movement in China. The course China is taking and which the countries of Southeast Asia are following is the only correct course before our people.

The Central Committee also proclaimed that it would work for the establishment of an "all-national united front headed by the working class" against imperialism and, to make matters quite clear, that it had adopted a resolution greeting Mao Tse-tung. Its future difficulties with Moscow, which will occupy us in the next chapter, are already foreshadowed, however, in the fact that one remark in its statement, to the effect that the CPI would rely on a revolutionary army of the peasantry,[98] was not reported in the Soviet press.

The causes of Ranadive's downfall. Thus the "left" period of Indian Communism under Ranadive's rule came to an end. It had been a period of almost unmitigated failure for the Party, and had resulted in its thorough weakening and disorganization. Yet it was not these factors that brought about Ranadive's downfall. As Borkenau says, "no Communist Party leadership has ever fallen as the result of a defeat, however severe, if its loyalties satisfied the men who were at the moment victorious in the Russian internal factional struggle."[99] To be sure, Ranadive's policy had made many enemies for him in the Party; but, much as they hated him and saw clearly that he was leading the Party to destruction, they could not remove him as long as he could claim that he enjoyed the support of Moscow and as long as Moscow did not openly contradict him. He could go so far as to insult Mao publicly and to ignore Liu's policy directives. But once Moscow spoke out by merely endorsing the latter, all his remaining power and his desperate maneuvers could not save him.

Although the internal situation of the CPI may have weakened Ranadive and determined his immediate successor, his fall was clearly due to what had become an irreconcilable divergence between the strategy he represented and that finally adopted by Moscow. Had Ranadive, during the two years when he controlled CPI policy, merely concentrated on opposition to the Congress and Socialist parties, that is, on a policy of the united front from below, which the "left" and neo-Maoist strategies have in common and which all the writers in Moscow have clearly favored since 1947, he might have been able to switch from the "left" to the neo-Maoist strategy without undue difficulty when Moscow made it clear that it desired the latter. Even his use of violent tactics, which are compatible with any of the three Communist strategies, during the preceding two years would have been no obstacle. But Ranadive had more and more committed himself on the very elements that distinguish the "left" from the neo-Maoist strategy—the present stage of the revolution, the nature of the main enemy, and the class composition of the enemy and friendly camps. On these elements, especially the last-mentioned, there were also differences in Moscow in 1947 and 1948; but, unfortunately for Ranadive, whereas his commitment was to the "left" strategy, Moscow resolved its differences in favor of the neo-Maoist strategy in 1949.

There is no doubt that among the factors responsible for Ranadive's extreme and persistent adherence to the "left" strategy was his inflexibility once he had become convinced, in December 1947, that this was the strategy required by the Zhdanov speech and that he enjoyed Moscow's support in pursuing it. He reached this conviction quite easily in view of his probable initial ignorance of the neo-Maoist alternative and the fact that there is a strong tradition in favor of the "left" strategy in the CPI. Although it was not used during long periods beween 1917 and 1947 and may now never be used again, the "left" strategy may, indeed, be regarded as the Communist strategy *par excellence,* as the strategy more congenial to the type of individuals who were likely to become leaders of Communist parties anywhere during the past decades than the "right" strategy of cooperation with other parties, particularly the hated Socialists, or the neo-Maoist strategy of appealing for capitalist support. Beginning with this attitude, Ranadive was driven further and further to the "left" by the logic of the situation in India. Strong governmental reaction to his policy of violence certainly tended to radicalize that policy further but would not necessarily have been solely responsible for a "left" as distinguished from a neo-Maoist orientation. It was, as we have seen, opposition to his strategy from within the Party, particularly from the Andhra Committee, that led to Ranadive's commitment.

Being engaged in a backward area of India in an armed uprising based on peasant support obtained through the appeal of agrarian reform, the Andhra Communists had no use for Ranadive's "proletarian" and anti-capitalist policies, which were in any case a practical failure, while their Telengana uprising was at first rather successful. They therefore quite naturally interpreted Zhdanov's call for abandonment of the "right" strategy of cooperation with the Congress in a neo-Maoist rather than "left" fashion, defining neo-Maoism strictly as the strategy and tactics followed by the Chinese Communists. Their main emphasis thus was on opposition to feudalism and reliance on the peasantry and on guerrilla warfare, the most striking aspects of the Chinese example and the ones most appropriate to their own situation, although opposition to foreign imperialism and inclusion of sections of the bourgeoisie in the united front also figured in their program. Interestingly enough, it was exactly these latter elements of Maoism that were stressed by Zhukov, the chief neo-Maoist interpreter of the Zhdanov thesis in Moscow, and that were destined to emerge as the essential elements of neo-Maoism.

Goaded by the Andhra opposition into making a theoretical statement of his strategy, Ranadive came out with an uncompromising "left" policy, concentrating on Indian capitalism rather than feudalism or foreign imperialism as the main enemy and rejecting all cooperation with the upper strata of the peasantry and any section of the bourgeoisie, and finally with an attack on the neo-Maoist strategy and on Mao himself. Just as the Andhra Communists' neo-Maoism had differed from that of the neo-Maoists in Moscow, so Ranadive's "leftism" went much farther than any "left" strategy ever advocated in Moscow between 1947 and 1949. Thus, when in the middle of 1949 Moscow finally accepted the neo-Maoist strategy, and when it subsequently decided to enforce that strategy on the Indian Communist Party, the CPI under Ranadive could not make a smooth and imperceptible shift to it, as had been done by some other Asian Communist parties. To be sure, in his Politburo statements of February and April 1950 Ranadive tried to make such a shift but he had become too closely and openly identified with opposition to neo-Maoism to remain acceptable to Moscow; his Andhra rivals, who considered themselves his legitimate heirs, were quick to take advantage of his weakness. The shift from the "left" to the neo-Maoist strategy, which is difficult to detect and identify in the history of many Communist parties, thus caused a major upheaval in the Indian Party, making the differences between the two strategies crystal clear— and thus making the case of the CPI a particularly valuable one for a study of the development of Communist strategy.

NOTES FOR CHAPTER 4

1. See pp. 65–66, above.
2. Translated in full in *Soviet Press Translations,* IV, No. 14 (July 15, 1949), 423–439. The quotations here are taken from the pamphlet Liu Shao-chi, *Internationalism and Nationalism.*
3. *Ibid.,* p. 47.
4. The revised transcript appeared as Ye. Zhukov, "Voprosy natsional'no-

kolonial'noi bor'by posle vtoroi mirovoi voiny," *Voprosy Ekonomiki*, No. 9 (September 1949; printed October 26), 54–61; translated in slightly condensed form in *Current Digest of the Soviet Press*, I, No. 49 (January 3, 1950), 3–6. A complete translation appeared as E. M. Zhukov, "Problems of National and Colonial Struggle after the Second World War," *Colonial Peoples' Struggle for Liberation* (Bombay: People's Publishing House, 1950), pp. 1–11. The quotations here are taken from this version.

5. *Ibid.*, p. 3.

6. *Ibid.*, p. 6.

7. *Ibid.*, p. 9.

8. *Ibid.*, pp. 9–11.

9. The revised transcript appeared as V. Maslennikov, "O rukovodiashchei roli rabochego klassa v natsional'no-osvoboditel'nom dvishenii kolonial'nykh narodov," *Voprosy Ekonomiki*, No. 9 (September 1949; printed October 26), 62–75. Condensed to about one third of its original length and translated in *Current Digest of the Soviet Press*, I, No. 49 (January 3, 1950), 6–7. Translated in full as V. M. Maslennikov, "On Leading Role of the Working Class in the National Liberation Struggle of the Colonial Peoples," *Colonial Peoples' Struggle for Liberation*, pp. 12–31.

10. *Ibid.*, p. 12.

11. *Ibid.*, p. 28; see also *ibid.*, pp. 18, 21 and 27.

12. *Ibid.*, p. 30.

13. V. Balabushevich, "Novy etap natsional'no-osvoboditel'noi bor'by narodov Indii," *Voprosy Ekonomiki*, No. 8 (August 1949; printed October 6), 30–48. Summarized at about one third of its original length in English in *Current Digest of the Soviet Press*, I, No. 49 (January 3, 1950), 8–10. Translated in full into German as W. Balabuschewitsch, "Eine neue Etappe im nationalen Freiheitskampf der Völker Indiens," *Neue Welt*, V, No. 4 (February 1950), 91–103, and No. 5 (March 1950), 95–106, and into English as V. V. Balabushevich, "New Stage in National Liberation Struggle of the People of India," *Colonial Peoples' Struggle for Liberation*, pp. 32–59.

14. *Ibid.*, p. 38.

15. *Ibid.*, p. 46.

16. *Ibid.*, p. 50.

17. *Ibid.*, p. 51.

18. *Ibid.* The emphasis on Telengana was supported by F. D. Gapchenko in the "discussion" of Balabushevich's report. "Peoples' Liberation Struggle in Colonial and Semi-Colonial Countries After Second World War," *ibid.*, pp. 95–96.

19. In the discussion of Balabushevich's report, the economists S. M. Melman and N. D. Grodko speak of the "Indian big bourgeoisie" as in a bloc with imperialism. *Ibid.*, pp. 92–95 and 96–98.

20. Balabushevich, "New Stage in National Liberation Struggle of the People of India," *ibid.*, p. 42.

21. *Ibid.*, p. 58.

22. "Peoples' Liberation Struggle in Colonial and Semi-Colonial Countries After Second World War," *ibid.*, p. 98.

23. "Speech by Mao Tse-tung to the Session of the Preparatory Committee for the New Political Consultative Council," *For a Lasting Peace, for a People's Democracy!*, July 1, 1949, p. 4; also in *Pravda*, June 22, 1949, translated in *Soviet Press Translations*, IV, No. 14 (July 15, 1949), 439–441.

24. Mao Tse-tung, "The Dictatorship of People's Democracy," *For a Lasting Peace, for a People's Democracy!*, July 15, 1949, p. 5. This article also appeared in *Pravda,* July 6, 1949, and is translated from there in *Soviet Press Translations,* IV, No. 15 (September 1, 1949), 454–461. Translations may also be found in Brandt, Schwartz, and Fairbank, *A Documentary History of Chinese Communism,* pp. 449–461, and in van der Sprenkel, *New China: Three Views,* pp. 180–198.

25. Chu-Teh, "Chinese People's Struggle for Liberation," *For a Lasting Peace, for a People's Democracy!*, September 1, 1949, p. 3.

26. "Great Victory of People's Democratic Revolution in China," *ibid.,* October 7, 1949, p. 1.

27. Akademiia nauk SSSR, *Krizis kolonial'noi sistemy natsional'no-osvoboditel'-naia bor'ba narodov Vostochnoi Azii* (Moscow, Leningrad: Izdatel'stvo Akademiia Nauk SSSR, 1949).

28. Published separately as a pamphlet (Bombay: People's Publishing House, 1950) and as a chapter in *Crisis of the Colonial System, National Liberation Struggle of the Peoples of East Asia.* Reports presented in 1949 to the Pacific Institute of the Academy of Sciences, USSR (Bombay: People's Publishing House, 1951), pp. 49–79.

29. *Ibid.,* pp. 50–51.

30. *Ibid.*

31. *Ibid.,* p. 74.

32. *Ibid.,* p. 78.

33. Published as a separate pamphlet (Bombay: People's Publishing House, 1950) and as a chapter of *Crisis of the Colonial System,* pp. 81–151.

34. *Ibid.,* pp. 105, 109–110, and especially pp. 143–146.

35. *Ibid.,* p. 146.

36. Published as a pamphlet, *New Stage in India's Liberation Struggle* (Bombay: People's Publishing House, 1950) and as a chapter, "Crisis of British Rule in India and the New Stage in the Liberation Struggle of her Peoples," *Crisis of the Colonial System,* pp. 1–48.

37. *Ibid.,* p. 38.

38. *Ibid.,* p. 46.

39. *Ibid.,* p. 48.

40. *Ibid.,* p. 45.

41. *Ibid.,* pp. 46–47.

42. The important speeches and documents of the Conference may be found in the organ of the WFTU, *World Trade Union Movement,* No. 8 (December 1949). The Conference is discussed at some length and a number of quotations are given in Milton Sacks, "The Strategy of Communism in Southeast Asia," *Pacific Affairs,* XXIII, No. 3 (September 1950), 231–236.

43. "Speech by Liu Shao-chi at the Conference of Trade Unions of Asia and Oceania," *For a Lasting Peace, for a People's Democracy!*, December 30, 1949, p. 2; also in *Pravda,* January 4, 1950, translated in *Soviet Press Translations,* V, No. 6 (March 15, 1950), 168–172. Though the speech is not mentioned in it, an editorial, "China's Revolution and the Struggle Against Colonialism," *People's China,* I, No. 4 (February 16, 1950), 3–5, is essentially an elaboration of it.

44. Extracts in Li Li-san, "The Chinese Labour Movement," *World News and Views,* XXX, No. 2 (January 14, 1950), 17–20. An article based on this report and almost identical with it appeared as "The Labour Movement in China," *People's China,* I, No. 2 (January 16, 1950), 9–10, 25–28.

45. "Manifesto of the Trade Union Conference of the Countries of Asia and Oceania," *For a Lasting Peace, for a People's Democracy!*, January 6, 1950, p. 1.

46. "Resolution on the Reports of the National Trade Union Centres of Asian and Australasian Countries," *World Trade Union Movement*, No. 8 (December 1949), 40.

47. Joshi, "Letter to Foreign Comrades," *Views*, pp. 2–3.

48. *Ibid.*, p. 9.

49. *Ibid.*, p. 7.

50. *Ibid.*, p. 12.

51. *Ibid.*, p. 11.

52. *Ibid.*, p. 14.

53. *Ibid.*, p. 15.

54. *Ibid.*, p. 27.

55. *Ibid.*, p. 6.

56. *Ibid.*, p. 9.

57. *Ibid.*, p. 14.

58. *Ibid.*, pp. 29–30.

59. "Mighty Advance of the National Liberation Movement in the Colonial and Dependent Countries," *For a Lasting Peace, for a People's Democracy!*, January 27, 1950, p. 1; reprinted in *Communist*, III, No. 2 (February–March 1950); extracts containing all important passages in "National Liberation Movement Advances," *World News and Views*, XXX, No. 7 (February 18, 1950), 74. Some paragraphs are quoted in Masani, *The Communist Party of India*, pp. 102–103, but the final paragraph allegedly quoted from the Cominform editorial by Masani on pp. 103–104 is not actually contained in that editorial. Rather, it comes from the CPI Politburo statement of February 1950 responding to the Cominform editorial and may be found in *Communist Review* (London), June 1950, p. 182. It is quoted in part on p. 108, above. Masani states, unfortunately without supporting documentation, that Palme Dutt later disclosed that the initiative for the Cominform editorial had originally come from the Communist Party of Great Britain.

60. Joshi, "Letter to Comrade Ranadive," *Views*, p. 41.

61. Jean A. Curran, Jr., "Dissension Among India's Communists," *Far Eastern Survey*, XIX, No. 13 (July 12, 1950), 135.

62. Joshi, "Letter to Comrade Ranadive," *Views*, p. 39.

63. *Ibid.*, pp. 39–40.

64. Joshi, "Extract from Letter to C. C. Communist Party of Pakistan," *ibid.*, pp. 46–47.

65. Joshi, "For Appeal Against Expulsion," *ibid.*, p. 51.

66. "Statement of the Editorial Board of the 'Communist,' Bombay, on the editorial article in the Organ of the Information Bureau on the National Liberation Movement in the Colonies," *Communist*, III, No. 2 (February–March 1950) quoted in part in Masani, *The Communist Party of India*, p. 104, and reprinted as "The Situation in India," *Communist Review* (London), June 1950, pp. 175–184.

67. *Ibid.*, p. 175.

68. *Ibid.*, p. 176.

69. *Ibid.*, p. 177.

70. *Ibid.*, p. 178.

71. *Ibid.*, p. 184.

72. *Ibid.*, p. 178.

73. *Ibid.*, p. 179.

74. *Ibid.,* p. 176.

75. *Ibid.,* p. 177.

76. *Ibid.,* p. 181.

77. *Ibid.,* p. 179.

78. See pp. 90–91, above.

79. "The Situation in India," *op. cit.,* p. 182.

80. "Defense of Peace and Struggle Against the Warmongers; Resolution of the Information Bureau," quoted in *For a Lasting Peace, for a People's Democracy!,* November 29, 1949, p. 1.

81. "The Situation in India," *op. cit.,* pp. 180–181.

82. *Ibid.,* p. 177.

83. *Ibid.,* p. 183.

84. Joshi, "Post Script" (written in late April or May 1950), *Views,* pp. 59–64.

85. *Ibid.,* pp. 59 and 61.

86. *Ibid.,* p. 63.

87. *Ibid.,* p. 62.

88. *Ibid.,* p. 63.

89. See p. 90, above.

90. See pp. 88, 92–93, above.

91. Joshi, "Post Script," *Views,* p. 62.

92. *Ibid.,* p. 63. Abbreviations and italics in the original.

93. *Ibid.*

94. Joshi, "Personal Explanation," *Views,* inside covers; see also "Post Script," *ibid.,* p. 59.

95. *Ibid.,* pp. 59–61.

96. Quotations from the document appear in Limaye, *Communist Party,* pp. 71–73, and it is summarized in Masani, *The Communist Party of India,* pp. 105–107. The original complete text has not been available to us.

97. "Statement of Central Committee of Indian Communist Party," *Pravda* and *Izvestia,* July 23, 1950, p. 3; translated in *Current Digest of the Soviet Press,* II, No. 30 (September 9, 1950), 31.

98. Reported in editorial, "Communism in India," *New York Times,* July 24, 1950, p. 16.

99. Franz Borkenau, "The Chances of a Mao-Stalin Rift," *Commentary,* XIV (August 1952), 119.

CHAPTER

—— 5 ——

THE SHIFT FROM VIOLENT
TO PEACEFUL NEO-MAOISM (1950–1951)

I. VIOLENT NEO-MAOISM AND THE SOVIET VIEW IN 1950

As we have just seen, the new Central Committee of the Communist Party of India, now dominated by the faction from Andhra Province, clearly proclaimed in its statement of July 19, 1950, its adherence to the neo-Maoist strategy. However, while Moscow, through the Peking WFTU Conference of November 1949 and the Cominform editorial of January 27, 1950, had demanded that the four-class element, but not the armed struggle element, of the "Chinese path" be applied in India, the Andhra Communists, thoroughly committed to their policy of peasant uprisings, felt that all the elements of the Chinese example were now to be followed by the CPI.

CPI statements favoring violent neo-Maoism, June–November 1950. This becomes quite clear in the message of greetings, dated June 30, 1950, which the new Central Committee sent to the Chinese Communist Party. Here "the Central Committee gratefully acknowledge the invaluable aid rendered by the leadership of the Communist Party of China, through their writings and speeches, to our present inner-Party discussions."[1] Without qualification, it is stated of the peoples of the colonial world that "they all see in the Chinese revolution the model of their own revolutions"[2] and that "the Communist Parties in the colonial world are looking upon the Communist Party of China as their model."[3] No doubt is left that the guerrilla warfare of the Chinese Communists is part of this model when it is emphasized that "the peoples of Viet Nam, Malaya, Burma, Philippines, Indonesia, have already taken to this path and other colonial people are going to take it,"[4] and that "the brave fighters of Telengana, Andhra, Mymensingh, etc., have already shown that the Chinese path is the path for India also."[5]

To get a full picture of the strategy of the Andhra leadership now that it was in control of the CPI we must also turn to two other documents published by it in the July–August issue of *Communist*[6] and intended to demarcate sharply its policies from those pursued by the CPI under Ranadive's leadership. Indicating the sources from which the new strategy was derived, these documents state that "the Editorial Board," that is, the CPI leadership, had, since Ranadive's first self-critical statement was made in February 1950, been conducting detailed discussions on the Cominform editorial in the light of the Manifesto and reports of the Peking WFTU Conference, articles and works of Mao Tse-tung, recent articles and speeches of Chinese Communist leaders, and documents of the Soviet academicians on the colonial revolutions.[7] As a result, the Editorial Board "has been reconstituted";[8] it has made "a complete turn" and chalked out "the broad lines of the new strategy and tactics of the present stage of the Indian revolution, which can serve as a basis for achieving unification of the Communist movement."[9] The new Editorial Board withdraws Ranadive's statement of February, saying that it was no honest self-criticism and that it took "a self-justificatory position,"[10] and withdraws also the four articles which set forth Ranadive's "left" strategy and attacked the Andhra Communists' neo-Maoist strategy, which were published in 1949 and which we discussed in Chapter 3, above.[11] It "requests the readers of *Communist* not to regard those articles as authoritative any longer."[12]

The new Andhra leadership of the CPI "unreservedly withdraws the entire criticisms of Comrade Mao Tse-tung" made in Ranadive's statement a year earlier and "tenders its deeply felt apologies"[13] to Mao and the Chinese Communist Party. To offer these humble apologies must have been very pleasing to the Andhra Communists. In doing so they were both defending their own position of the past few years and seizing an opportunity to attack the Ranadive Politburo as being guilty of "a criminal violation of the principle of fraternal cooperation among Communists of all countries," of "a base slander," and of "disrupting solidarity of the anti-imperialist democratic front."[14] The old leadership had "dishonestly pitted the authority of the Nine Communist Parties' Conference against Comrade Mao in order to declare his great work as revisionist," and "went to the length of suggestively mentioning the names of Tito and Browder in the same breath as that of Com. Mao."[15] This attack on Mao had been "one of the most serious of the many mistakes committed by the Editorial Board"[16] and "a necessary part of the Trotskyite-Titoite conceptions which dominated the mind of the Editorial Board" and which it thought were "the last word in the application of Marxist-Leninist theory to the problems of the new stage of the national liberation movement."[17]   The Ranadive leadership is also accused of having "distorted Zhdanov's report and turned a blind eye to the valuable articles of the brother Parties,"[18] of slanderous criticism of brother Communist parties in the article on Revisionism, and failure to publish articles by Chinese Communist leaders in *Communist*.   It is accused of suppression of the Peking Manifesto, of delay in the publication of the Cominform editorial,[19] and of having "remained deaf to the clarion call of the Peking Conference" until finally roused by the Cominform editorial.[20]

In setting forth its own strategy, the new Andhra leadership of the CPI repeatedly refers to the document of the Andhra Provincial Committee of June 1948, which we have discussed earlier,[21] and concurrently attacks Ranadive for not having adopted its proposals.   It thus presents us with another summary of the differences between the "left" and the neo-Maoist strategies, this time from the neo-Maoist point of view.   We now find that, although he had made ample use of quotations from Lenin and Stalin, Ranadive "threw overboard all the teachings of Lenin and Stalin on imperialism and colonial revolutions, produced a full-fledged Trotskyite thesis of one stage revolution."[22] The Andhra leadership, following the Chinese model, on the other hand, proclaims that the New Democratic Revolution is one of all anti-imperialist classes culminating in the People's Democratic Dictatorship. Only this paves the way for the second stage of the revolution, the building of a socialist society.   They point out that Mao had warned against uniting the two stages—that is, against the Trotskyite theory of a single revolution.[23]   This "left" theory of a one-stage revolution had led the CPI to ignore imperialism and feudalism as its main enemies and, instead, to regard the entire bourgeoisie as such.   "The Editorial Board negated the anti-imperialist, anti-feudal, and national liberationist character of the present stage of the revolution in India."[24]   It had made an analysis of the agrarian question denying the dominance of feudal relations,[25] and "systematically neglected and disrupted the developing of the anti-feudal struggle of the peasantry."[26]   Lastly, the former leadership is charged with having stuck dogmatically to its "left-opportunist" conception that the entire bourgeoisie had gone collaborationist, refusing to see that the imperialist–big bourgeois–landlord combine injured the interests of sections of the middle bourgeoisie.[27] To support this charge the new leadership quotes at length the passage from Maslennikov's report to the Soviet Academy of Sciences, which we have quoted above,[28] and it stresses that the task of bringing the middle bourgeoisie into the common front is a very important one for the final victory.[29]

There is hardly a page in the two statements of the new leadership that does not hail Mao's *New Democracy* or the experience of the Chinese Communists as containing "the most valuable lessons for the proletariat and the Communist parties in India and the other colonial countries."[30] Following Mao's "The Dictatorship of People's Democracy," this Chinese experience is defined in terms of three factors, the party, the army, and the united front; and it is then claimed that the Cominform editorial "emphasized exactly these main lessons of the rich experience of the Chinese revolution."[31] As we have seen, however, the Cominform editorial definitely did not emphasize the use of an army for the Indian Communists. Similarly, Mao is quoted as summing up the essence of the Chinese experience when he said: "In China without armed struggle there will be no place for the proletariat, no place for the people, no place for the Communist Party and no victory for the revolution,"[32] and this is followed by a long quotation from Mao on the need to turn backward remote rural areas into military, political, economic, and cultural revolutionary strongholds.[33] Such may indeed have been the essence of Communist experience in China, but the Andhra leaders were wrong in regarding it as the essence of what was now known as the "Chinese path," that is, the neo-Maoist strategy. Since it apparently never occurred to them to distinguish between a particular Chinese tactic and the neo-Maoist strategy, they were following the former as rigidly as the latter. Thus, in a policy statement of November 15, 1950, quoted by the Indian Home Minister to Parliament, the Politburo is reported to have proclaimed: "Finally it is necessary to clearly grasp the truth that the armed struggle has become the principal form of struggle in the present agrarian revolutionary stage that our national liberation movement has grown to."[34]

The new leaders of the CPI from Andhra were undoubtedly trying hard to follow the new line, but their background and policy commitments prevented them from understanding exactly what was expected of them by Moscow, and they were not entirely successful in fulfilling the promise implied in the conclusion of their statement:

> The warning voice of the editorial of the organ of the Information Bureau and the clarion call of the Peking Conference of Trade Unions of Asia and Australasia have awakened us. The leadership and the ranks of our movement are now engaged in a mighty collective effort to correct the past Left-opportunist mistakes, to sharpen and finalize our understanding of the new political line in the light of self-criticism. . . .[35]

Further disintegration of the CPI. To repair the disorganization and low state of morale in the CPI inherited after the two long years

of Ranadive's dictatorial misrule would in any case have been a difficult
task for the new leadership.   As it developed, its policy seemed designed
to aggravate rather than to overcome these difficulties, for, at a time
when not only Ranadive's tactics of throwing bombs in large cities
but also the Andhra Communists' guerrilla tactics in Telengana had
substantially failed, it continued Ranadive's emphasis on violent
methods, although shifting their focus entirely from urban to rural
areas.   The new Andhra leaders of the CPI thus had to contend with
the opposition not only of the adherents of Ranadive's tactics of urban
violence, whom they had just replaced, but also of all those who favored
a return to peaceful tactics, including both Joshi and those leaders in
the large northern cities who sought to base Communist strength
largely on the trade unions.   The Andhra leaders' efforts to spread
guerrilla warfare from Telengana to other areas therefore created
further factionalism and deterioration of morale in the CPI, with the
difficulties apparently centering on discussions of the nature and future
of the Party's activities in Telengana.   Thus a Politburo circular of
December 16, 1950 noted a strong trend in the CPI "casting doubts
on Andhra partisan actions whether they are in the nature of individual terrorist actions."[36]

Within a few months after Rajeshwar Rao's and the Andhra Committee's assumption of power, the Party had been reduced to such
a state that the Politburo, in a circular dated September 16, 1950,
declared:

> A state of semi-paralysis leading to lack of mass activities is now
> a general picture inside the Party, though exceptions are also there.
> Since the last CC meeting in May, the inner Party crisis has further
> accentuated and it has assumed the most acute form leading to
> organizational deadlocks and extreme financial crisis at all levels of
> the Party organization.[37]

The only way out the leadership could suggest was the convening of
a Party congress; and it stated that preparations for it were in progress
—although, as we shall see, such a congress was not to meet until over
three years later.   It appears that, unlike Ranadive, who had by strong
measures managed to maintain himself in power in spite of his Party's
disintegration and had to be removed by foreign intervention, Rajeshwar Rao was on the verge of losing control over the Party.   In a
situation of this sort the eyes of all the factional leaders undoubtedly
turned to Moscow. So, therefore, must ours.

The absence of advice from Moscow, June–November 1950. It has
become clear by now that although Moscow had succeeded, a year after
it had itself wholly accepted the neo-Maoist strategy and half a year

after it had declared its use to be obligatory for all Asian Communist parties, in imposing it on the CPI, it had not succeeded in getting the CPI to follow that particular tactic of the neo-Maoist strategy desired by Moscow. Both the intra-Party situation, which had made it almost inevitable that the Andhra faction would fall heir to Ranadive's power, and Moscow's tendency to express its wishes in rather obscure language were undoubtedly important factors explaining this continued difference between the CPI and Moscow on the use of violence.

Since Ranadive and the "left" strategy lost power in the CPI, adherence to the essential element of the neo-Maoist strategy, the inclusion of a section of the bourgeoisie in the united front, has not been an issue between Moscow and the CPI. Its advocacy in Moscow need therefore no longer be traced but may be taken for granted without any further emphasis on our part.[38] Having completed the treatment of the principal subject of our investigation—the shift of Moscow and consequently of the Indian Communist Party to the new strategy of world Communism with its appeal to the capitalists—we now have to trace the adjustment of the CPI's tactics in accordance with Moscow's wishes.

As has often been true of its relations with the CPI, Moscow seemed to be in no hurry to clarify its own policy and to impose it on the CPI. It appears that in the case of a Communist party like the Indian, whose immediate usefulness to Soviet objectives is in any case limited, Moscow prefers to assume a minimum of responsibility for its guidance and is quite content to let the factional struggle take its course, intervening only when the party's policy becomes quite incompatible with Moscow's and even then just to the extent necessary to make it move in the right direction again, but not giving it specific instructions as to exactly what is desired. Thus, beyond the purely negative guidance on the use of violence in India provided by the Peking WFTU Conference and the Cominform editorial, little seemed to be forthcoming from Moscow on that subject, perhaps simply because Moscow did not feel strongly enough about it, perhaps because it hoped that the intra-CPI developments would force matters in the proper direction anyway.*

* At the time the Andhra Committee replaced Ranadive in the CPI leadership, there even appeared an editorial in the Cominform journal which—perhaps because the writer very carelessly listed a fact simply because it was a fact though not a desired one, perhaps because he was of the same persuasion as Balabushevich and Dyakov at the time of their reluctant conversion to neo-Maoism in 1949—listed armed struggle "in a number of districts in India" along with other Asian countries where Communists were engaging in warfare and stated that "in the present conditions, as shown by the experience of China, armed resistance to the imperialist plunderers is the most effective form of the national liberation movement in

A warning against violent neo-Maoism from Peking, June 1950. A statement that may well have been intended as a directive to the CPI appeared at the time of the Andhra Committee's assumption of the Party's leadership in the Chinese Communists' chief organ, in the form of a reply to a reader from the editor. Undoubtedly to indicate its significance, and probably to make it available to the Indian Communists, it was reprinted in the Chinese Communist English-language periodical.[39] After dealing with Communist peasant warfare in China, this statement declares that this characteristic of the Chinese revolution "can under certain historical conditions become the common characteristic of all revolutions of other colonial and semi-colonial countries."[40] It then quotes from Liu Shao-chi's opening address to the Peking WFTU Conference on the desirability of armed struggle on the part of "many colonial and semi-colonial peoples" and from the Cominform editorial of January 27. It proceeds to quote a statement made by Ranadive, identifying him as the General Secretary of the CPI, fully accepting the conclusions of this editorial and the lessons of the Chinese Revolution as an infallible compass for the CPI. Having thus sharply focused on India a discussion that began as one of armed struggle in general and the Chinese Civil War in particular, the article makes this statement on the applicability of the Chinese example, which it had just quoted the CPI as accepting wholeheartedly:

> Armed struggle against imperialist aggression is essential for the liberation of many colonies and semi-colonies. But the time and place for conducting this kind of revolutionary armed struggle must be decided according to concrete conditions. It can by no means be conducted in any colony or semi-colony at any time without the necessary conditions and preparations.[41]

Just as Ranadive had had the rug pulled out from under him by an editorial in the organ of the Cominform, on which he had relied in the defense of his "left" strategy, so the Andhra Communists are here told by the chief organ of the Chinese Communist Party, to whose example they constantly referred in justifying their policy of rural violence, that this policy is not a necessary part of the Chinese example. The immediate effect, however, was not the same. For, although the Andhra Communists looked to Peking for their example, they apparently looked quite as much as the other Indian Communists to Moscow

---

colonial countries." Editorial, "The Peoples of the Colonial and Dependent Countries in the Struggle against the Warmongers," *For a Lasting Peace, for a People's Democracy!*, May 19, 1950, p. 1. However, the acknowledged quality of a directive of the Cominform editorial of January 27 or the pronouncements of the Peking WFTU Conference cannot be attributed to such a remark.

for their directives. The editorial in Moscow's Cominform journal had brought almost immediate results; the editorial in Peking's *People's Daily* was ignored. It brought forth no self-critical statements, let alone the fall of the Andhra leadership. As we have seen, that leadership continued to propound and pursue its policy of violent neo-Maoism for several months, although its position was at least as weak in the latter half of 1950 as Ranadive's had been in the early part of that year.

Palme Dutt's open letter in favor of peaceful neo-Maoism, December 1950. When, by the end of 1950, the situation within the CPI had gone from bad to worse, advice from the West finally arrived. It was in the form of a reply to questions on India, dated December 20, by the British Communist expert on India and the CPI's old guide, Palme Dutt.[42] For the first time some positive guidance was now provided as to how the CPI was expected to implement Moscow's year-old directive to adopt the four-class strategy, a task which the Party had obviously shown itself to be incapable of fulfilling by its own devices. Its forms of struggle, Dutt advises the CPI, may vary from the collection of signatures and the holding of meetings and demonstrations to local limited mass struggles such as strikes and campaigns on special issues, "reaching to the highest forms of popular struggle" wherever the conditions are ripe. The term "highest forms of struggle" always refers to armed struggle, although the latter phrase is not used by Dutt. However, in sharp contrast to the CPI's Andhra leaders, who placed their main emphasis on armed violence in rural areas, Dutt continues: "It is evident that the present paramount task is the initial mobilization of mass support and activity on the most elementary issues, the development of working class unity, the promotion of the alliance of the working class and the peasantry, and the building of the peace movement and the broad democratic front." Here we have a listing of objectives the CPI has been pursuing since 1951 and one that omits armed violence as of no applicability at the present time.

Palme Dutt's statement is particularly emphatic on the need for a broad united front and a strong peace movement. To make the formation of the Democratic Front a reality, Dutt suggests that its program not be laid down beforehand by one section (meaning the Communist Party) and imposed on the others or made a condition of their cooperation, but that the program be simple and concrete and, at the outset, be limited to a few points corresponding to the real wishes of the masses. In his stress on the peace movement, Dutt opened up a new perspective to the CPI, revealing that Moscow was now beginning to appreciate the fact that Nehru's neutralist foreign policy at times, in

effect, aided Soviet foreign policy objectives. Ever since the abandonment of the "right" strategy in Moscow in the middle of 1947 and in
India at the end of that year, both Moscow and the CPI had virulently
denounced the Nehru government and all its works. They had in particular again and again "unmasked" its "third path" foreign policy
as merely hiding its subservience to Anglo-American imperialism, implying that only two paths were possible, each leading straight to one
of Zhdanov's two "camps." Now, however, Dutt proclaims that the
"indications of a divergence, even though still hesitant and limited,
of Premier Nehru . . . from the reckless aggressive war policy . . . are
a very important development." "Supporters of peace in India, while
welcoming every step towards disentanglement of India from the
Anglo-American war-bloc, will press forward with unsparing vigour
for the further steps which are necessary in order that India shall fulfill
a firm and consistent peace policy." Thus the CPI was to remain
opposed to the Nehru government—there was no thought of replacing
the united front from below with a united front from above with the
Congress—but to welcome those of its steps that moved in the direction
of "peace," that is, were favorable to Moscow objectives.*

II. The Shift of the CPI to Peaceful Neo-Maoism

*Central Committee meeting of December 1950: The ascendance of
peaceful neo-Maoism.* In December 1950, the month in which Dutt
wrote his open letter, the CPI's Central Committee met. We do not
know whether the Dutt letter was available to it at that time and
cannot be sure that it would, in any case, have been considered as
authoritative as a direct Moscow statement. Certainly no immediate
self-critical statement was forthcoming from the CPI leadership, and
the divisions within the Party persisted. Nevertheless, the effect of the

---

* Correspondingly, as we shall see, the Communist-led "peace" movement was to
differ from the Communist-led "national liberation" movement in that it could
include people who differed with the CPI on some issues. The CPI was now
placed in a somewhat ambiguous situation which, being essentially incompatible
with its totalitarian creed of naturally dividing the world and all its people into
black and white (or red) camps, has plagued it to the present day. Indeed, generally speaking, the relation of the party to the peace movement has been the chief
internal problem of Communist parties everywhere in recent years.

M. R. Masani summarizes at some length, unfortunately without indicating its
source, another letter sent during this period by Palme Dutt to the CPI. Its contents do not seem to differ substantially from those of Dutt's open letter discussed
above, but it is far more explicit in its emphasis on the essential characteristics of
the neo-Maoist strategy and on the necessity of abandoning the use of armed
violence for the present. Masani, *The Communist Party of India*, pp. 109–111.

new line, whether it had been received through Dutt's letter or otherwise, was clearly visible in the decisions of the Central Committee. The intra-Party situation was apparently such that the leadership could not hope to conceal the existence of factional divisions. A communique of the Party's central headquarters[43] openly announced that it had not been possible "to thrash out the main political differences and evolve an agreed political line" and that "differences on vital tactical issues have yet to be resolved." Final decisions would be taken by a Party congress that "will be convened as soon as possible to work out the political line of the Party."

This Central Committee meeting marked the end of the short and turbulent period of the Andhra Committee's undivided rule over the CPI. Although, as the communique expressly noted, Rajeshwar Rao, the Andhra leader, continued as General Secretary, the Central Committee was enlarged and the Politburo once again reconstituted in order, it was claimed, to represent all major trends in the Party. In reality this reshuffle indicated the admission to power of the faction in the Party standing for peaceful neo-Maoism, which must have consisted in part of former adherents of the "right" strategy, but not the return of any advocates of Ranadive's "left" strategy. In a special resolution the Central Committee invited the "very large number of comrades . . . suspended or expelled from the Party on the basis of flimsy or baseless charges" during Ranadive's regime to rejoin the Party,[44] and it also granted Joshi's request for a retrial, while at the same time setting up a commission to inquire into the conduct of Ranadive and bring charges against him.[45] It is interesting to note that the followers of both violent and peaceful neo-Maoism were now sharing power, an arrangement inconceivable when the shift from the "right" to the "left" and from the "left" to the neo-Maoist strategy took place. This situation indicates that differences in the Party over the use of violent or peaceful tactics are not so deep as differences on strategy.

In a compromise between the adherents of the new peaceful neo-Maoist tactics emphasized by Dutt and the adherents of the old violent tactics of the Andhra Communists, the Central Committee agreed on the one hand, to redouble the Party's efforts in the peace campaign and in the creation of labor unity and a broad united front of all "left" parties and, on the other hand, "to make every effort to popularize the cause of the heroic peasants of Telengana and other areas who are waging a glorious struggle for land and freedom."[46] However, the new tactics were in the ascendancy already, for little seems actually to have been said about Telengana, while a special resolution was passed "On

United Front."[47]   It begins with the typically neo-Maoist assertion, to which Ranadive used to object so strongly, that the acquisition of independence by India had changed nothing, that foreign imperialism therefore remained the main enemy, and that the Congress was subservient to the imperialists and to "foreign capitalists and Indian big business, princes, landlords."   Having thus defined the enemies as not including the entire bourgeoisie, it opposes to them in equally good neo-Maoist fashion the "united revolutionary struggle by all anti-imperialist classes, sections, parties and groups."   That the Congress is not considered one of these anti-imperialist parties is obvious; and the Socialist Party leadership, too, is denounced as supporting imperialism.   To these two large parties the CPI is to have typical united front from below relations, and it is even stated that united front relations are to be established with the anti-imperialist rank and file of the Socialist Party.

United fronts from below and from above.   Palme Dutt had been thinking primarily in terms of such a united front from below, of winning mass support away from the other parties by means of a simple concrete program appealing to people's immediate needs.   The most striking aspect of the new Central Committee's resolution on the united front, however, is that it clearly conceives of this united front primarily in terms of one from above, of "top alliances" with what it calls the "left" parties—small non-Congress, non-Socialist Party groups more or less sympathetic to the Communists—and that it wants to establish united action among these parties on the basis of a common program emphasizing such by no means elementary and immediate issues as a Democratic People's Government, confiscation of all foreign capital and landlord's holdings, etc.   It proclaims that the "left" parties, including the CPI, had in the past often been guilty of a sectarian approach and that this disunity must now be ended.   The first step in the establishment of unity among all anti-imperialist classes, parties, groups, and organizations is the united front between "left" parties.   While this is in no sense a return to the "right" strategy of a united front from above with the Congress and the Socialists and is, in fact, part of the united front from below against these parties, since the "left" parties are largely splinters that seceded from them, the preference of the CPI leadership for the approach "from above" to these small "left" parties rather than an approach "from below" to the rank and file of the large parties is noteworthy.   To some extent it may be due to the fact that at that time former adherents of the "right" strategy of the united front from above were regaining some influence in the Party, and the "left" strategy of the united front from below associated with Ranadive was thoroughly discredited. The main reason for the preference is more likely to have been that it appeared easier to the CPI leadership to expand its power by means of deals with the leaders of various splinter groups than by making an effective appeal directly to the people.

The peace movement and its difficulties. Emphasis on the "peace" movement, just as on the "Democratic Front," became very prominent in the CPI after the policy change, indicated by Dutt's letter, at the end of 1950. By early 1951 "peace" had become the major theme of the Party's weekly newspaper *Cross Roads,* in which far more space was devoted to the peace movement than to the CPI itself. At the end of March it was officially announced that the paper would change its appeal in accordance with the new line.[48] Apparently referring not only to the more distant past under Ranadive but also to the more immediate past under Andhra leadership, the announcement stated that "everywhere our voice was muffled and gagged by a narrow sectarian outlook," but now "the New Crossroads . . . will be the voice of ALL sections in that democratic front, and not the voice of any one section or group . . . [and] will be devoted above all to the cause of Peace." The Communist Party newspaper, having thus characterized itself as sectarian because it had been the voice of the Communist Party, now promises to introduce such features as humor, art, cinema, short stories, sports, and household hints as well as a feature page on Asia.*

Just as Palme Dutt had done in December, so the CPI discovered in January that Nehru was not a lackey of imperialism after all, and that it would be wise from the Communist point of view to encourage rather than "unmask" his neutralist foreign policies. Reporting on the Commonwealth Prime Ministers' Conference,[49] *Cross Roads* states approvingly: "Pandit Nehru has taken a firm and forthright stand on the steps necessary to ensure world peace"; he "forcefully demanded recognition of People's China and its inclusion in the United Nations" and "promotion of world peace by cooperation with the Soviet Union." The report speaks of India's "present independent peace stand" and urges Nehru to "break with these mercenaries of the dollar" and strike a blow for peace. Three weeks later this remarkable change in the CPI's attitude was made official in a statement of the Central Committee saying that "The Communist Party of India welcomes the forthright refusal of Prime Minister Nehru . . . to associate India with the

---

* Another event closely related to the growing emphasis on the peace movement is the formation, during the same period, of a China-India Society in Calcutta. "Calcutta Heralds: China-India Society," *Cross Roads,* March 2, 1951, p. 4.

American plan to unleash a third world war on Asian soil by branding People's China as an aggressor."[50]   That there was opposition to this new attitude in a party that had regarded Nehru as its chief opponent during the past three years is obvious.   It is clear from an article by the editor of *Cross Roads*[51] referring those who continue to say that Nehru is a puppet of imperialism to a number of his actions, including those in favor of peace in Korea and of the admission of Communist China to the U. N. and those in opposition to rearmament and the atom bomb.   "Nehru's peace role" is to be understood and appreciated —although it is pointed out that the Party is not blind to his "reactionary" home policy or to such "danger signals" in his foreign policy as India's continued membership in the Commonwealth and Nehru's silence on Malaya and Vietnam.

We have already alluded to the difficulties entailed in the sponsorship of a supposedly broad and non-partisan peace movement by a Communist party.   These are graphically illustrated by resolutions on the "Misuse of the Peace Platform," adopted by the preparatory committee of the Second National Peace Congress at New Delhi, March 3–4, 1951, which indicate that there was a tendency on the part of CPI members to regard the peace movement as but another Communist Party organization.   The committee, it was reported,[52] took serious note of two types of mistakes made by certain peace committees.   The first of these was the use of the peace platform for purposes other than that of peace between nations.   Such use must be avoided, for "on our platform we want all who believe in peace irrespective of where they stand on other issues"; it must not become the platform for any one party.   The discussion of issues other than peace will alienate some people.   The second mistake is that of passing resolutions that go beyond the agreed views of all elements in the Indian peace movement[53] and represent the viewpoint of only a section, however large.*   Specifically, not all Communist Party resolutions must find their way to the platform of peace committees.   The hope is then expressed that, armed with these resolutions on the Misuse of the Peace Platform, the peace movement can really widen into a movement embracing millions of all shades of opinion.   In fact, however, as we shall see, the Party found it necessary to continue, on the one hand, to warn its members against "sectarianism" in relation to the peace movement and, on the

---

* This is illustrated by the following example: all agree on peaceful settlement in and withdrawal of foreign troops from Korea, and a large majority feel that the Americans were the aggressors in the Korean War.   This latter view should not be embodied in peace resolutions, since it would alienate some of those already in the movement as well as potential future followers.

other, to make that movement palatable to them, even though non-Communists were in it and it was not revolutionary.[54]

The CPI Program of April 1951 and the 1951 May Day Manifesto. In April 1951 the Communist Party of India published a new Program.[55] It is not surprising that, at this late date, it is a thoroughly neo-Maoist document. It attacks the Indian government for protecting foreign capital, the landlords, and the princes and for being subservient to and dependent on British imperialism. It characterizes the present stage of the Indian Revolution and the revolutionary forces in typically neo-Maoist fashion when it says that the

> . . . Communist Party is not demanding the establishment of Socialism in our country. In view of the backwardness of the economic development of India and of the weakness of the mass organizations of workers, peasants and toiling intelligentsia, our Party does not find it possible at present to carry out socialist transformations in our country. But our Party regards as quite mature the task of replacing the present anti-democratic and anti-popular Government by a new Government of People's Democracy, created on the basis of a coalition of all democratic anti-feudal and anti-imperialist forces in the country.

The bourgeoisie takes its place among these forces. It is listed, along with the workers, peasants, and the petty bourgeoisie, as a victim of the government's policies: "Even the industrialists, manufacturers, and traders are hit by the policies of this Government which is totally in the grip of monopoly financiers, landlords, and princes and their foreign British advisers." And, along with the other classes, the native bourgeoisie is appealed to in the new Program by the inclusion of a plank for the protection of national industries against foreign competition. How the Party envisaged its united front to be one from below directed against the Congress and the Socialist Party, and how workers and capitalists—the antagonists of the Marxian class struggle—are, under the neo-Maoist strategy, to be united by the Communist party, are made very clear by a passage in the CPI's May Day Manifesto, published almost simultaneously with the new Program. After referring to those socialists who oppose their anti-Communist leaders, it says: "The Party desires to declare on this May Day that it will be its sincere endeavour to unite all these Socialists, other Leftists, honest Congressmen, and above all, the lakhs of workers, peasants, middle classes, intellectuals, non-monopoly capitalists and other progressives in a mighty Democratic Front."[56]

The Statement of Policy of April 1951. Being directed to the general public, both the Party's Program and the May Day Manifesto state its opposition to the government and set forth its own general objectives, but not the methods by which these latter are to be attained. In other words, these two documents are based on the general neo-Maoist strategy, on which the CPI leadership was agreed, but are silent on the question of the use of violence, on which the leadership had been, as recently as December 1950, deeply divided. However, we have seen how, since that split was openly acknowledged at the December meeting of the Central Committee, the new tactics of emphasis on the peace movement and a broad united front had pushed aside the old ones of peasant guerrilla warfare. Without the aid of a Party congress, which in December had been regarded as the only way to resolve the differences, but no doubt with the aid of Palme Dutt's letter and possibly other new hints from Moscow and perhaps from Peking as well as a restudy of old hints, the CPI leadership was by April 1951 sufficiently consolidated around the Moscow line to tackle the problem of tactics openly.* It did this in a Statement of Policy[57] issued by the Politburo and designed expressly to deal with the methods by which the objectives of the Party's new Program were to be achieved. This Statement marks the defeat of the policy of violent neo-Maoism sponsored by the Andhra Communists and the final victory of the policy of peaceful neo-Maoism, which was to be in effect during the following years. It is thus the last one of the many fundamental CPI documents analyzed in this book as marking the shifts in the Party's line and, like the others, is worthy of some detailed attention.

As is necessary for a party which changes its line as frequently as the CPI, the Statement, like many of its predecessors, first of all distinguishes the new policy from the old ones, in this case both from Ranadive's "left" strategy, discarded only a year earlier, and especially from the even more recent violent tactic of the Andhra Communists' neo-Maoism:

> After the Second Party Congress, differences and controversies arose inside the Party about the path that the Indian revolutionary

* According to one report—for or against which we have no evidence—the Moscow line was imposed on and agreement on it was reached among the CPI leadership through an "underground" trip to Moscow early in 1951 of four CPI leaders, including General Secretary Rajeshwar Rao, who represented the Andhra faction standing for rural violence, S. A. Dange, the foremost Communist trade union leader, and Ajoy Ghosh, a representative of the faction standing for peaceful neo-Maoism. Democratic Research Service, *Communist Conspiracy at Madurai*, also published in identical form as *Communist Conspiracy in India* (Bombay: Popular Book Depot, 1954) , pp. 19–20, and Masani, *The Communist Party of India*, p. 115. That the new CPI line was indeed of Moscow origin is clear from our analysis; its manner of transmission from Moscow to India is of less interest to us.

movement must adopt. For a time, it was advocated that the main weapon in our struggle would be the weapon of general strike of industrial workers followed by countrywide insurrection as in Russia. Later, on the basis of a wrong understanding of the lessons of the Chinese Revolution, the thesis was put forward that, since ours is a semi-colonial country like China, our revolution would develop in the same way as in China, with partisan war of the peasantry, as its main weapon.[58]

Just as the Andhra Committee had proclaimed less than a year earlier, so now the new group in control of the Party announced that, while all preceding "paths" had been wrong, it had finally hit upon the "correct" one:

> After long discussion, running for several months, the Party has now arrived at a new understanding of the correct path for attaining the freedom of the country and the happiness of the people, a path which we do not and cannot name as either Russian or Chinese. It should be, and is, one that conforms to the teachings of Marx, Engels, Lenin and Stalin, and that utilizes the lessons given by all the struggles of history, especially the Russian and Chinese, the Russian because it was the first Socialist Revolution in the world carried out by the working class under the leadership of the Communist Party of Lenin and Stalin in a capitalist and imperialist country, and the Chinese because it was the first People's Democratic Revolution in a semi-colonial, dependent country, under the leadership of the Communist Party in which even the national bourgeoisie took part. At the same time one has to remember that every country has its own peculiarities, natural and social, which cannot fail to govern its path to liberation.[59]

From the description of prerevolutionary Russia as capitalist and imperialist and of China as semi-colonial and dependent, it is clear that the Chinese example is held more applicable to India than the Russian; and it is interesting to note that the only feature of the Chinese revolution stressed is the participation in it of the national bourgeoisie. That its other chief feature, peasant warfare, which the Andhra Communists had stressed, is not to serve as an example is not left to inference, however; for, although no more is said about the Russian example, an entire section of the Policy Statement is devoted to the similarities and differences between India and China.[60]

The similarity lies simply in the general Maoist and neo-Maoist definition of the main enemy: "Like the Chinese, we have to fight feudalism and imperialism. Our revolution is anti-feudal, anti-imperialist." But the Central Committee finds that to conclude from this that the CPI should rely mainly on peasant partisan warfare "would mean neglecting to look at other factors of the Chinese Revolution and also neglecting to look into our own specific conditions." Thus it is pointed out that the Chinese Communists already had an army when they turned to the countryside, and that the absence of a good communications system in China made it difficult for the enemy to attack the guerrilla forces. But India has such a system; in India, moreover, there is a far bigger working class than there was in China. Further, the Chinese Communist army was again and again threatened with annihilation until it reached Manchuria, where, with the industrial base in hand and the friendly Soviet Union in the rear, it could rebuild and launch its final offensive. The geographical situation in India is quite different. Finally, it is pointed out, the Chinese Communists stuck to peasant partisan war alone out of sheer necessity and not out of principle, and the CPI should not make a principle out of that necessity.

For the CPI the correct path is to be "the grand alliance of the working class and the peasantry, acting in unison, the combination of workers' and peasants' struggles,"[61] which had in practice been ignored both in the "left" period with its emphasis on the working class and in the Andhra period with its concentration on the peasantry.* Reliance on both the working class and the peasantry is hailed as "this great lesson of history, a lesson which is neither only the Russian path nor the Chinese path, but a path of Leninism applied to Indian conditions," while "all our previous understandings have to be discarded as being one-sided and defective."[62]

Having clearly rejected exclusive reliance on peasant guerrilla warfare, the Statement turns to the question of the use of violence in general, but in a far less forthright manner.

> The understanding will also show to comrades that the main question is not whether there will be armed struggle or not, the main question is not whether to be non-violent or violent. It is the reactionary ruling classes who resort to force and violence against the people and who pose for us the question whether our creed is violence or non-violence. Such a poser is a poser of Gandhian ideology, which in practice, misleads the masses and is a poser of which we must steer clear. Marxism and history have once and for all decided the question for the Party and the people of every country in the world long ago. All action of the masses in the defence of their interests to achieve their liberation is sacrosanct. History sanctions

---

* Just as Ranadive had done, the new leaders criticize the Andhra Communists because under them "the working class remained leader only 'in theory,' only through the Party, because the Party is defined as the Party of the working class." Like Ranadive, who, however, had at least wanted to attack all of neo-Maoism and not just its Andhra variant, they hit well beyond the target with this attack, which, as we discussed on pp. 71–73, above, goes to the very heart of Leninism itself.

all that the people decide to do to clear the lumber-load of decadence and reaction in their path to progress and freedom.[63]

The Statement had already pointed out that "even a liberal would now feel ashamed to maintain, let alone the Communist Party and other democrats and revolutionaries, that this Government and the classes that keep it in power will ever allow us to carry out a fundamental democratic transformation in the country by parliamentary methods alone"[64] and that the road leading to the realization of the Party's program would therefore have to be found "elsewhere." Violence is thus clearly justified in principle, and its ultimate use seems to be envisaged.* However, we are not interested here in the Communists' principles since they themselves are not guided by them, nor in their visions of the ultimate seizure of power since many changes in line can intervene between now and the time when such a seizure might take place. Just as in Palme Dutt's letter, which set the tone for the CPI's new policy, violence is mentioned as one of the Party's possible methods but has no place among its immediate tasks.

Describing the "Immediate Situation and Tasks,"[65] the Policy Statement declares that, although the crisis of the government is deep and growing and Communists cannot "move and work as if they are living in a democracy with rights and liberties, and nothing need be done to protect that Party and the leadership of mass organizations from onslaughts of the law run mad," yet "it would be gross exaggeration to say that the country is already on the eve of armed insurrection or revolution." Such a reading of the situation would lead the CPI into "adventurism," isolate it from the people, and "hand over the masses to reformist disruptors." It is admitted that the Party is too weak and that it has not been able to mobilize all anti-government dissatisfaction in its favor: "The growth of the mass movement has not kept pace with the growth of discontent against the present Government" and "this weakness of the mass movement is due, above all, to the weakness

---

* However, a special section of the Statement of Policy (pp. 7–8) is, as an attack on the Andhra Committee, directed against the use of individual terrorism, which, it is said, is not sanctioned by history because in it the masses are not in action. That this and subsequent condemnations of individual terrorism were, in fact, aimed at the Andhra Communists is borne out by a statement of Dange at a press conference in answer to a question as to what deviations there were from the Party line in "the Telengana question," that is, the Andhra Communists' conduct of the fighting in Telengana: "The only deviation was individual terror." "Press Conference of Dange, Member of Indian Communist Party Central Committee," *Pravda*, November 28, 1951, p. 3; *Izvestia*, November 28, 1951, p. 4, in *Current Digest of the Soviet Press*, III, No. 48 (January 12, 1952), 22–23, also in *Soviet Press Translations*, VII, No. 3 (February 1, 1952), 90–92.

of our Party." The immediate task of the Party, therefore, far from engaging in violence, is to build "unity in action," to "grow into a mass Party," and, particularly, to participate in the coming parliamentary elections. This quite non-violent theme is elaborated in the concluding sections of the Policy Statement on "Working Class Unity" and the "Struggle for Peace."[66] There it is stressed that united workers' and peasants' organizations must be formed, the latter "including rich peasants," by "the most intense, patient and daily work among the masses" and appeals to their "immediate, simple demands." Finally, "one of the key tasks . . . is the building of the peace movement. The struggle for peace must become an integral part of our work in all mass organizations." The Party, it is stated, supports any move for peace, including those of the government, but it has no illusion that the government is pursuing "a consistent and honest policy for peace."

The CPI's Statement of Policy of April 1951 served two important functions: First, it brought into the open for the first time the question of the extent of the applicability of the Chinese example to India, making it crystal clear that armed struggle on the Chinese model is not applicable to India and that it is thus not an essential aspect of the neo-Maoist strategy, a point that both Moscow and Peking had been making at least since the Peking WFTU Conference a year and a half earlier. Second, the Statement of Policy adopts in full Palme Dutt's ideas on the methods to be followed by the Party, notably those of the broadest possible united front against the Congress and Socialist Parties and of great reliance on the peace campaign. Thus it makes clear, especially if it is read in conjunction with the CPI's new Program adopted at the same time, that the essential aspect of the neo-Maoist strategy, the four-class appeal, was firmly anchored in CPI policy.

The Statement of Policy, then, marks the point where, after at least a year and a half but possibly two or more years of divergence, the strategy and policy of the Indian Communist Party had once again been brought into full agreement with those favored by Moscow. We have seen that, beginning at the end of 1947, as a result of the Zhdanov speech, the CPI moved farther and farther to the "left" while Moscow moved in a neo-Maoist direction, with both being committed to sharply different positions by the middle of 1949; that the "left" strategy was finally replaced by the neo-Maoist strategy in the CPI in the first half of 1950; and that the neo-Maoist strategy was followed until the end of 1950 in its violent form, not approved of by Moscow for India. Now, finally, the CPI understood what was expected of it. Since 1951 it successfully followed the Moscow line in respect to those of its fundamental aspects with which we are here concerned.

The "Tactical Line" of early 1951. We must now deal briefly and parenthetically with the "Tactical Line," reportedly a secret Communist document brought back from Moscow by CPI leaders early in 1951 on which the Statement of Policy and, indeed, Communist strategy in subsequent years were based.* Like the Statement of Policy, it rejects the view that peasant warfare on the Chinese model should be the CPI's main weapon,[67] but it is far more outspoken than the published statement in its advocacy of violent methods, favoring a combination of peasant guerrilla warfare with workers' uprisings in the cities.[68] This is a striking feature of the "Tactical Line," but it does not make it essentially different from the Statement of Policy, since it envisages armed action not for the present but "when the maturing crisis gives rise to" it.[69] Like the published document, the "Tactical Line" states expressly that "it would be gross exaggeration to assert that India is already on the verge of armed insurrection or revolution,"[70] and it admits that "if the crisis bursts out in the near future the Party in its present and disorganised and weak state will not be able to fully utilise it to lead the people to revolution."[71] The immediate tasks listed in the two documents are the same: the creation of "a broad nationwide United Front of all anti-imperialist classes (including the national bourgeoisie), sections, groups, parties and elements";[72] unity in workers' and peasants' organizations;[73] strengthening the Party;[74] participation in the forthcoming elections;[75] and, above all, building the peace movement by abandoning all manifes-

---

* This document was published by the Democratic Research Service, an anti-Communist propaganda organization in Bombay, early in 1954 (*Communist Conspiracy at Madurai*, pp. 35–48) and is reprinted as an appendix by M. R. Masani, one of the chief figures in this organization, in *The Communist Party of India*, pp. 252–263. The authenticity of the document seems to have been widely accepted, and we have no reason to doubt it, although its sources remain unknown to us. Its content and style, at least, make it appear entirely possible that it is genuine. Nevertheless, we shall not examine the "Tactical Line" in detail, not only because to do so would be a departure from our policy to rely for basic documentation on what are unquestionably the Communists' own published words—a source entirely adequate for the purposes of the analysis here carried on—but also because it contains substantially and often almost verbatim the same message as the published Statement of Policy.

Some important quotations from this document may be found in Atreya, "Indian Communists Plan for Revolution," *The New Leader*, XXXVII, No. 10 (March 8, 1954), 3–5, where it is wrongly referred to as a memorandum brought by Harry Pollitt, General Secretary of the British Communist Party, to the 3rd Congress of the CPI, held at Madurai from December 27, 1953 to January 3, 1954.

tations of sectarianism.[76] All of these are to be accomplished not by violent means but by "patient day to day work"[77] on the basis of the people's immediate demands—although the building of underground units in the cities and villages is also mentioned.[78]

It is clear that there is no need to refer to a secret Communist document, even if there is no question about its authenticity, to prove that the Indian Communists under their current policy do not in principle reject the use of violence. They have made that point quite clear in their published Statement of Policy. We have seen, particularly with regard to the neo-Maoist strategy, that the use of violence is for them a matter merely of tactics and not of strategy, let alone of principle. The secret "Tactical Line" does not prove that the Indian Communists will necessarily eventually engage in armed violence. It can only show that in early 1951 their leaders believed or professed to believe that such would ultimately be the case (although for the more immediate future they themselves advocated the peaceful tactics the CPI has in fact employed since 1951). However, we know very well that future CPI policy will be determined not by the leaders' past opinions but by Moscow's future desires.

Furthermore, we cannot be entirely certain that the secret rather than the published statement represents the true views of the leaders, and that they said little about future violence in the published one in order to make their policy more acceptable to the Indian people. It is just possible that, on the contrary, they did not in truth expect armed violence but emphasized it in the secret document to make their current peaceful policy acceptable to those factions of the Party, notably the Andhra one, which were deeply committed to the use of violence. If Communist leaders are unprincipled and untruthful, as they obviously are, we must expect them to be so in relation to their own party as well as to the general public; and we must not place any greater reliance on a secret than on a published party document as an indication of the party's policy in the relatively distant future—especially when the two do not differ essentially.

The replacement of the Andhra leadership and the end of fighting in Telengana. In May 1951, just after the adoption of the Statement of Policy, the CPI's Central Committee met[79] and ratified the defeat of the Andhra faction, heralded in that Statement, by replacing its leader, Rajeshwar Rao, by Ajoy Ghosh as the Party's new leader.* The

* Formally, the position of General Secretary was left vacant and Ghosh was named as the Secretary of the Secretariat of the Central Committee, this Secretariat being identical with the Politburo. Ghosh was later elected General Secretary at a Party Conference in October 1951.

Central Committee also directed Party units and members to concentrate on the work of forging "unity," announced that the Party would participate in the coming elections, and once again stressed that "Communists cannot have anything to do with the tactics and methods of individual and squad terrorism."[*]

The entire Party leadership had now officially been brought into line behind the policy of peaceful neo-Maoism, but in Telengana the partisan war, which had begun in 1946 and continued through the periods of Joshi's "right" strategy, Ranadive's "left" strategy, and Rajeshwar Rao's neo-Maoist strategy, was still going on. The Party had to attack the difficult problem of liquidating this venture if it wanted to make its practice accord with its new policy. In a resolution passed by the Central Committee at its session in May 1951[80] it did so in a rather gingerly fashion. The resolution began by saying that, while the Party had to make suggestions on tactics, it could not decide on or call off the people's struggles, that the decision was up to the people of Telengana, and that the Party wanted to protect them and their hard-won gains. But, getting to the point, it continued: "At the same time, the CC wishes to state that it is prepared to solve the problem by negotiation and settlement, intended to preserve and protect the interests of the peasantry and the people and to restore peaceful conditions in the area." To pave the way, it asserted that the fighting, which had begun before the Nehru government was in existence, had not been intended to overthrow that government but merely to end feudal oppression, a distinction that had not been drawn in the past when the government was described as representing and serving the feudal interests. A number of conditions for settlement were then set forth.

Subsequently the Communist press reported that Communist negotiators had arrived in Hyderabad on July 18, listing somewhat fewer conditions than before,[81] but by the end of July the government appar-

---

[*] P. C. Joshi, CPI leader during the "right" period up to 1947, who had denounced both Ranadive's "leftism" and Rajeshwar Rao's violent neo-Maoism, returned to the fold with the adoption of the strategy of peaceful neo-Maoism. He became editor of an unofficial Communist monthly, *India To-Day*, whose appearance as "a new democratic monthly" was announced in an advertisement in the CPI's *Cross Roads*, April 13, 1951, p. 3. B. T. Ranadive, the "left" leader, was apparently not restored to grace until 1953, when some articles of his on economic questions—a non-controversial matter in terms of the strategy differences that had torn the Party and in which he figured so prominently—appeared in CPI organs. "India's Economic Crisis," *New Age* (Bombay), II, No. 2 (February 1953), 49–65; No. 3 (March 1953), 39–55; "Why this Crisis in India's Economy," *Cross Roads*, August 16, 1953, p. 10.

ently had refused to negotiate.[82] This must have put the Communist
leaders on the spot, since, with Moscow's demands always coming first
and the actual situation in India only second, in order to be faithful
to their new policy they were obliged to call off the fighting whether
the government met their conditions or not. They finally did this
on October 22, 1951 in a press conference statement[83] made on behalf
of the Central Committee and the Andhra Committee (under whose
provincial jurisdiction the Telengana fighting had been going on). In
an effort to make this, in effect, unconditional surrender—due as much
to Moscow's as to the Indian government's policy—appear as an attack
on the government, they implied that they would now deprive the
government of all excuses for not holding elections in Telengana, an
intention of which they had accused it. Then, saying no more about
conditions for a settlement, the statement announced that "the Central
Committee as well as the Andhra Committee have decided to advise
the Telengana peasantry and the fighting partisans to stop all partisan
actions and to mobilize the entire people for an effective participation
in the ensuing general election to rout the Congress at the poll." That
the CPI succeeded in that election in inflicting heavy defeats on the
Congress in the Telengana area is evidence that its activities there had
not been unpopular. But election victories could not in any real way
compensate the Party for having had to surrender its "liberated areas"
and its base for guerrilla activities, which had played such a large part
in the CPI's theoretical and programmatic discussions and which had
once been held to be the example and the starting point for the conquest of power in all of India.

　*The CPI Election Manifesto and the Ghosh article and Conference
of October 1951.* Two other CPI documents of the period immediately
following the adoption of the policy of peaceful neo-Maoism are characteristic of that new line and worthy of mention. One is the Party's
Election Manifesto of August 6, 1951,[84] which furnishes a good example
of the neo-Maoist four-class appeal. Not only does it define the
"people's democratic government," which it favors as "a government
consisting of all democratic parties, groups and individuals, a government representing workers, peasants, the middle classes and the national bourgeoisie which stands for genuine industrialization of the
country, for the freedom and independence of India." It also includes
in the many promises it makes to various groups the following: "The
people's democratic government will develop India's industry . . .
cooperating with private industrialists who will be guaranteed profits
stipulated by law and whose interests will be guaranteed." Thus,
under the neo-Maoist strategy, the Communist party promises to guar-

antee by law, when it comes to power, what under earlier strategies it had condemned as exploitation of the workers.*

The second document is a long article by the CPI's new leader, Ajoy Ghosh, in the Cominform journal of October 18, 1951,[85] apparently chiefly designed to apologize to international Communism for and to explain the Party's failure during the past years "to make use of all the tremendous possibilities that developed in these years . . . to develop a united mass movement of the people." Ghosh, in a single long sentence, attacks the mistakes of the past, beginning with a condemnation from a neo-Maoist point of view of the "left" strategy, but shifting in the middle to a condemnation of the Andhra Communists' wrong application of the neo-Maoist strategy:

> This, to a great extent, was due to the failure of the party leadership to evolve a correct revolutionary line, the prevalence of a left-sectarian outlook, policies and methods, the attempt to skip over the democratic stage of the revolution and refusal to see the semi-colonial nature of our country which demanded the unification of all anti-imperialist classes and forces for carrying out the anti-feudal and national liberation tasks, the attempt to run ahead, the failure to build unity . . . the revolutionary phrasemongering and the issuing, in many cases, of calls and slogans unrelated to realities and the existing relations of class forces, minimizing the role of consciousness and organization, the attempt to draw mechanical parallels with other countries and failure to take into account the specific features of the Indian situation—in brief, to our failure to master and correctly apply the great teaching of Lenin and Stalin, our failure to learn from the rich experience of the international Communist movement, from the great victory of the Chinese people under its glorious leader, Comrade Mao Tse-tung, from our history and from the masses of our people.

Making quite clear that the Andhra as well as the "left" period is included in his condemnation, Ghosh states: "It is only recently that, with the adoption of a new Draft Program and policy by the Central Committee, the mistakes of the past began to be corrected. . . ."

Ghosh promises to do better than his predecessors and, in doing so,

* Masani, *The Communist Party of India*, p. 138, quotes a CPI *Discussion Pamphlet* No. 1, which, dealing with the rural reform program of the Communists' election platform, contains the following statements typical of the neo-Maoist pro-capitalist approach: "As regards the capitalist landlords . . . adequate land will be left to them to pursue capitalist farming. . . . The revolution will not harm the rich peasants. They, too, to some extent suffer from feudal exploitation and from usury and will therefore gain from the revolution. . . . The Communists admit . . . that these reforms as contemplated will not effect a socialist transformation in the country."

demonstrates that the abandonment of the "left" strategy and of violent neo-Maoism is not, in any sense, tantamount to a return to the "right" strategy. He says that neo-Maoism is, in fact, a third strategy which must fight "on two fronts" against the deviations of both the "right" and the "left" strategy, attacking the "left" for its "sectarianism"—that is, its refusal to form a broad united front, and the "right" for its "opportunism"—that is, its attempt to form that front through an alliance with "reformist" parties instead of "under its own banner."

> Learning from the experience of the past, the Communist Party is determined to root out all remnants of sectarianism from its outlook, its policies and methods. At the same time it will fight against all opportunist tendencies, legalist illusions, against all rejection of militant actions, against relapse into reformism, that is, against all that worked havoc in the period immediately preceding the Second Party Congress and prevented the Party from mobilizing the people under its own banner and from carrying out a revolutionary policy.
>
> In waging this battle on two fronts, the teaching of Lenin and Stalin, the experience of the international Communist movement, the writings of the leaders of the Chinese Communist Party—Comrade Mao Tse-tung, Liu Shao-chi and others— . . . will be invaluable weapons.

The shift from violent to peaceful neo-Maoism, which had been begun at the Central Committee meeting of December 1950, found theoretical expression in the Program and Policy Statement of April 1951 and practical expression in the termination of Communist-led fighting in Telengana by the fall of 1951. It was confirmed by the replacement of Rajeshwar Rao by Ghosh at the Central Committee meeting of May 1951 and was finally officially ratified by an All-India Conference of the CPI held in October 1951.[86] This Conference unanimously elected a new Central Committee, which selected a new Politburo with Ghosh as General Secretary, and also unanimously approved the Party's new Program and Statement of Policy. The Politburo hailed these events as settling all disputes and differences that had existed in the Party over the past few years.

III. The Soviet View, 1951–1952

The preceding section has shown how in early 1951 CPI policy once again came into agreement with the policy propounded for the CPI in Moscow. We now turn, for the last time, to Moscow in order to document the fact that Moscow had not only settled on the neo-Maoist strategy, as became clear in the last chapter, but wanted that strategy to be applied in a peaceful manner in India.

Publication of CPI statements in the Cominform journal. Perhaps the most obvious indication of Moscow's approval of the new CPI policy, is the publication in the Cominform and Soviet press of CPI documents and statements by the CPI leaders. We have already remarked on the strange silence in that press on the Second CPI Congress of March 1948, which had most strikingly marked the Party's turn from the "right" to the "left" strategy. During the following three years not a single CPI document was reprinted in the Cominform journal; nor did a single article by Ranadive, the "left" leader, or Rajeshwar Rao, the violent neo-Maoist leader, appear in its pages during their combined rule of the Party of over three years. In contrast, major articles by their successor, General Secretary Ajoy Ghosh, appeared at the rate of about two a year.[87] As noted in the last section, the CPI's new Program of April 1951 was reprinted not only in the Cominform journal but also in American, British, and probably other Communist periodicals and its Election Manifesto of August 1951 appeared in the Cominform journal, thus obviously enjoying Soviet blessing. Furthermore, the Cominform organ reported CPI Politburo statements on the May 1951 Central Committee meeting and the October 1951 Party Conference, which formalized the shift to the strategy of peaceful neo-Maoism.

Approval of CPI policy by Dutt and Soviet writers. Soviet approval of the new CPI line was also expressed in other ways. One of the first to voice it was, not surprisingly, Palme Dutt,[88] who had done much to bring about its adoption. He hails the Party's new Program as a "political landmark in India" and as providing the basis of the solution of the very acute problems of strategy, tactics, and leadership the CPI had faced; and he welcomes the Politburo's decision "to radically reorientate its tactical line." Dutt stresses the neo-Maoist character of the new Program when he emphasizes that it is a program not for socialism but for people's democracy on the basis of a coalition of "all democratic anti-feudal and anti-imperialist forces"; but he also points to the limitations of the Chinese example by stating that, "while the lessons of international experience are of the greatest importance and value for India, no mechanical analogies can be drawn from the conditions of other countries to the specific conditions of India. The Indian people will have to advance along their Indian path. . . ." A year later, in an article in the Cominform journal,[89] Dutt again speaks of the CPI's "historic programme indicating the path of liberation of the Indian people towards the aim of people's democracy in India."

The CPI, which had so often been told to learn from the Chinese Communists, is now itself set up as an example for Communists in other underdeveloped areas:

> In the colonial countries the greatest successes have been won where a united national front has been effectively established. . . . The Programme of the Communist Party of India is of especial significance in indicating the path of political development in semicolonial countries towards the aims of people's democracy.

Soviet writers, too, gave their blessing to the Indian Communist Party's new line. One of them, speaking of the Party Conference of October 1951, says that "a firm foundation was laid for the consolidation of ideological, political, and organizational unity within the Party," and specifically praises the new Program, the Statement of Policy, and the Election Manifesto.[90] He makes their neo-Maoist character very clear by preceding these remarks with a denunciation of the CPI's earlier "right" opportunist and "left" sectarian errors "which gravely impaired the Party's work—in particular its failure to understand the question of unifying all anti-imperialist classes and forces in the antifeudal struggle of national liberation." Similarly, an article in *Bolshevik*,[91] speaking of the CPI's new Program, states: "After overcoming the grave opportunist errors of the right and the sectarian views of the left which prevented the development of a correct political line, the Communist Party managed to plot the true course for the liberation of the people." It goes on to summarize the Program, quoting verbatim the paragraph saying that the CPI does not call for socialism but for people's democracy through a coalition of all anti-imperialist forces. The Indian national elections in early 1952 and the relative success of the Communists in them gave the Cominform and Soviet press a further opportunity to praise the CPI and to ascribe its successes to its "correct" program of peaceful neo-Maoism.[92]

The meeting of the USSR Academy of Sciences of November 1951. As we have seen earlier, sessions of the Soviet Academy of Sciences are, for our purposes, among the most important and revealing indications of what Communist strategy is favored by Moscow. Thus the session of June 1947 heralded both the abandonment of the "right" strategy and the ensuing indecision in Moscow between the "left" and the neo-Maoist strategies, whereas the session of June 1949 indicated the complete adoption of the neo-Maoist strategy in Moscow. From November 12 to 23, 1951, at a time when the Indian Communist Party had finally settled on the policy of peaceful neo-Maoism, there took place a conference "On the Character and Attributes of People's Democracy in Countries of the Orient" at the Institute for Oriental Studies of the

USSR Academy of Sciences,[93] the report of which is by far the clearest Soviet statement of this period on Communist strategy both in under-developed countries in general and in India in particular. More than any preceding document, it brings out the distinction between the four-class appeal as the essential element of the neo-Maoist strategy and armed violence as its non-essential element.

As usual, E. M. Zhukov delivered the opening and chief report to the meeting. He, as well as several speakers in the ensuing "discussion," analyzed the tasks of people's democracy in the Orient and thereby expressed the concept which underlies the neo-Maoist strategy. These are the national liberation, or anti-imperialist, and the anti-feudal tasks, the "all-national" and "all-democratic" tasks of the bourgeois revolution. They are not the tasks of building socialism, the tasks of the dictatorship of the proletariat, which second stage of people's democracy follows the first one much later than it does in the Euro-pean people's democracies. It follows that people's democracy in the Orient is, in Zhukov's words, "based on a wide coalition of anti-imperialist and anti-feudal forces, including not only the workers, the peasants, and the petty-bourgeoisie of the towns, but also the national bourgeoisie (middle and small manufacturers and merchants)."* This is true not only of China, Mongolia, North Korea, and Vietnam, the four areas regarded as the oriental people's democracies, but is also

---

* Subsequently, Zhukov "examined the concept of the national bourgeoisie—excluding the comprador bourgeoisie as closely connected with imperialism and dividing the national bourgeoisie into big and middle bourgeoisie, of which the first is closely linked with the landlords, is inclined toward making a deal with the imperialists, and is the most short-lived and unreliable participant in the united front." Zhukov here follows the Chinese practice of distinguishing between the "comprador" and the "national" bourgeoisie, while it had hitherto been Soviet practice to refer to the entire native bourgeoisie as "national" and to divide it into the pro-imperialist "big" and the anti-imperialist "middle" bourgeoisie. Now both "big" and "middle" bourgeoisie are part of the anti-imperialist united front, although the former is less anti-imperialist than the latter. That these distinctions are essentially only verbal ones, the real one being simply between the pro-American bourgeoisie and the pro-Soviet bourgeoisie, was stated by Zhukov himself; see p. 91, above.

At least by 1951 Zhukov had come to appreciate the importance of the peasantry to the united front, which had not been true of his earlier statements: "The more vigorously the peasantry, which constitutes the overwhelming majority of the popu-lation in the colonial countries, is drawn into the anti-imperialist struggle, the more powerful this front becomes. The resolving of the agrarian question and the struggle against feudalism and feudal survivals are the most important content of the national liberation movement in the colonial and semi-colonial countries." Here Zhukov approaches the views expressed by Balabushevich and Dyakov after their reluctant conversion to neo-Maoism; see pp. 89–90 and 94, above.

repeated with special reference to India when Zhukov speaks of "the formation of an extremely broad anti-imperialist front including, as the program of the Communist Party of India points out, millions of working people, the working class, the peasantry, the working intelligentsia and the middle classes, as well as the national bourgeoisie interested in the freedom of the country and in establishing a well-to-do life."   Finally, Zhukov makes clear that this four-class appeal is to be used in all underdeveloped areas: "The experience of the national liberation movement shows that the creation of a united anti-imperialist front is of cardinal importance for a successful struggle for independence in colonial countries."

Having thus set forth the essential elements of the neo-Maoist strategy—the anti-imperialist and anti-feudal nature of the coming revolution and the four-class alliance that is to bring it about—Zhukov goes on, with a frankness unusual in Soviet writings on the subject, to point out that the other outstanding element of the Maoist strategy as it was applied in China, its country of origin—armed struggle—is not an essential element of neo-Maoism:

> The experience of the Chinese revolution is of immense significance.   Traces of its fruitful influence can easily be found in the documents of the Communist Party of India and the Workers' Party of Viet-Nam.   But remembering the first tactical principle of Leninism—the principle of obligatory consideration of the particularly and specifically national elements in each individual country—it would be risky to regard the Chinese revolution as some kind of "stereotype" for people's revolutions in other countries of Asia.
>
> In particular, it is difficult to presuppose that other countries of the Orient following the path of people's democracy could necessarily calculate on acquiring the vitally important advantage of the Chinese revolution—a revolutionary army such as there is in China.
>
> All this of course by no means signifies that there will not be thousands of problems during the resolving of which the advanced peoples of India, Indonesia or any other country of the Orient will require consideration of the concrete experience of the Chinese revolution or of the experience of the October revolution in Russia.*

Although Zhukov spoke here in general terms about Asia, though significantly singling out as examples India and Indonesia, the two prin-

---

* The excerpts of the report of the session of the Academy appearing in the CPI's *Cross Roads* include a full quotation of this passage and are preceded by the following note of the editor: "The discussions will also reveal how the various Communist Parties, while drawing valuable lessons from the rich experience of the peoples of other lands who have carried through their revolutions successfully, base themselves on the concrete conditions and specific features of their own country. It is on this basis alone that any Communist Party could draw a correct programme for its country," *Cross Roads*, July 20, 1952, pp. 16, 13.

cipal Asian countries where the Communist parties were following the peaceful variant of the neo-Maoist strategy, the discussion became more sharply focused when several subsequent speakers took up the subject. Most of them stressed the significance of the Chinese experience for other countries, G. N. Voitinsky noting its special influence on the CPI's new Program, and G. I. Levinson listing the Philippines, Burma, Malaya, and Vietnam as countries that had followed the Chinese example in creating revolutionary armies.

Then V. N. Nikiforov expressly disagreed with Zhukov on the latter's crucial point. According to him, revolutionary armies arise because of the domination of imperialism and feudal relationships. Since the conditions created by these prevail also in other oriental countries such as India, these countries, too, will create revolutionary armies of their own.

The task of refuting this view was assigned to two specialists on India, Nasenko and, of all people, Balabushevich, who, as we know, not only had been a stubborn advocate of the "left" strategy until 1949 but also had, when he was then converted to neo-Maoism, emphasized exactly the non-essential armed struggle element of that strategy in preference to its essential four-class appeal. These two now replied to Nikiforov that the Chinese revolution is no obligatory model for other countries of Asia, which they demonstrate by the example of India "where we have seen the full error of mechanically applying the experience of the Chinese Revolution to Indian circumstances without consideration of India's specific features—and, what is more, the interpretation of the Chinese experience applied was incorrect." As distinguished from this "error" of the Andhra leadership, the CPI's latest Program is "a genuine program of struggle for a people's democracy and the creation of a broad popular front in the concrete conditions of India." This statement again implies that the four-class appeal is applicable everywhere, but that armed struggle is to be used only where the "concrete" conditions are suitable for it, which was not the case in India. Whether Nikiforov, in expressing a different view, represented a dissenting faction in Moscow or was merely made to state it to have it publicly disavowed, we cannot know. The latter possibility appears more likely. In any case, the session of the Academy made it quite clear that the view supported by both Zhukov, the most authoritative Soviet academic voice on Asian affairs, and by Balabushevich, one of the outstanding experts on India who had for so long represented different opinions, was the official one.

Three months after this important session of the Soviet Academy of Sciences the Cominform journal carried an editorial that made essentially the same point, though as usual in more obscure form, and that was duly reprinted in the Indian Communists' *Cross Roads*.[94] It states that the alliance of the working class with the peasantry is "also joined by the intelligentsia, by all progressive sections of town and countryside and by patriotic elements of the national bourgeoisie. A brilliant example of the united people's democratic front is offered by the struggle of the Chinese people." After thus setting up China as an example of the use of the four-class appeal, the editorial shows that the Chinese Communist use of armed forces is not of equally universal applicability: "The nature of the liberation movement varies in the different colonial and dependent countries. In some it has developed into open armed struggle." Here Vietnam, Malaya, Burma, and the Philippines are praised and even the Japanese are said to be intensifying their struggle, but of India the Cominform editorial merely says that "the Communist Party strives to rally all the progressive national forces into a united democratic front and for a people's democratic government" and it hails the Communists' recent election success. Similarly, another Cominform editorial,[95] a year later, expresses approval of the CPI's present strategy when it says that "the Communist Party of India is inspiring and organizing the popular struggle against the domination of foreign imperialism, against British imperialism in the first instance."

NOTES FOR CHAPTER 5

1. "Greetings to Communist Party of China on its 29th Anniversary, July 1, 1950," *Communist*, III, No. 3 (July–August 1950), 3–5, on p. 4.
2. *Ibid.*, p. 3.
3. *Ibid.*, p. 4.
4. *Ibid.*, p. 3.
5. *Ibid.*, p. 4.
6. "Statement of the Editorial Board," *ibid.*, pp. 1–2; "Statement of Editorial Board of *Communist* on Anti-Leninist Criticism of Comrade Mao Tse-tung," *ibid.*, pp. 6–35. Page numbers in the following footnotes will indicate which of the two statements is referred to.
7. *Ibid.*, p. 1.
8. *Ibid.*, p. 2; see also *ibid.*, p. 12.
9. *Ibid.*, p. 2.
10. *Ibid.*, p. 1. See pp. 106–110, above.
11. See pp. 63–76, above.
12. *Communist*, III, No. 3 (July–August 1950), p. 2.
13. *Ibid.*, p. 6.
14. *Ibid.*, see also *ibid.*, pp. 1–2.
15. *Ibid.*, p. 8.
16. *Ibid.*, p. 6.
17. *Ibid.*, p. 7.

18. *Ibid.*, p. 1.

19. *Ibid.*, p. 11.

20. *Ibid.*, p. 26.

21. See pp. 61–63, above.

22. *Communist*, III, No. 3 (July–August 1950), p. 1.

23. *Ibid.*, p. 13.

24. *Ibid.*, p. 12; see also *ibid.*, p. 7.

25. *Ibid.*, p. 10.

26. *Ibid.*, p. 26, see also *ibid.*, p. 28.

27. *Ibid.*, p. 22.

28. See p. 89, above.

29. *Communist*, III, No. 3 (July–August 1950), p. 24.

30. *Ibid.*, p. 13.

31. *Ibid.*, p. 14.

32. *Ibid.*, p. 26.

33. *Ibid.*, pp. 27–28, from "The Chinese Revolution and the Communist Party of China," *China Digest*, V, No. 10, 16.

34. Quoted in Robert Trumbull, "New Delhi Scorns Reds' Peace Offer," *The New York Times*, March 11, 1951, p. 3, and in Masani, *The Communist Party of India*, p. 114.

35. *Communist*, III, No. 3 (July–August 1950), pp. 33–34. For a similar statement on the shift of the Communist Party of Ceylon from the "left" to the neo-Maoist strategy as a result of the Cominform editorial of January 27 and the WFTU Peking Conference, see the report on the 4th Congress of the Ceylon Communist Party, held in August 1950, N. Sanmugathasan, "Ceylon Communist Congress," *World News and Views*, XXX, No. 42 (October 21, 1950), 501.

36. Quoted in Limaye, *Communist Party*, p. 62.

37. Quoted *ibid.*, p. 75, and in Masani, *The Communist Party of India*, pp. 107–108.

38. A few of the more important statements advocating the four-class strategy for Asian countries that appeared in Soviet publications or that of the Cominform between 1950 and 1953 may be listed here: Editorial. "The Peoples of the Colonial and Dependent Countries in the Struggle against the Warmongers," *For a Lasting Peace, for a People's Democracy!*, May 19, 1950, p. 1; V. V. Vassilieva, "Leninist-Stalinist Teaching on Nations and the National and Colonial Revolution," *Communist*, III, No. 3 (July–August 1950), 88–112; V. Avarin, "The Economic Plight and the Struggle for National Liberation in the Colonies of Southeast Asia," *Voprosy Ekonomiki*, No. 7, 1950, in *Soviet Press Translations*, VII, No. 7 (October 1, 1952), 355–362; Peng Chen, "Great Chinese People in Camp of Peace and Democracy," *For a Lasting Peace, for a People's Democracy!*, April 27, 1951, p. 2; Lu Ting-yi, "World Significance of Chinese Revolution," *ibid.*, June 29, 1951, p. 2, also in *People's China*, IV, No. 1 (July 1, 1951), 9–12, and in *World News and Views*, XXXI, No. 28 (July 14, 1951), 309–311; Li Wei-sen, "Communist Party of China and People's Democratic United Front," *For a Lasting Peace, for a People's Democracy!*, July 6, 1951, p. 2, also in *People's China*, IV, No. 1 (July 1, 1951), 35–39 (where the author's name is given as Li Wei-han); W. Rogov, "Confusion Over Important Matters," *Izvestia*, January 27, 1952, p. 3, in *Current Digest of the Soviet Press*, IV, No. 4 (March 8, 1952), 7–9; I. Plyshevsky, "National Liberation Struggle of Working People in Colonial and Dependent Countries," *Pravda*, April 30, 1953, p. 3, condensed in *Current Digest of the Soviet Press*, V, No. 17 (June 6, 1953), 26–27.

39. "An Armed People Opposes Armed Counterrevolution," *People's Daily* (Peking) , June 16, 1950; *People's China,* II, No. 1 (July 1, 1950) , 11–13.

40. *Ibid.,* p. 12.

41. *Ibid.,* p. 13.

42. "Palme Dutt Answers Questions on India," *Cross Roads,* January 19, 1951, p. 7. Important sections are quoted in Limaye, *Communist Party,* pp. 78–80.

43. "Central Committee of C.P.I. Reconstituted," *Cross Roads,* December 29, 1950, p. 5.

44. "Resolutions of Central Committee on CPI," *ibid.,* January 5, 1951, p. 6.

45. "Central Committee of C.P.I. Reconstituted," *op. cit.*

46. *Ibid.*

47. "Resolutions of Central Committee of the Communist Party of India," *Cross Roads,* December 29, 1950, p. 6.

48. "Announcing the New Crossroads," *ibid.,* March 30, 1951, p. 16.

49. "London Talks Expose C'wealth War Face," *ibid.,* January 12, 1951, p. 1.

50. "C.P.I. Welcomes Nehru's Stand on Peace," *ibid.,* February 2, 1951, p. 2.

51. Romesh Thapar, "Nehru's Foreign Policy," *ibid.,* March 30, 1951, pp. 3, 12.

52. "Peace Belongs to All," *ibid.,* p. 8.

53. "We Must March Together in India's Peace Movement," *ibid.,* April 6, 1951, pp. 8–9.

54. "India's Peace Movement and the West," *ibid.,* June 22, 1951, pp. 3, 8.

55. Supplement to the CPI's Bengali daily *Swadhinata* (Calcutta) , April 29, 1951; reprinted as "Draft Programme of the Communist Party of India," *For a Lasting Peace, for a People's Democracy!,* May 11, 1951, p. 3, and in *Political Affairs* (New York) , XXX, No. 9 (September 1951) , 55–64. Substantial extracts appear in *World News and Views,* XXXI, No. 23 (June 9, 1951) , 253–256, and in *Cross Roads,* May 4, 1951, pp. 3, 14.

56. "May Day Manifesto of Communist Party of India," *ibid.,* April 27, 1951, p. 3. One lakh equals one hundred thousand.

57. Most of the important passages are reprinted in Democratic Research Service, *Communist Conspiracy at Madurai* (Bombay: Popular Book Depot, 1954) , pp. 20–23, and in Masani, *The Communist Party of India,* pp. 117–120. The full text appears as "Policy Statement of Communist Party of India: India will Strike its Own Path to Freedom and People's Rule," *Cross Roads,* June 8, 1951, pp. 3, 6, 16, and as *Statement of Policy of the Communist Party of India* (Bombay: Jayant Bhatt, November 1951) .

58. *Ibid.,* p. 3.

59. *Ibid.,* pp. 3–4.

60. *Ibid.,* pp. 4–6.

61. *Ibid.,* p. 6.

62. *Ibid.,* p. 7.

63. *Ibid.*

64. *Ibid.,* p. 2.

65. *Ibid.,* pp. 8–9.

66. *Ibid.,* pp. 10–12.

67. *Communist Conspiracy at Madurai,* p. 36.

68. *Ibid.,* p. 37.

69. *Ibid.,* p. 38; see also *ibid.,* p. 40.

70. *Ibid.,* p. 43.

71. *Ibid.,* pp. 44–45.

72. *Ibid.,* p. 35.

73. *Ibid.,* pp. 39–40.

74. *Ibid.,* p. 44.

75. *Ibid.*

76. *Ibid.,* pp. 45–48.

77. *Ibid.,* pp. 39, 40.

78. *Ibid.*

79. "Statement by Political Bureau of Communist Party of India," *For a Lasting Peace, for a People's Democracy!,* June 15, 1951; also in *Cross Roads,* June 8, 1951, p. 2.

80. "C.P.I. Ready for Negotiated Settlement in Telengana," *ibid.,* June 15, 1951, p. 3.

81. "C.P.I. States Basis for Telengana Settlement," *ibid.,* July 27, 1951, pp. 1–2.

82. "Congress Game in Telengana: Keep Pot Boiling and Grab 5 Million Votes," *ibid.,* August 10, 1951, p. 8.

83. "C.P.I. Advises Stoppage of Partisan Action in Telengana," *ibid.,* October 24, 1951, pp. 1, 3.

84. "Election Manifesto of Communist Party of India," *For a Lasting Peace, for a People's Democracy!,* August 31, 1951, pp. 3–4. Also reported, but not given in full, in *Cross Roads,* August 24, 1951, pp. 6, 7, 8.

85. Ajoy Ghosh, "Communist Party of India in Struggle for United Democratic Front, for People's Democratic Government," *For a Lasting Peace, for a People's Democracy!,* October 19, 1951, pp. 2–3.

86. "Statement by Political Bureau, Communist Party of India," *ibid.,* November 2, 1951, p. 6; also in *Pravda,* October 29, 1951, translated into German in *Ost-Probleme,* III, No. 47 (November 24, 1951), 1448–1449.

87. Ajoy Ghosh, *op. cit.;* "Concerning Results of General Election in India," *ibid.,* March 28, 1952, p. 3; "Some of Our Main Weaknesses," *ibid.,* November 7, 1952, p. 5; "Third Congress of Communist Party of India," *ibid.,* February 5, 1954, p. 5; "Next Tasks of the Communist Party of India," *ibid.,* May 21, 1954, pp. 3, 4. Another member of the CPI Politburo published two articles on the Indian peasant problem in the Cominform journal in 1952 and 1953. E. M. S. Namboodripad, "Indian Peasantry in Struggle for Food, Land and Peace," *ibid.,* September 19, 1952, p. 5; "Present Stage of Peasant Movement in India," *ibid.,* December 18, 1953, pp. 3–4.

88. R. Palme Dutt, "Political Landmark in India," *World News and Views,* XXXI, No. 24 (June 16, 1951), 264–265; also in *Cross Roads,* June 29, 1951, p. 5.

89. R. Palme Dutt, "Growing Crisis of Colonial System of Imperialism," *For a Lasting Peace, for a People's Democracy!,* May 2, 1952, pp. 3–4.

90. I. Lemin, "Fruits of Imperialist Domination in India and Pakistan," *Voprosy Ekonomiki,* No. 1 (January 1952; published in February), 73–89, translated in full in *Soviet Press Translations,* VII, No. 8 (April 15, 1952), 211–220 and condensed in *Current Digest of the Soviet Press,* IV, No. 11 (April 26, 1952), 26–28.

91. Orestov, "The Parliamentary Elections in India," *Bolshevik,* No. 5 (March 1952), translated in *Soviet Press Translations,* VII, No. 11 (June 1, 1952), 263–267.

92. "Success of People's Democratic Front in Indian Elections," *For a Lasting Peace, for a People's Democracy!,* January 25, 1952, p. 4; "Elections in India," *Trud,* January 30, 1952, translated into German in *Ost-Probleme,* IV, No. 8 (February 23, 1952), 232–233; "Election Successes of People's Democratic Front in India," *For a Lasting Peace, for a People's Democracy!,* February 15, 1952, p. 4; R. Palme Dutt,

"The Indian Elections," *World News and Views*, XXXII, No. 9 (March 1, 1952), 102–104, also in *Cross Roads*, March 7, 1952, pp. 8–9; Orestov, *op. cit.*

93. *Izvestia Akademii Nauk SSSR*, History and Philosophy Series, IX, No. 1 (January–February 1952; published in May), 80–87. Translated in full in *Current Digest of the Soviet Press*, IV, No. 20 (June 28, 1952), 3–7, 43, and in *Labour Monthly*, XXXV, No. 1 (January 1953), 40–46, No. 2 (February 1953), 83–87, No. 3 (March 1953), 139–144.

94. Editorial, "National-Liberation Movement of Peoples in Colonial and Dependent Countries," *For a Lasting Peace, for a People's Democracy!*, February 29, 1952, p. 1; reprinted in *Cross Roads*, March 14, 1952, pp. 8–9.

95. Editorial, "Growing Upsurge of National-Liberation Movement in Colonial and Dependent Countries," *For a Lasting Peace, for a People's Democracy!*, January 9, 1953, p. 1; reprinted in *Cross Roads*, January 25, 1953, p. 15.

THE PEACEFUL NEO-MAOIST STRATEGY
IN INDIA (1952–1954)

I. PROBLEMS AND TACTICS OF NEO-MAOISM IN INDIA

At this point we have carried the story of the CPI through October 1951. To continue it in strictly chronological order would involve us in considerable repetition and would not result in the kind of history of the evolution of Communist strategy in which we are here interested. The period in the CPI's history that began at the end of World War II, when every year and often every few months brought a striking development in the Party's strategy, came to an end in 1951. We have already shown in the last chapter how the Indian Communist Party became firmly committed to its strategy of peaceful neo-Maoism, and that this policy enjoyed full Moscow support. With the neo-Maoist strategy and its peaceful application fully accepted, there remained for the CPI only questions of tactics. We can discuss these best in the form of a brief survey of the major themes appearing in CPI documents during 1952 and 1953. In conclusion, we shall deal with the Party's Third Congress at the beginning of 1954. While the questions of tactics, though of great significance for the CPI, are of relatively minor importance in the context of our discussion, which has been concerned with Communist strategies, in some instances they offer interesting illustrations of the problems with which the application of the neo-Maoist strategy confronts a Communist party.

CPI statements on the weakness of the Party and its fronts. Although the CPI's internal factional struggles over strategy were now over and it had emerged from the general elections at the beginning of 1952 with some results rather favorable to it,[1] the Party continued to be dissatisfied with its own weakness. A resolution adopted by the Politburo at its meeting of August 11–17, 1952, declares that "the fact that must be grasped is that the single biggest factor that is preventing the development of the movement is organizational weakness of the

Communist Party itself, its weakness among the basic masses of the people—the working class and the peasants in many areas . . .";[2] and it admonished the Party that "we have to combat all manifestations of frustration and demoralization in our own ranks" and "we have to combat all tendencies to undermine the organizational discipline of the Party, immediately . . . restore discipline inside the Party. . . ."[3] The Cominform journal, reporting on this meeting of the Politburo,[4] also stated that the latter had resolved on steps to strengthen the Party organizationally.

The subject evidently aroused some concern in Moscow. Soon after this meeting there appeared a special article on it in the Cominform journal, written by Ajoy Ghosh himself and entitled "Some of our Main Weaknesses,"[5] which is practically a confession, though not a personal one. In it Ghosh admits the Party's lack of trained cadres and the fact that in several Indian states the Party's membership amounted to far less than one per cent of the vote gained by the CPI, and even that not properly organized and only a fraction of it "ideologically-politically developed." The absence of the convenient excuse available to Party leaders in the past that all troubles were due to the "incorrect" strategies followed by their predecessors is noted by Ghosh when he states that, in the past, explanations for the Party's weaknesses had been sought in incorrect slogans and forms of struggle, but, these being correct now, the difficulties are due to organizational weakness. Although differences on strategy are always finally resolved in line with Moscow's desires, the disastrous consequences of frequent shifts cannot be overcome in a few months, a fact that is made clear by such remarks as the following, made by Ghosh in the course of his demand for the restoration of "Party forms and Party discipline, which were seriously undermined in the period before the adoption of the Programme of the Party." "Anarchistic concepts of inner-party democracy manifest themselves in many units." "In some units past prejudices, a legacy of the period of inner-party struggle, stand in the way of unified functioning." "We must put an end to present planlessness in work, an end to the looseness of discipline and to the scant regard for Party forms."

The Indian Communist Party itself, even if it had been organizationally strong, would still have been numerically weak. What mass influence it had was exercised through its so-called mass organizations, the peace movement, and the "United Front." The Party was greatly concerned with strengthening all three of these. Ghosh repeatedly complained about the weakness of the mass organizations, that is, the Communist-dominated trade unions and peasants', women's, youth, and student organizations. In one of his articles in the Cominform journal,[6] he referred to them as "still extremely weak" and bemoaned the disunity of the working class and the trade union movement, which the Party should overcome, establishing leadership "in its own class." Equally important was the strengthening of the Party's base among the peasant masses, "vast numbers of whom, except in areas of Andhra, Telengana and Kerala, have not yet been drawn into the democratic movement." Elsewhere Ghosh stated that "only the building of united mass organizations can rally the people against the Congress,"[7] thus indicating that the organizations he has in mind are not really to be united in the sense of including Congress-affiliated organizations, but are, on the contrary, to be built up "from below" as against the Congress. Considering that the term "democratic parties" does not in the Communist vocabulary include parties opposed to the Communists, such as the Congress and the Socialist Parties, this is also made clear by an appeal of the Central Committee to "all democratic parties, organizations, groups and individuals . . . to come together and form united trade unions, united kisan sabhas [peasant organizations], united student and youth organizations, united women's organizations, united organizations of intellectuals, etc., so that every factory, every town and village, every institution where people come together in daily life can be transformed into a fortress against imperialism, feudalism and monopoly capital."[8] This is a typically neo-Maoist formulation both in its characterization of the enemy and in its stress on the broad united front from below.

Several meetings of the CPI leadership dealt with the problem of strengthening the mass organizations.[9] Their success can be judged from the fact that the communiqué of one of the later ones still had to state that "the Central Committee resolved that the work of building united mass organizations should be taken up in right earnest . . . ."[10] We have already noted that beginning in early 1951 the peace movement became the CPI's chief concern.* Like the development of the mass organizations, its strengthening was a subject of re-

---

* In 1952 an Asian and Pacific Peace Conference was held in Peking that set up a Peace Liaison Committee of the Asian and Pacific Regions of twelve members representing various countries, including some on the West coast of the Western hemisphere. Like the WFTU Asian and Australasian Liaison Bureau in Peking and often in conjunction with it, this organization has frequently been referred to as the equivalent of an Asian Cominform and/or as evidence of Chinese, as distinguished from Soviet, domination of the Asian Communist parties. Our skeptical comments on the WFTU Liaison Bureau in the footnote on p. 100, above, fully apply to it *mutatis mutandis*. See "Documents of the Peace Conference of the Asian and Pacific Regions," *People's China*, No. 21 (November 1, 1952), supplement.

peated admonitions and complaints in the resolutions of the CPI leadership.[11]

The united fronts from above and from below. It has already been mentioned that when, after Palme Dutt's letter of December 1950, the CPI began to pay serious attention to the formation of a united front with non-Communist elements, it concentrated in practice not so much on appeals "from below" to the rank and file of the Congress and Socialist Parties, although such were made, as on arrangements "from above" with the leadership of various small so-called "left" parties. This tendency was further strengthened by the general elections of early 1952, which led the Party to enter into various electoral alliances with such groups.[12]   It was strongly confirmed by the relative success of many of these alliances.   Following the elections the Central Committee triumphantly stated that their results showed that the unity of "all freedom-loving democratic classes and their parties, organizations and individuals" was "an eminently practical objective."[13]   In making such "top-alliances," the CPI has always been concerned with keeping its own independence intact.   A Politburo resolution of August 1952 specifically warns that "we have to combat all tendencies which, in the name of fighting sectarianism, minimize the importance of maintaining the independence of the Party, advocate tactics which would reduce the Party to an appendage of the petty-bourgeois parties . . . ."[14]

United front agreements "from above" with small "left" parties are entirely compatible with the neo-Maoist strategy of the united front from below and must be clearly distinguished from the "right" strategy. Under the latter the Communist party united or sought to unite with parties differing widely from it, such as socialist and "bourgeois" parties like the Congress, the CPI's enemies under neo-Maoism against whom the united front from below is directed.   The CPI's allies under the neo-Maoist strategy were often groups quite close to it ideologically and by no means necessarily to its "right."*

There was, however, some awareness among the CPI leadership that

---

* Thus, according to its program as reported in *Cross Roads,* January 11, 1953, p. 15, the Forward Bloc, one of these allies, proclaims itself a Marxist party which supports the cause of peace, democracy, and socialism headed by the Soviet Union, New China, and the People's Democracies and will fight tooth and nail against the third force, "the screen under which the right Socialists hide their alliance with imperialists and war-mongers." Its difference with the CPI, *Cross Roads* notes, is that while the latter aims at People's Democracy in India, the Forward Bloc considers conditions ripe for a socialist revolution, a formulation which the Communist paper calls dangerous. It would seem, then, that this particular ally of the CPI is nothing but a Communist party which does not follow the current Party line but rather one close to Ranadive's "left" strategy.

alliances with "left" parties were not a sufficient means for carrying out the neo-Maoist four-class strategy of forming a united front "embracing all the anti-imperialist strata of the population."   Writing in the Cominform journal, Ghosh admits[15] that such a united front is yet to be built; that otherwise it is only a top alliance between leaders. Similarly, the Politburo emphasizes that building this front remains the Party's key task, which cannot be fulfilled by reliance on top alliances but only by struggle for the immediate demands of the people, and by unity in action.   "The task today is that of broadening the mass movement by drawing into it all strata and sections including the national bourgeoisie and Congressmen,"[16] and it calls for "extensive agitation among ALL classes."[17]

The approach "from below," especially toward the Congress Party, was a necessity if capitalists were to be included in the united front, as is essential under the neo-Maoist strategy, for not many of these were likely to be found in the "left" parties, which could be approached "from above."   That the Party very definitely was to appeal to capitalists was made clear by the Politburo in its resolution of August 1952.   Condemning the government, it states that "opposition has grown rapidly not merely amongst the workers, peasants, and intelligentsia, but also amongst new strata and sections, including sections and elements of the national bourgeoisie."[18]   It registers some successes of its neo-Maoist strategy when it continues: "The attendance of a number of industrialists and businessmen at the Moscow Economic Conference, the proposals made by several businessmen that closer trade relations should be established between India and the Socialist and People's Democratic countries, are also significant factors."*   But how is the Party, which throughout its history has been based on the principle of the class struggle, to appeal to the workers on the basis of their immediate demands without thereby alienating the capitalists?

* "Post Election Situation And Our Tasks," *New Age,* I, No. 1 (September 1952), 35. See also the passage written by an Indian fellow traveller or Communist after his return from China in 1952: "Supposing, therefore, Communism of the Chinese type comes to India, a majority of our capitalists and, particularly, the industrialists would not only survive but receive every possible encouragement from Government in the interest of production. In fact, the national bourgeoisie, or patriotic capitalists who have not tied themselves with Anglo-American cartels, would have every reason to welcome such a changeover. The axe of the new regime would fall only upon half a dozen of the bigger cartel kings of India—the compradors with powerful foreign alliances, the zemindars, the blackmarketeers, speculators and moneylenders. These would probably be sent to reformatories. The rest of our bourgeoisie would be allowed to coexist, cooperate, and coprosper together with the people." R. K. Karanjia, *China Stands Up; the Wild Men of the West* (Bombay: People's Publishing House, 1952), p. 160.

By forgetting its principle and by emphasizing the community of interest between capital and labor. The Politburo suggests that "the demands of the working class in each industry should be linked with demands of the industry itself so that the working class can come before the people as the builder and defender of national economy, which monopoly interests subservient to foreign Powers are ruining."*

While we have now focused on the distinction between the approaches from above and below used by the CPI in following its neo-Maoist strategy, the Party itself generally obscured this distinction by speaking of a united front both of parties, that is, from above, on the basis of the demand for a government of the United Democratic Front, and of individuals, that is, from below, on the basis of their immediate demands. In language borrowed from the Peking WFTU Conference and the January 1950 Cominform editorial, which initiated the neo-Maoist strategy in India, the Party was constantly exhorted to "strive ceaselessly to build up a United Front of all democratic parties, organizations, groups and individuals."[19] Ajoy Ghosh proclaimed: "We maintain that the power that replaces the Congress, which represents the monopolists and landlords, must be the power of all democratic classes and sections. Only a United Front of all democratic parties and individuals can represent such a power." "Only the development of a united mass movement for the immediate rights and demands of the people . . . can rally the people against the Congress."[20] And again: "Never were the possibilities of a broad and powerful United Front embracing all patriotic parties, all patriotic sections and strata of our people including the national bourgeoisie and millions of followers of the Congress, so bright as it is today."[21] To have "unity of action" with other parties, Ghosh claims, the CPI does not demand that they agree with it on all issues: "What the Communist Party wants to emphasize is that its attitude towards these parties would be determined primarily by their attitude towards the Government."[22] These three last-quoted passages make it amply clear that, whether through alliances from above with anti-government parties or through appeals

---

* "Post Election Situation And Our Tasks," *op. cit.*, p. 44. A British Communist reporting on India also stresses that "even sections of the bourgeoisie are affected and are beginning to understand, for instance, that peace and trade with China would be in their interest . . . ." "The task of finding concrete ways and means of uniting different strata of the population . . . in a progressive democratic front with the leadership of the working class . . . and uniting all sections of the workers, peasants, professional and intellectual sections and the urban middle class as well as patriotic elements from the bourgeoisie . . . is seen by the Indian Communists as the key to further advance." Phil McCann, "New Political Trends in India," *World News and Views*, XXXIII, No. 29 (July 25, 1953), 344–346.

from below to the "millions of followers of the Congress," the purpose of the Communists' neo-Maoist united front is always to "rally the people against the Congress" and the Socialist Party. It is thus, in effect, a united front from below against these two and is as different from the old "right" strategy of a united front from above with the Congress as it is from the old "left" strategy of a united front from below against the bourgeoisie.

Sectarianism: the chief obstacle to the neo-Maoist strategy. We have now seen that under its neo-Maoist strategy the CPI sought to strengthen not only its organization, as would be true under any strategy, but also its mass organizations, its peace movement, and its united front, these three being widely overlapping and to a considerable extent only different ways of uniting the same people. The peace movement in particular is closely related to the neo-Maoist strategy. Like the latter, its appeal is directed to all strata of the population regardless of class; it concentrates on an external enemy, war, which, like the neo-Maoist enemy imperialism, is generally identified with the United States. Any persistent obstacle to the development of the peace movement found by the CPI within its own ranks is, therefore, symptomatic of a difficulty of the neo-Maoist strategy itself.

We have already noted that the great enemy of the peace movement within the CPI has been what the Communists call sectarianism. The strengthening of the peace movement and of the mass organizations and the united front obviously requires some cooperation of Communists with non-Communist elements and therefore a certain degree of tolerance. But tolerance is a quality utterly alien to Communists and one for any display of which they, at other times, condemn themselves as opportunists. Sectarianism, that is, the unwillingness to cooperate with non-Communists, and opportunism, that is, the willingness to cooperate with non-Communists, are, indeed, the Scylla and Charybdis between which Communists must always seek to steer their precarious course. However, they are not always equally dangerous. During periods when the "left" strategy is in effect warnings are sounded primarily against opportunism; during "right" periods sectarianism is regarded as the chief evil. When they are supposed to be following the neo-Maoist strategy, Communists could theoretically be guilty both of the opportunism of working with allegedly pro-imperialist parties, such as the Congress and the Socialists, and of the sectarianism of being unwilling to work with all strata of the population, especially the bourgeoisie. In practice, however, the Indian Communists and, it is suspected, all Communists are by nature much more prone to be sectarian than opportunists, more prone to denounce

than to cooperate with non-Communists.   In 1939 and in December
1947 they switched with alacrity to the "left" strategy away from
cooperation with the Congress; none of them, including even Joshi,
the leader in the "right" period, for years showed any inclination
of returning to that policy of cooperation.   But in 1935, when they
were ordered to abandon the "left" for the "right" strategy, apparently
it took months and even years to make the change effective; and in
June 1941, when the "left" period of the Hitler-Stalin Pact was followed by the "right" period of the "people's war," half a year was
required by the Party to make the shift in spite of the urgency of the
situation.   Similarly now, several years after the Party's shift to the neo-
Maoist strategy, it still encounters the danger of sectarianism in its
midst.

In April 1952 Ghosh exclaimed that "the narrow and restricted outlook which has been a characteristic feature of the Left movement as
a whole . . . this outlook has to go."[23]   The following month the Con-
vention of the All-India Trade Union Congress, the CPI's labor front,
adopted a unity resolution which "liquidates all traces of sectarianism
in relation to the problem of unity."[24]   The Politburo resolution of
August 1952 warned against tactics leading to the isolation of the
Party,[25] saying that "in evolving forms of struggle we have to get rid
of all dogmatic and preconceived notions."[26]   At the end of 1953 a
CPI Politburo member, in the pages of the Cominform journal, attacked sectarianism in the peasant movement, although ostensibly
speaking of groups outside the CPI:

> There are certain political groups in India which call themselves
> "Marxists" and even "Marxist-Leninists," who argue that our agrar-
> ian reform should be so organized as to fully eliminate not only
> landlord exploitation, but the exploitation by the rich peasant as
> well. Distorting the lessons of the Russian Revolution, they call for
> a plan for the immediate organization of collective cultivation and
> oppose land distribution.
>   Only if these and other distortions of the tasks of agrarian reform
> are resolutely combated can the peasantry be rallied in their millions
> and united into a mighty force under the guidance of the working
> class for successful struggle against imperialism and feudalism.[27]

"Bracketing the rich peasant with the landlord," we are told, is a
distortion of "a 'left' disruptionist character."

It is obviously difficult for a party raised on the principles and vocabulary of the class struggle suddenly to recognize opposition to what it
has long been taught was the workers' and poor peasants' exploitation
by the capitalists and rich peasants as disruption and distortion and
to appeal to the "exploiters" on the basis of a community of interest

with the "exploited." Yet this is exactly what is expected of good Communists under the neo-Maoist strategy. Clearly, sectarianism is the chief difficulty faced by Communist parties in the application of that strategy.

The CPI's attitude towards the USSR and Communist China. . We now turn to a brief consideration of the CPI's attitude towards the Soviet Union and Communist China during the recent past, a subject which has aroused great interest and one on which this study may help throw some light. We have seen that the question of the applicability of the methods of the Chinese Communists to Indian conditions had been at the very heart of the differences that divided the CPI. Ranadive, leading the Party in 1948 and 1949, rejected both the rural armed struggle and the four-class appeal aspects of the Chinese strategy, whereas the Andhra Communists, who succeeded him in control of the CPI during 1950, wholeheartedly embraced both. In 1951 the four-class appeal without armed struggle emerged as the approved strategy. Throughout this period, however, there was never any question that the CPI, even under Ranadive, welcomed the Chinese Communist victories as important and highly desirable events from which it expected to benefit. On the other hand, as the facts we have adduced clearly demonstrate, there is no question that at all times, even under the Andhra Communists, effective external control of the CPI, insofar as it existed at all, came from Moscow rather than Peking.

It is our impression that, although the elusive problem of the relative role of Moscow and Peking in the affairs of Asian Communist parties can be attacked through an analysis such as ours of the changes in each party's strategy and of related changes in Moscow and Peking, it cannot be successfully studied from the party's attitude towards the Soviet Union and Communist China as exhibited in its own propaganda. So long as the present situation of complete outward amity between Moscow and Peking prevails, an Asian Communist party has nothing to lose and everything to gain from impartially playing up the supposed successes of both countries and basking in their reflected glory.

Thus during the period under review here—1951, 1952, and 1953— innumerable articles on the "achievements" both of the Soviet Union and of "New China" appeared in the CPI's *Cross Roads,* some of them being glowing reports of visitors returned from these countries. Much space was also devoted to various "cultural" delegations coming to India from the Soviet Union and China, to Soviet films, and, when the occasion arose during the International Industries' Fair in Bombay early in 1952, to the Chinese, Soviet, Czechoslovak, and Hungarian pavilions. Chinese Communist English-language periodicals, such as *People's China,* are widely advertised in the Indian Communist press as available in India along with numerous Soviet publications such as the Cominform journal and *New Times.* Pamphlets by Mao Tse-tung, Liu Shao-chi, and other Chinese Communist leaders and writers are sold along with the works of Lenin and Stalin. *Communist,* the Party's "theoretical" monthly, was completely dominated in 1949 and even 1950 by reprints of Soviet articles and even statements of eastern European Communist leaders, but *New Age,* which succeeded it in 1952, contains a fair proportion of translations of articles by Chinese Communists.

There may well be some conflict between Peking's and Moscow's claims to serve as the example for and leader of the Asian Communist parties. The Chinese tend to claim greater originality for Mao's theories than Moscow is willing to accord to them. For example, Lu Ting-yi, a Chinese Communist Party Central Committee member, writes that "Mao Tse-tung's theory of the Chinese revolution is a new development of Marxism-Leninism in the revolution of the colonial and semi-colonial countries . . . . It is, indeed, a new contribution to the treasury of Marxism-Leninism."[28] The latter phrase used to be exclusively reserved in the Soviet press to describe Stalin's works, and there was a tendency in that press to characterize the Chinese Communist victory as the result of the correct application of Leninist-Stalinist, rather than any original Maoist, theory, as "a new triumph for Marxism-Leninism, a triumph for the Lenin-Stalin strategy and tactics . . . "[29] Also, the statement by Lu just cited not only claims that the Chinese revolution serves as an example for all colonial countries, which, as we have seen, has long been conceded and even propagated by Moscow. It also confines the applicability of the model of the Russian October Revolution to the imperialist countries, which has never been conceded by Moscow:

> The classic type of revolution for the imperialist countries is the October Revolution.
> The classic type of revolution in the colonial and semi-colonial countries is the Chinese revolution, the experience of which is invaluable for the peoples of these countries.*

Yet even this extreme Chinese statement was reprinted in the Cominform journal and so could not have aroused any very strenuous objections in Moscow. On the other hand, the Chinese themselves more

---

* A recent newspaper report relates that Chen Yun, a CCP Politburo member, asserted in a speech on the anniversary of Stalin's death that China, and not the Soviet Union, is the champion of Communism in Asia and the fount of revolution

usually couple their own claims to being the example for Asia with the recognition that the Soviet Union is the example for the entire world, not excluding Asia, as in the following typical passage:

> . . . the oppressed people of Asia . . . see the path to the future of all mankind charted by the Great October Socialist Revolution. They see before them the shining example of the victory of the Chinese Revolution, the prototype of revolution in a semi-colonial and semi-feudal country . . .[30]

This convenient formula recognizing both the Soviet Union and China as examples for India, one of more general and one of more immediate applicability, was used by the CPI as far back as the Political Thesis of the Second Congress in early 1948.* It still represents the Party's line on this subject, making it possible for the Party to avoid the question as to which of the two examples is primary. Thus in May 1953 the Communist All-India Trade Union Congress could send a message to the All-China Federation of Trade Unions including the standard phrase: "Your experience in the liberation struggle has shown the path to the colonial, semi-colonial, and dependent countries,"[31] and three months later an editorial in *Cross Roads* could hail the Communist Party of the Soviet Union in the following words: "The struggle of the Russian people under the leadership of this Party has offered invaluable lessons for the peoples of all countries of the world, who have today come to look upon it as the model on which they have to build their own parties."[32]

That Chinese Communism is a model for other colonial countries means that their Communist parties follow the neo-Maoist strategy. This strategy, however, as we have seen, was adopted by Moscow as well as Peking, has been used by Communist parties in underdeveloped areas far from Asia and even in the West, and was embraced by the CPI on orders not from Peking but from Moscow. The question of which country—China or the Soviet Union—serves as an example to the CPI must therefore not be confused with the question of which country directs the CPI. Conceivably, the CPI could look solely to one country as a model and yet do so on orders of the other country, as, indeed, the Andhra Communists thought they were doing during their short-lived rule of the CPI. Although both China and the Soviet

---

in the Orient. Volney D. Hurd, "Peking-Vietminh Rift Rumored," *The Christian Science Monitor*, March 9, 1954, p. 1.

* The *Political Thesis* (Bombay, 1949), p. 93, spoke of "the Soviet Union as the leader of humanity," while it emphasized the "glorious achievements of the Chinese Revolution, underlining its international significance, particularly its significance for the peoples of Asia."

Union are today models to the CPI, the fact, documented in this study, remains that the Indian Communist Party has, from its beginnings, executed every change in its strategy in response to direction from Moscow and in a manner which it thought—not always rightly— accorded with Moscow's desires. It is therefore very likely to owe its first loyalty to Moscow and not to Peking—despite such statements as Ghosh's, made shortly after he came to power in the Party in 1951 in a letter to Mao Tse-tung, that "People's China, under your leadership, stands forth today as the leader of the resurgent peoples of Asia."[33]

Two declarations of loyalty to the rulers in Moscow issued at critical junctures in 1953 tend to support this conclusion. The first was a cable sent by Ghosh to Malenkov after the latter succeeded Stalin saying: "We declare our solidarity and pledge the support of the Indian working people and the Indian Communist Party in the common struggle for common objectives."[34] The second was a resolution adopted by the CPI's Central Committee at a meeting held July 23–31, shortly after the ouster of Beria. In it

> . . . the Central Committee of the Communist Party of India joins the Communist and Workers' Parties throughout the world in expressing its deep respect and affection for the Communist Party of the Soviet Union (CPSU). The Central Committee expresses its satisfaction that the Central Committee of the CPSU has proved itself strong and vigilant enough to unmask in time the real face of Beria . . .[35]

And, to make sure that Malenkov could not harbor any suspicions on the CPI's loyalty, its Central Committee called on all Party members and units

> . . . to carry on a ceaseless campaign among the people pointing out the fact that Beria pitted himself not against Malenkov, as is slanderously asserted by the enemy, but against the entire Central Committee, against the entire Communist Party of the Soviet Union. It is only by doing this that we, Indian Communists, will be able to prevent the enemy succeeding in discrediting the Model Party of the world working class in the eyes of the Indian people.

It is not surprising that when Ajoy Ghosh suffered from a "leg ailment" he went to Moscow and not to Peking "for treatment,"[36] to remain there for half a year and not to return until less than three weeks before the CPI's Third Congress.

II. THE THIRD PARTY CONGRESS

Agreement on the peaceful neo-Maoist strategy. Unlike the Second Congress of the CPI, held six years earlier, its Third Congress, which convened in Madurai from December 27, 1953 to January 4, 1954, did not mark the adoption of a new strategy. Its approach, as S. A. Dange said in the debate on the Political Resolution,[37] was the same as that of 1951, and the strategy of peaceful neo-Maoism then worked out by the CPI was now again given the seal of approval by Ghosh's recent return from Moscow and the attendance at the Congress of Harry Pollitt, General Secretary of the British Communist Party. The very divisions within the Party—and there are indications that these were very deep*—are, in a sense, evidence of the Party's unity on the neo-Maoist strategy, for they were all on issues arising within that strategy rather than on any choice between different strategies, and they did not run along the lines that had, in years past, split the adherents of various strategies.[38] The most serious splits at the Third Congress apparently occurred over the question of who was the main enemy and over the form of the united front. However, in the first case the question was not, as it had been in the conflict between the "left" and the neo-Maoist strategy, the fundamental one whether the main enemy was the Indian bourgeoisie or foreign imperialism, but merely which foreign imperialism—British or American. And in the second case the question was not, as it had been in the conflict between the "right" strategy and the "left" and neo-Maoist strategies, whether the united front should be one from above with the Congress and Socialist Parties or one from below against these parties, but rather merely one of the approach to be used and the role to be played by the CPI in the anti-Congress united front from below. This does not mean that the splits in the CPI could not have been very important, but it does mean that there was general agreement by all factions on the postulates of the neo-Maoist strategy.

Britain vs. the U. S. as the main enemy. In a secret document, published by the Democratic Research Service,[39] the Andhra faction of the

* Democratic Research Service, *Communist Conspiracy at Madurai* (Bombay: Popular Book Depot, 1954), pp. 12–19. If there be any question as to the authenticity of the secret Communist documents on which the work of the Democratic Research Service is based (see footnote on p. 141, above), the CPI's own publications, on which we found our analysis of the Third Congress, leave no doubt of the existence of factionalism. Its existence is also clear from a parting message given to the CPI in an interview with *New Age* by Harry Pollitt after the Congress, "to rally round your new Central Committee in complete unity so that the line of march ahead as laid down in the Political Resolution of the 3rd Congress can be implemented. There have been important and protracted discussions at your Congress, but now the line of policy has been voted upon and accepted in a democratic manner . . . ." "Britain's 'Shameful Heritage'," *World News* (London; this succeeded *World News and Views* at the beginning of 1954), I, No. 6 (February 6, 1954), 115.

Party, still led by Rajeshwar Rao, vigorously championed the view at the Third Congress "that British imperialism is the chief enemy of our national progress and therefore of our national independence." "So when we talk of anti-imperialist revolution it specifically means, in the present set-up, a fight against British imperialism for national independence and freedom, but not against Anglo-American imperialism or world imperialism in general."[40]   It is admitted that as "part of the world working class," that is, the international Communist movement, it "is our inviolable international obligation" "to fight against American imperialism," for, "internationally speaking, America is the spearhead of world reaction as the main enemy of Peace and Freedom for all the people."   But, interestingly enough, the Andhra Communists do not really want to speak "internationally," that is, they do not want to put Soviet interests ahead of their own.   They say: "We, situated as we are in a country under a particular State, have some concrete tasks to perform.   The chief enemy of our national freedom today is British imperialism."[41]

Even if this secret "Andhra Thesis" is not authentic, it is clear that the view set forth in it was advanced at the Congress, as must also have been the opposite view that the United States was the main enemy, since Ghosh, in his report on the Congress, refers to both of them as deviations.[42]   In seeking to compromise between them, he asserts that the struggles against Britain and the United States "have to be conducted simultaneously"[43] and that it "is an incorrect approach" to ask which of the two tasks should be taken up first since they are not opposed to each other.[44]   Rather, he says,

> We have to win full freedom from the British but we also have to defend our existing freedom from the increasing menace of the U. S.
> Unless we defend it from the U. S., we can never win complete freedom from the British.[45]

Apparently pleased with this argument, he declares: "This way, with an integrated and comprehensive understanding, we can avoid both deviations."[46]

However, Ghosh, both in his review of the Congress and in a speech to it, does go so far as to say that "the basic struggle in our case is the struggle against British domination."[47]   The Political Resolution that emerged from the Third Congress, in a paragraph not contained in the secret draft resolution submitted to it,[48] also seeks to compromise between the anti-British and the anti-American positions and is weighted in favor of the former:

> Thus the question of defeating the war plans of the American imperialists and India's struggle for peace is closely linked with the

question of India's struggle for full and unfettered national freedom, which means first and foremost, freedom from control of the British who continue to be the dominant imperialist power and of liquidating feudalism. . . .[49]

We have earlier expressed our belief that to Moscow the essence of the neo-Maoist strategy and the chief reason for its adoption was its anti-Americanism. One may strongly suspect, therefore, that the stand adopted by the Indian Party on this issue at the Third Congress, which gave somewhat greater emphasis to the anti-British than to the anti-American position, went against Moscow's wishes. This suspicion is confirmed by the fact that in Ghosh's report on the Third Congress in the Cominform journal[50] which otherwise closely follows the lines of his review of the Congress published in India, there is no hint that the anti-British struggle is regarded as more basic than the anti-American, but the overestimation of the danger from either imperialist enemy at the expense of the other is condemned and both views are said to have been decisively rejected by the Congress. Ghosh's report to Moscow and international Communism thus distorts the actual state of affairs in order to conceal what would be displeasing to his masters.

National liberation movement vs. peace movement. The question of whether the CPI should concentrate on the British or the American enemy is not an academic one nor is it so new to us as may at first appear. As is noticeable from the passage of the Political Resolution just quoted, the anti-American attitude is identified with the peace movement, the anti-British with the so-called struggle for national liberation. Ghosh, who discusses the entire question under the heading "Struggle for Peace and Freedom," makes this quite clear when he says that "in our country the struggle for peace has its main edge directed against the American imperialists while the struggle for freedom has its main edge directed against the British."[51] What is implied in the conflict between the anti-American and the anti-British factions is stated quite bluntly in his report in the Cominform journal, which says that to concentrate on the British enemy "meant the total minimization of the significance of the peace movement" and "would have the peace movement relegated to a position of minor importance."[52] This is, in other words, but another form of the old conflict between those who want to follow the present Moscow line of emphasizing the peace movement, with its all-class approach and its concentration on a foreign enemy, and the more old-fashioned Communists. This latter group has greater interest in the Party, even if it is a four-class party, than in this milk-and-water peace movement, and greater interest in the internal more immediate enemy, even if that enemy is not the native bourgeoisie but only feudalism and British capital, than in the more distant United States. It is not surprising that this latter policy should have been championed by the Andhra Communists, whose neo-Maoist policy of peasant, that is, anti-feudal, warfare and terrorism had been succeeded by the present one of peaceful neo-Maoism with its stress on the anti-American peace movement.

That this conflict existed in the terms we have just used, as well as in its anti-British vs. anti-American form, is confirmed by Ghosh when he states that there has come "to the forefront the question of the relation between the peace movement and the national libera-tion movement which had for so long been argued out inside the Party."[53] He defines the relation of the two movements to each other by explaining that

> . . . the struggle for peace and the struggle for national liberation are not identical or co-extensive. All those who are in the struggle for freedom will join the struggle for peace, but many in the struggle for peace may not join the struggle for full freedom.[54]

However, this explanation does not succeed in resolving the conflict. Those Communists who dislike the peace movement do so precisely because it is broader than the "liberation" (i.e., Communist) move-ment and because in it they are forced to cooperate with "many" who are unwilling to join their Communist struggle. Ghosh, consistent with long-established CPI leadership practice, deplores that "there has been, so far, a very serious underestimation inside the Party about the importance of the peace movement"[55] and, in particular, takes the trade unions and peasant organizations to task for "the biggest negli-gence" in this field.[56] The Political Resolution speaks of "the impera-tive need to broaden, extend and strengthen the peace movement."[*]

If Moscow favored the anti-American view and the peace movement related to it, why then was the faction that emphasized hostility to

---

[*] *Political Resolution* (New Delhi: Jayant Bhatt, 1954) , p. 6. American military agreements with Pakistan, coming at the time of the Third Congress, which were characterized as "a grave menace to the Indian people, a menace against which the entire country must be mobilized" (*ibid.,* p. 4) in view of their apparently wide-spread unpopularity in India, gave the Communists a golden opportunity to pose as Indian patriots and to emphasize the importance of their peace movement. Moscow's interest in the Indian peace movement is clearly indicated by the fact that the Cominform journal, too, eagerly seized upon this issue, playing it up in two articles in the space of two weeks. "Peace Movement in India Gaining Momentum," *For a Lasting Peace, for a People's Democracy!*, January 8, 1954, p. 1; "Sharp Protest in India against USA-Pakistan War Pact," *ibid.,* January 22, 1954, p. 6.

Britain and was antagonistic to the peace movement not sharply condemned at the Third Congress, and why was it treated with such caution by the Ghosh leadership? One reason no doubt was the strength of the anti-British faction in the Party. However, we have learned that, in the past, internal Party politics had never been a factor sufficiently strong to override what appeared to be Moscow's wishes, and there is no reason to explain the situation revealed at the Third Congress by an assumption of a weakened hold of Moscow on the CPI. Rather, the Party Congress could not faithfully reflect Moscow's attitude vis-à-vis the United States and the peace movement because the CPI felt that to do so would lead to the abandonment of another basic policy also approved by Moscow, the policy regulating the Party's relationship with the Nehru government.

The CPI's attitude toward the Nehru government. As has been true ever since Palme Dutt's letter of December 1950, the Party recognized the usefulness to itself (and the Soviet Union) of certain of Nehru's foreign policies. Speaking of the government's denunciation of the atom bomb, its help in ending hostilities in Korea, and its opposition to the U. S.-Pakistan agreement, the Third Congress said that it played "a role appreciated by the peace-loving masses and states";[57] and Ghosh admonished the Party as follows: "When the Nehru Government takes a good step for peace . . . we must welcome it wholeheartedly, without any 'buts' and 'ifs.' "[58] The Party clearly felt that basically Nehru was pro-British and anti-American. Once this was assumed, too great emphasis on opposition to the United States and on the peace movement on the part of the CPI would logically have led it to a policy of cooperation with the Nehru government. This was actually made quite explicit by Ghosh: "If U. S. imperialism is looked upon as the main enemy not only of peace but also of national freedom, then the tendency would increasingly be of lining up behind the Nehru Government on the plea of fighting the American threat."[59] In his Cominform article, too, Ghosh explained that the anti-American position would lead to "full support" of the government.[60]

Ghosh recognized very clearly that here the Party was up against a basic question of strategy, the question of whether its relation to the government and the Congress should be one of the united front from above or of the united front from below:

> As a matter of fact, there can be only two basic lines: cooperate with the Government but criticize specific acts; or, oppose the Government but support specific acts. Here is not a question of different emphasis only. These are two different lines.[61]

Faced with this choice of two different lines or strategies, the Party did not hesitate which to adopt. The government was found to follow "a policy of collaboration with feudalism and imperialism, as it represents certain classes,"[62] and therefore "our attitude towards the Government continues to be one of general opposition,"[63] "even in the international sphere . . . because the Indian Government does not follow consistently a policy of peace and democracy."[64]

Here, then, seems to have been the underlying reason for the CPI's inability to go all out in a stand naming the United States as its main enemy and condemning the faction that wanted to concentrate on the British enemy and, by implication, to minimize the importance of the peace movement. Concentration on the American enemy and on the peace movement is a natural policy for Communist parties in countries where the governments are relatively strongly pro-American. In India the government was sufficiently anti-American for the Communists to feel that such a policy would have led them to support the government. Clearly, however, Moscow did not consider the Nehru government sufficiently anti-American to make CPI support for it seem appropriate. This view does not exclude the possibility that, if the Nehru government feels further alienated by United States policy or attracted by Soviet policy, such support may be appropriate in the future, involving the Communist party, as in Guatemala (under President Arbenz) and Indonesia (during the rule of the Nationalist Party) , in a united front from above with the governing party, or at least in efforts to form such a front, unsuccessful as they may be. This would mean a new policy shift for the CPI, returning it close to the "right" strategy of the united front from above with the Congress which was abandoned at the end of 1947.*

* *Postscript:* The above paragraphs were written and our research was completed in mid-1954. It would seem in 1955, just after Nehru's return from a visit to Moscow where he was being feted by the Soviet leaders now strongly interested in encouraging "neutrality," that during the past year the CPI has traveled farther along the path indicated above. It has, however, not yet abandoned the neo-Maoist strategy in favor of a return to the "right" one of a united front from above with the Congress. The trend begun with Palme Dutt's letter of December 1950 (see pp. 129–130 and 133–134, above) of support for certain phases of Nehru's foreign policy has continued to the point where only a few are still subjected to CPI criticism. On domestic policy, however, the Party has substantially remained in opposition to the Congress government, although it has recently given its support to some aspects of the government's economic planning. "Reds Back Nehru on Foreign Policy. Indian Party Shifts After His Moscow Trip, But Scores Domestic Program," *The New York Times,* June 30, 1955, p. 4. See also the discussion of the CPI's attitude toward Nehru in Madhu Limaye, "Indian Communism: The New Phase," *Pacific Affairs,* XXVII, No. 3 (September 1954) , 205–207 and 212–213, and Randolph Carr, "Conflicts Within the Indian CP," *Problems of Communism,* IV,

The neo-Maoist strategy is essentially an adjustment of Communist policy to a situation in which the major parties, both bourgeois and labor, are relatively pro-American and anti-Soviet and where the Communists yet want to unite all the classes represented by these parties against the United States. Where this situation changes by such a party's becoming relatively anti-American and pro-Soviet, there is no reason to assume that Communist strategy will not accordingly change back to the "right" strategy in relation to that party. The direct appeal of the Communists to the bourgeoisie is likely to continue, however, and since, in any case, some efforts to win over individuals and groups to Communism "from below" are always being made, even in periods of the united front from above, the four-class appeal, the essential element of what we have defined as the neo-Maoist strategy, will probably remain a feature of Communist policy.

The united fronts from above and below. Although the Third Congress seemed agreed on the necessity of continuing the policy of the united front from below against the Congress and Socialist Parties, disagreements on the form of the CPI's united front, which had been going on during the preceding years, continued. The utility of united front agreements with other parties and organizations was generally recognized, and the CPI Congress resolved that "it is necessary for the Communist Party to continue and intensify efforts for such agreements on each issue."[65] But Ghosh noted the existence of a "liquidationist" tendency favoring the submersion of the Party in the united front;[66] and the secret draft resolution devoted a long paragraph to the condemnation of "a United Front having a programme, organization and discipline of its own" and "a united front that circumscribes the independent role of the Communist Party."[67] The draft was corrected by the substitution of an even longer and more specific section demanding

---

No. 5 (September–October 1955), 7–13, on pp. 11–12. This attitude was summarized by the Party's Central Committee meeting in Delhi in June 1955: "Although the foreign policy of the Government of India has undergone a welcome change in recent years, no such change has taken place in its internal policies. These policies, on the contrary, continue to be, in the main, reactionary and undemocratic." Quoted in G. S. Bhargava, "Communists change their tactics," *The Manchester Guardian Weekly*, January 12, 1956, p. 3.

As these pages went to the printer early in 1956 the CPI was about to hold its Fourth Congress at Palghat. Coming after the visit of the Soviet leaders Khrushchev and Bulganin to India and the rich praise they bestowed on Nehru and the Indian government, this was likely to become the occasion for the CPI to move closer to the "right" strategy of advocating a united front from above with the Congress Party. The CPI may thus be approaching the completion of the circle begun in 1947 from the "right" to the "left" to the neo-Maoist to the "right" strategy.

that united front committees be merely coordinating and *ad hoc* bodies and not permanent organizations,[68] but this was completely dropped in the final published resolution, which stated only that "it should be remembered that the growth of the United Front depended, above all, on the independent role of the Party in uniting and mobilizing the working class and the working people."[69]

It is difficult to believe that any significant segment of the CPI actually favored dissolving the Party organizationally in a broader United Front, as Ghosh charged, although it is quite likely that some of the Party's allies in the United Front desired this[70] and that the Third Congress faced the problem of furnishing Party members with arguments against such a course and at the same time trying not to alienate its present and potential future allies. Within the Party the real issue was probably, as it had been since 1951, between those who wanted to confine their united front activities to cooperation "from above" with "left" parties and those who felt that, in addition, much greater emphasis must be given to the united front from below, especially against the Congress and the Socialists. It is doubtful that on this issue any faction stood openly for the former point of view. Victory went clearly to the latter position, which had been that of the Party leadership all along, thus further emphasizing the fact that relations between the CPI and the Congress Party remained essentially hostile. The Third Congress went on record against "reliance on top negotiations and manoeuvres."[71] Ghosh said: "There is the tendency of looking upon 'Left unity'—unity of Left parties—as a necessary precondition to the building of broad democratic unity. This concept is wrong."[72] In but slightly different words, both Ghosh's report on the Third Congress published in India and the one in the Cominform journal as well as the Political Resolution of the Congress all hammered home the message that "eschewing sectarianism does not merely mean the adoption of a friendly attitude towards the 'Left parties'; the united front in today's context means the drawing in of the vast masses who are getting disillusioned with the Congress and also with the Socialist Party but who are not yet prepared to subscribe to the entire Programme of our Party."[73] The point that the united front must pre-eminently be one from below is also made when it is "emphasized that the unity that has to be built is unity of the masses in action";[74] that, "if the Party wants to get strong, it has to base itself, above all, on the economic and other immediate demands of the people."[75]

That the CPI's united front, following the neo-Maoist pattern, was to include sections of the bourgeoisie hardly needs any further documentation. It seems to have been taken for granted at the Third

Congress. In its analysis of the economic situation the Congress found that "contradictions between imperialism and the Indian bourgeoisie are becoming sharper and even sections of the big bourgeoisie have begun raising their voices on this issue."[76] Perhaps indicating some practical difficulties met by the Party in appealing to both workers and capitalists, the Congress again resolved, as the Politburo had already done in 1952, that "the working class must come out for the protection of national industries against the competition of the imperialists."[77] In a letter from the Party's Central Committee to two fellow-travelers in Hyderabad, published by the Democratic Research Service, the theory underlying the neo-Maoist strategy of the predominance of common interests between labor and capital is clearly stated:

> The Communist Party's conception of United Front is basically a front of classes. . . . Although these classes may have mutually conflicting interests, nonetheless the fact remains that imperialism and feudalism constitute the common enemies of all and constitute the biggest obstacle standing in the way of our country's progress. Our concept of United Front arises from this common interest between these various classes.[78]

Sectarianism and the weakness of fronts and the Party. Just as the Party leadership had done throughout 1951–1953, the Third Congress called for the strengthening not only of the peace movement and the united front but also of the Communist mass organizations of workers, peasants, students, youth, and women, which were admitted to be "still weak and in many places nonexistent."[79] In particular, it called for trade union "unity," that is, the winning over "from below" of members and organizations affiliated with non-Communist trade unions.[80] However, Ghosh does not even seem aware that he is condemning his own Party, which claims to speak for the working class, when, in his report in the Cominform journal, he mentions in passing "the traditional weakness of the Party in the major industrial and mining areas."[81] Facing the problem of strengthening its peace movement, its united front, and its mass organizations, the Party still considered sectarianism in its ranks as a serious obstacle. "The Congress drew the attention of the entire Party to the fact that a firm struggle against sectarianism is not being carried out by the Party units."[82] The Congress deplored both the tendency in the Party to regard all members of the Congress and the Socialist Party as reactionary and "the failure to distinguish between the platform of the Front and the Party Forum,"[83] that is, the tendency to treat the united front like a Communist Party organization and thus to alienate non-Communists. In particular, the leadership at the Third Congress seemed to be upset

about sectarianism in the trade unions, which, it declared, in many
cases "has led to unions being reduced to Party groups, to absence of
democratic functioning and, ultimately, to loss of mass basis."[84]   Sectarianism being, as we have pointed out, a trait natural to Communists,
it can be safely predicted that this type of preaching will both continue
and remain ineffective for quite some time.

Just as the Third Congress echoed all the other major demands made
upon Party members that we have found had characterized CPI statements since 1951, indicating that none of them had yet been fulfilled,
so it also called for "the rapid strengthening of the Party."*   Ghosh
speaks of "glaring shortcomings which persist in our organization and
functioning"[85] and which were apparently sharply revealed by the
very inadequate preparations for the Congress itself.   The "extremely
weak"[86] Party center, manned by only two or three members of the
Politburo, received the major blame for this state of affairs and was
described as having "reached a critical stage . . . on the point of total
breakdown."[87]   Ghosh also says that an "attitude of neglecting Party
jobs, an attitude bordering on irresponsibility, is one of the appalling
shortcomings that came to the forefront in the Party Congress, most
strikingly in the political preparations for it."[88]   Finally, he feels im-
pelled to apologize for the fact that differences within the Party, some
of which we have just discussed, had been "allowed to accumulate"
so "that there was no escape from them at the Party Congress: they
had to be faced and thrashed out";[89] and he blames this on an "attitude
of indifference and even liberalism . . . towards differences, towards
deviations from the Party line."[90]   However, while a better organized
party would no doubt have been able to squelch or compromise these
differences before they came out into the open at the Congress, they
had, as we have seen, persisted in one form or another since the adoption of the neo-Maoist strategy in its peaceful form early in 1951 and
are, indeed, of the kind that one would expect to arise under that
strategy.

The CPI in 1954 and the three strategies of Communism.   It would
be a mistake to assume that the men whom we have in the course of
our story met as the leaders of the CPI during the various periods when
it followed its different strategies are principled enough still to adhere
to the strategies that they championed while they were in power.   We

---

* *Political Resolution,* p. 33.   Ghosh, *On the Work of the Third Congress of the
Communist Party of India* (New Delhi: Jayant Bhatt, 1954), p. 19, gives the CPI's
strength as "50,000 members and about 20,000 candidates," indicating that it was not
even approaching the strength of 90,000 listed early in 1948 and dissipated in the
three subsequent years of violent tactics and factionalism.

have ourselves seen that Joshi, the "right" leader, became an advocate of peaceful neo-Maoism long before the Party leadership then in power realized that this was the "correct" line to take; that Ranadive, the "left" leader, was quite willing to switch to neo-Maoism in order to maintain himself in power; and that Rajeshwar Rao, the "violent neo-Maoist" leader, was apparently himself involved in carrying out the Party's turn to peaceful neo-Maoism. They all seemed to be converted to this latter strategy of the CPI and, at most, displayed their individuality by taking different stands on issues arising within this strategy. However, in the mind of the Party's rank and file and of the general public they remain identified with the strategies in effect when they led the CPI, and for this reason their position in the Party, as revealed at the Third Congress, may be regarded as symbolic of the position occupied by the CPI in 1954 in relation to the three strategies of Communism. Ajoy Ghosh, who led the Party since its adoption of peaceful neo-Maoism, appeared, after his return from Moscow, to be more firmly in the saddle than ever.[91] Rajeshwar Rao, the leader of the Andhra Communists, continued as a member of the CPI's top leadership.[92] On the other hand, both P. C. Joshi and B. T. Ranadive remained outside the Central Committee. However, while Ranadive was not even a delegate to the Third Congress,[93] Joshi's influence was said to be increasing, and he was reported to have declined a seat in the Central Committee as a gesture of unity.[94]

That neo-Maoism in its peaceful form continued to be the policy of the Indian Communist Party was, in any case, clear from the pronouncements of the Third Congress, and Ghosh's strengthened position merely confirms this conclusion. Rajeshwar Rao's uninterrupted continuance in the Party's leadership, as contrasted to the position of the other two deposed General Secretaries, Joshi and Ranadive, indicates that differences between the violent and peaceful forms of one strategy are considered much less important by the Communists than differences between strategies. While the neo-Maoist strategy was thus firmly entrenched in the CPI in 1954, with its peaceful form dominant, both the "right" and the "left" strategies were rejected. The "left" one, however, was rejected much more decisively not, it appears, because, as was widely concluded from Ranadive's exclusion from the Congress, it had been applied in its violent form during the latter's rule—for in that case Rajeshwar Rao, who had been no less violent than Ranadive, would also have had to be excluded—but because of its negative attitude towards the bourgeoisie, which is its main point of difference from the neo-Maoist strategy. The "right" strategy, on the other hand, agrees with the neo-Maoist one on the desirability of cooperation with the bourgeoisie, but differs from it in its approach to the bourgeois and socialist parties, substituting that "from above" for the neo-Maoist one "from below." Though still rejected, it seemed likely in 1954 that this strategy was somewhat closer to the CPI's neo-Maoism than was the anti-bourgeois "left" strategy.

NOTES FOR CHAPTER 6

1. We do not have to deal with the election results in this book. For a good presentation and discussion of them, see three articles by Richard L. Park, "Indian Democracy and the General Election," *Pacific Affairs*, XXV, No. 2 (June 1952), 130–139; "India's General Elections," *Far Eastern Survey*, XXI, No. 1 (January 9, 1952), 1–8; "Indian Election Results," *ibid.*, No. 7 (May 7, 1952), 61–70. See also "The Indian General Elections," *Indian Press Digests* (Berkeley: Bureau of International Relations of the Department of Political Science, University of California), I, No. 4 (September 1952), 45–85; and Masani, *The Communist Party of India*, pp. 156–164.

2. "Post Election Situation And Our Tasks," *New Age*, I (Madras; subsequent volumes appeared in Bombay), No. 1 (September 1952), 31–45, on p. 38.

3. *Ibid.*, p. 45.

4. "Decisions of Political Bureau of the Communist Party of India," *For a Lasting Peace, for a People's Democracy!*, September 5, 1952, p. 2.

5. *Ibid.*, November 7, 1952, p. 5.

6. Ghosh, "Concerning Results of General Election in India," *For a Lasting Peace, for a People's Democracy!*, March 28, 1952, p. 3. See also Ghosh, "Some of our Main Weaknesses," *ibid.*, November 7, 1952, p. 5.

7. Ajoy Ghosh, "United Front—a New Force in Indian Politics," *Cross Roads*, April 25, 1952, pp. 2, 8.

8. "Central Committee of Communist Party Meets," *ibid.*, April 4, 1952, pp. 4, 5, 10, on p. 10.

9. *Ibid.*; "Meeting of Central Committee, Communist Party of India," *For a Lasting Peace, for a People's Democracy!*, May 2, 1952, p. 3; "Post Election Situation And Our Tasks," *op. cit.*

10. "Communiqué on Meeting of C.P.I.'s Central Committee," *Cross Roads*, April 12, 1953, p. 3.

11. "Central Committee of Communist Party Meets," *op. cit.*, p. 4; "Post Election Situation And Our Tasks," *op. cit.*, pp. 36 and 42–43; "Communist Party's Call for United Action," *New Age*, II, No. 2 (February 1953), 13–14.

12. For a listing of electoral blocs entered into by the CPI with various groups in different provinces, see Masani, *The Communist Party of India*, pp. 153–154.

13. "Central Committee of Communist Party Meets," *op. cit.*, p. 5.

14. "Post Election Situation And Our Tasks," *op. cit.*, p. 45.

15. Ghosh, "Concerning Results of General Election in India," *op. cit.*

16. "Post Election Situation And Our Tasks," *op. cit.*, p. 40.

17. *Ibid.*, p. 41; capitalization in the original.

18. *Ibid.*, p. 34.

19. "Communist Party's Call for United Action," *op. cit.*

20. Ghosh, "United Front—a New Force in Indian Politics," *op. cit.*

21. Ajoy Ghosh, "Broaden and Strengthen the Popular Movement," *Cross Roads*, August 31, 1952, pp. 3, 2.

22. *Ibid.*

23. Ghosh, "United Front—a New Force in Indian Politics," *op. cit.*

24. "Working Class unity can and must be achieved!," *Cross Roads*, June 22, 1952, pp. 7, 10.

25. "Post Election Situation And Our Tasks," *op. cit.*, p. 39.

26. *Ibid.*, p. 41; see also "Decision of Political Bureau of the Communist Party of India," *For a Lasting Peace, for a People's Democracy!*, September 5, 1952, p. 2.

27. E. M. S. Namboodripad, "Present Stage of Peasant Movement in India," *ibid.*, December 18, 1953, p. 4.

28. Lu Ting-yi, "World Significance of Chinese Revolution," *For a Lasting Peace, for a People's Democracy!*, June 29, 1951, p. 2; also in *People's China*, IV, No. 1 (July 1, 1951), 9–12, and in *World News and Views*, XXXI, No. 28 (July 14, 1951), 309–311.

29. Editorial, "National-Liberation Movement of Peoples in Colonial and Dependent Countries," *For a Lasting Peace, for a People's Democracy!*, February 29, 1952, p. 1.

30. "The October Revolution and Asia," *People's China*, IV, No. 9 (November 1, 1951), 3.

31. "New China Inspires Indian Working Class," *Cross Roads*, June 14, 1953, p. 14.

32. "50 Years of the Soviet Communist Party," *ibid.*, August 9, 1953, p. 2.

33. "China's Advance—an Inspiration to all Asia," *ibid.*, September 21, 1951, p. 1.

34. "CPI Greets Comrade Malenkov," *ibid.*, March 22, 1953, p. 2.

35. "Take Political Lessons of Beria's Expulsion," *ibid.*, August 9, 1953, p. 3.

36. "Ajoy Ghosh Leaves for Moscow for Treatment," *ibid.*, May 31, 1953, p. 2.

37. Democratic Research Service, *Communist Conspiracy at Madurai* (Bombay: Popular Book Depot, 1954), p. 24.

38. The present divisions in the CPI are summarized in Marshall Windmiller, "Indian Communism Today," *Far Eastern Survey*, XXIII, No. 4 (April 1954), 49–56.

39. Reprinted in Masani, *The Communist Party of India*, pp. 264–269, from *Communist Conspiracy at Madurai*, pp. 49–54. See also *ibid.*, pp. 12–14 and 16–18.

40. *Ibid.*, p. 51.

41. *Ibid.*, pp. 51–52.

42. Ajoy Ghosh, *On the Work of the Third Congress of the Communist Party of India* (New Delhi: Jayant Bhatt, 1954), p. 5.

43. *Ibid.*, p. 7.

44. *Ibid.*, p. 23.

45. *Ibid.*, p. 9.

46. *Ibid.*, p. 10.

47. *Ibid.*, p. 7; see also "Tasks before the Communist Party of India," *ibid.*, p. 23.

48. *Communist Conspiracy at Madurai*, pp. 55–86.

49. *Political Resolution* (New Delhi: Jayant Bhatt, 1954), p. 8.

50. Ajoy Ghosh, "Third Congress of Communist Party of India," *For a Lasting Peace, for a People's Democracy!*, February 5, 1954, p. 5.

51. Ghosh, *On the Work of the Third Congress*, p. 7. See also *ibid.*, pp. 7–10.

52. Ghosh, "Third Congress of Communist Party of India," *op. cit.*

53. Ghosh, *On the Work of the Third Congress*, p. 5.

54. *Ibid.*, p. 10. Ghosh made the same point in his speech to the Congress, *ibid.*, p. 24.

55. *Ibid.,* p. 7; see also *ibid.,* p. 23.

56. *Ibid.,* p. 10; see also *ibid.,* p. 23 and *Political Resolution,* p. 4.

57. *Political Resolution,* p. 3; see also *ibid.,* p. 6.

58. Ghosh, *On the Work of the Third Congress,* pp. 9–10; see also *ibid.,* pp. 24–25.

59. *Ibid.,* p. 6.

60. Ghosh, "Third Congress of Communist Party of India," *op. cit.*

61. Ghosh, *On the Work of the Third Congress,* p. 6.

62. *Ibid.,* p. 9; see also *ibid.,* pp. 7 and 25.

63. *Ibid.,* p. 7.

64. *Political Resolution,* pp. 6–7; see also Ghosh, *On the Work of the Third Congress,* p. 24.

65. *Political Resolution,* p. 23.

66. Ghosh, "Third Congress of Communist Party of India," *op. cit.*

67. *Communist Conspiracy at Madurai,* pp. 74–75.

68. *Ibid.,* pp. 85–86. For other secret documents favoring a loose united front leaving the CPI independent, see *ibid.,* pp. 102–114 and 142–156.

69. *Political Resolution,* p. 23.

70. See *Communist Conspiracy at Madurai,* pp. 29–31.

71. *Political Resolution,* p. 22.

72. Ghosh, *On the Work of the Third Congress,* p. 14.

73. *Ibid.,* p. 15; see also Ghosh, "Third Congress of Communist Party of India," *op. cit.,* and *Political Resolution,* pp. 23–24.

74. Ghosh, *On the Work of the Third Congress,* p. 15.

75. *Ibid.,* p. 12; see also *ibid.,* pp. 28–29, and *Political Resolution,* p. 22.

76. *Ibid.,* p. 10.

77. *Ibid.,* pp. 28–29.

78. *Communist Conspiracy at Madurai,* p. 144.

79. *Political Resolution,* p. 30.

80. *Ibid.,* p. 26.

81. Ghosh, "Third Congress of Communist Party of India," *op. cit.*

82. *Ibid.*

83. *Political Resolution,* p. 24; see also Ghosh, *On the Work of the Third Congress,* p. 15.

84. *Political Resolution,* p. 27; see also Ghosh, *On the Work of the Third Congress,* p. 16, and "Third Congress of Communist Party of India," *op. cit.*

85. *Ibid.*

86. Ghosh, "Third Congress of Communist Party of India," *op. cit.*

87. Ghosh, *On the Work of the Third Congress,* p. 4.

88. *Ibid.*

89. *Ibid.,* pp. 4–5.

90. Ghosh, "Third Congress of Communist Party of India," *op. cit.*

91. Associated Press, "Indian Communist Order: Avoid Terrorist Tactics," *The Christian Science Monitor,* December 28, 1953, p. 4.

92. See *Communist Conspiracy at Madurai,* pp. 157–158 or Masani, *The Communist Party of India,* pp. 270–271 for the results of the elections to the CPI Central Committee held at the Third Congress.

93. "India's Reds Mapping Non-Violence Policy," *The New York Times,* December 27, 1953, p. 5.

94. Associated Press, "India Reds Choose Leaders," *The Christian Science Monitor,* January 4, 1954, p. 10.

SUMMARY AND CONCLUSIONS

I. SUMMARY

The story of the development of Indian Communist Party strategy having been set forth in some detail, it may be useful to summarize it here and present some general conclusions which have explicitly or implicitly emerged at various points in this study.

The three strategies of Communism. It has been our purpose to trace the evolution of the strategy of the Communist Party of India and to determine the roles of Moscow and Peking in that process. To do this it has been necessary to distinguish clearly between the various Communist strategies according to a scheme of classification which is illustrated and validated by our study. The "right" strategy regards imperialism and feudalism (or, in western countries, fascism) as the Communists' main enemies and therefore envisages first a bourgeois-democratic and only later a proletarian-socialist revolution. It calls for an alliance of the Communist party with anti-imperialist and anti-feudal (or anti-fascist) parties, both labor and bourgeois, that is, a united front "from above" or popular front. The "left" strategy, on the other hand, considers capitalism and the native bourgeoisie to be enemies at least as important as foreign imperialism and feudalism and therefore looks forward to an early socialist revolution merging with or even skipping the bourgeois-democratic revolution. It seeks a united front "from below" by appealing to workers and also the petty bourgeoisie and poor peasantry as individuals or in local organizations to leave labor and bourgeois parties and work with the Communists and by denouncing the leaders of these parties as traitors to their followers.

During World War II the Chinese Communists developed a third strategy which we call the neo-Maoist strategy. Like the "right" strategy, it primarily opposes imperialism and feudalism and thus

183

expects two separate revolutions. Also like the "right" strategy, it seeks an alliance of workers, peasants, petty bourgeoisie, and the anti-imperialist bourgeoisie; but, unlike the "right" and like the "left" strategy, it approaches these groups not "from above" through their principal parties but "from below" in opposition to these parties. Thus, the Communist party itself now claims to be the true representative of the interests not only of the exploited classes but also of the capitalists. A united front from below including sections of the bourgeoisie is the characteristic distinguishing the neo-Maoist strategy from its "right" and "left" predecessors. Either violent or peaceful methods may be combined with any of the three strategies. Although important, such methods are mere tactics and therefore not a principal criterion for the classification of Communist strategies.

CPI strategy from its beginnings to 1947. The Communist Party of India (CPI) has always sought to follow the lead of Moscow in making changes in its strategy, although it has not always been equally quick or successful in doing so. Organized in 1933 during a "left" period of international Communism, the CPI, following the strategy of the united front from below, violently denounced the National Congress and particularly its left wing as a bourgeois organization, only to shift, after Moscow shifted to the "right" strategy in 1935, to a policy of unity from above with the Congress and Congress Socialist Parties. The Stalin-Hitler Pact of 1939, opposed by the Communists' anti-fascist Popular Front partners in the West, also brought about a shift back to the "left" strategy in India. The Nazi invasion of Russia in 1941 once more returned the international line to the "right" strategy, changing the war from an "imperialist" one to a "people's war," and forcing the reluctant CPI into cooperation, this time not with the anti-British Congress and Socialists but with the British, until then regarded as "imperialists," against Germany and Japan.

In the immediate postwar years, and in keeping with the continuance of the Soviet alliance with the West, Moscow still favored the "right" strategy of cooperation between the Communists and major labor and bourgeois parties, but, not being vitally interested in Asia at that time, Moscow gave little specific guidance to the CPI. The latter, therefore, by and large sought a united front from above with both the Congress, or at least its "progressive" (Nehru) wing, and the Muslim League, but was so unsure of its proper course that in August 1946 it suddenly shifted to the "left" strategy of the united front from below against these organizations—only to revert to the "right" strategy by the end of the year and to continue to adhere to it until the end of 1947.

The shift from the "right" strategy, 1947. In 1947, with the deterioration of Soviet relations with the West, Moscow gave up the "right" strategy for international Communism. A session in June 1947 of the Soviet Academy of Sciences strongly denounced the entire Congress, including Nehru, as an ally of imperialism and opposed to it an anti-imperialist movement led by the Communists. This session, however, also marked the emergence of a disagreement, probably not even noticed at the time. One view, represented by the academicians Dyakov and Balabushevich, identified the entire bourgeoisie with imperialism and thus favored a return from the "right" to the "left" strategy with its proletarian, anti-capitalist approach. The other, advanced by Zhukov, the head of the Academy's Pacific Institute, condemned only the "big" bourgeoisie and thus left the way open for a united front from below, including some sections of the bourgeoisie, against the Congress. This latter view represents the first appearance, at least in relation to India, of the neo-Maoist strategy in Moscow.

Zhdanov's report to the first Cominform meeting of September 1947 was the chief signal from Moscow for the abandonment of the "right" strategy, but it said little about Asia and failed to make clear whether the "left" or the neo-Maoist strategy was to succeed the "right" one. The Zhdanov speech, however, was given a clearly neo-Maoist interpretation by Zhukov in an important article applying it to the colonial areas that openly advocated the inclusion of sections of the bourgeoisie in the united front from below. Nevertheless, Dyakov and Balabushevich continued to champion the "left" strategy in India, and the Cominform journal, intentionally or unintentionally, concealed Mao Tse-tung's pro-capitalist statements in its report of his speech of December 1947. The uncertainty as to which of the two strategies should be followed was not resolved at the Calcutta Southeast Asia Youth Conference of February 1948, which served to popularize the shift away from the "right" strategy among the Asian Communist parties.

In December 1947, as a reaction to the Zhdanov speech and six full months after the session of the Academy of Sciences, the CPI Central Committee met to execute what it interpreted to be the change of line desired by Moscow. "Leftist" by nature and probably quite ignorant of the neo-Maoist strategy, the CPI leadership was not bothered by or even aware of Moscow's indecision and substituted a full-fledged "left" strategy for the discarded "right" one. Its resolution sharply attacked both the entire Congress and the entire bourgeoisie as allies of imperialism, favored a united front from below against these, looked forward to an early anti-capitalist revolution, and implied that the use of violent methods was in order. The CPI leadership thus lined up with Balabushevich and Dyakov in Moscow, but it is more likely to have misunderstood Zhukov than to have opposed him, and certainly must have been sure that it was correctly interpreting the Zhdanov speech and therefore enjoying Moscow's support.

The "left" strategy in India, 1948–1949. The new "left" policy was confirmed by the Second Congress of the CPI in March 1948, where Joshi was replaced as General Secretary by Ranadive, a man fanatically convinced that the Zhdanov speech heralded a sharp turn of Moscow to the "left" and the imminent outbreak of revolution in India and throughout the world. Moscow maintained virtually complete silence on the Second Congress, obviously displeased with or uncertain about it for some reason. Throughout 1948 it neither clearly approved nor disapproved of the CPI's new "left" strategy. Both the "left" and the neo-Maoist strategies continued to find advocates in Moscow, indicating that the differences between them had still not been recognized as important.

After his assumption of power in the CPI, Ranadive embarked on a policy of violent strikes and terrorism, especially in large urban areas, which resulted in heavy loss of support for the Party and growing dissatisfaction and factionalism within it. The Andhra Provincial Committee of the CPI, in charge of the Communist-led peasant uprisings in the backward Telengana district of Hyderabad, submitted an anti-Ranadive document to the Politburo in June 1948 advocating the neo-Maoist strategy. Basing itself completely on the Chinese Communist example, it stood for both the specifically Chinese elements of that strategy—rural guerrilla warfare and chief reliance on the peasantry—and its essential elements: concentration on imperialism and feudalism as the main enemies, a revolution in more than one stage, and the inclusion of a section of the bourgeoisie as well as the "middle" and even the "rich" peasantry in the united front from below.

Ranadive replied with a series of Politburo statements drawn up at the end of 1948 and published between January and July 1949. In them he took an uncompromising "left" position, insisting on the Soviet Union as the chief example for the CPI, on the expectation of an early socialist revolution, and on regarding the Indian bourgeoisie rather than foreign imperialism and feudalism as the main enemy. Ranadive's united front from below against the Congress, therefore, could be based only on the urban and rural proletariat and the poor peasantry and could include some middle peasants and petty bourgeois elements, but not any part of the bourgeoisie or the rich peasantry. While the issue between the neo-Maoist and the "left" strategies was thus clearly joined in the CPI, Ranadive did not attack the Andhra Committee's advocacy or the Chinese example of the use of violent methods, although he continued to place his emphasis on urban rather than rural violence.

Ranadive also assailed various unnamed other Communist parties and certain elements in the CPI for their "revisionism." In the Politburo statement published in July 1949 he not only characterized the Andhra document as "anti-Leninist" but went so far as to attack Mao Tse-tung himself by name, ridiculing the assertion that Mao was an authoritative source of Marxism, mentioning him in one breath with Tito and Browder, and describing some of his passages advocating the promotion of capitalism as "horrifying" and "reactionary and counter-revolutionary." Clearly, Ranadive must have felt sure of Moscow's support. Whether he actually enjoyed it and whether Moscow or one faction in Moscow was opposed to Mao and approved of or even encouraged Ranadive's attack on Mao are questions on which we can only speculate.

The shift to the neo-Maoist strategy, 1949–1950. Whatever may have been Moscow's attitude toward Mao, it is clear that by the middle of 1949, even before Ranadive launched his assault on Mao, the decision between the "left" and the neo-Maoist strategies had finally, after two years of uncertainty, been made in Moscow in favor of the latter. The adoption of the neo-Maoist strategy is marked by the publication in *Pravda* in June 1949 of a vigorous assertion by Liu Shao-chi that all Asian Communist parties must cooperate with sections of the bourgeoisie and by a number of reports to the Soviet Academy of Sciences in which not only Zhukov, but also the former adherents of the "left" strategy, Dyakov and Balabushevich, now favor the inclusion of some bourgeois elements in the united front from below.

With Ranadive now committed to an extreme "left" strategy and Moscow having settled on the neo-Maoist strategy, a showdown became inevitable. The Peking WFTU Conference of November 1949 proclaimed that the use of the neo-Maoist strategy was now obligatory for all Asian Communist parties, defining it clearly as the inclusion of sections of the bourgeoisie in the united front, while requiring the use of armed force only "wherever and whenever possible." Even this call was completely ignored by Ranadive, who continued with his "left" strategy, thus necessitating a more direct intervention by Moscow. This finally came in the form of an editorial in the Cominform journal of January 27, 1950, telling the CPI to take the "Chinese path" of forming the broadest united front with all anti-imperialist classes and elements, but again mentioning the use of armed force only in

connection with countries other than India. Openly deprived of
Moscow's support, Ranadive's fate seemed to be sealed, but from
February through April 1950 he fought desperately to retain the
Party's leadership by issuing statements combining decreasing doses
of self-justification with increasing doses of self-criticism. Moscow
would not acknowledge them, however, thus permitting his intra-
Party enemies to press forward to the kill. During May and June
1950 the Central Committee met and Ranadive was replaced by
Rajeshwar Rao, the leader of the Andhra Communists. The neo-
Maoist strategy was taking the place of the "left" strategy.

The shift from violent to peaceful neo-Maoism, 1950–1951. The
CPI's new leadership, deeply committed to the type of peasant guerrilla
warfare it had been carrying on in Telengana, and misunderstanding
Moscow's and Peking's references to the "Chinese path" as including
the specifically Chinese Communist tactics as well as the essential four-
class element of the neo-Maoist strategy, championed that strategy in
its violent form. Although the Party, already brought to the brink
of ruin under Ranadive's leadership, disintegrated further as a result,
no advice was forthcoming from Moscow; and a warning in June 1950
from Peking against the necessary identification of the use of armed
force with the neo-Maoist strategy was ignored by the CPI. Finally,
in December 1950 Palme Dutt, who had in years past often served as
Moscow's voice for the CPI, wrote an open letter to the Party advising
it to concentrate on building a broad united front and a strong peace
movement and, in effect, to shift to a policy of peaceful neo-Maoism.
In the same month the CPI's Central Committee met and reconstituted
the Politburo to include adherents of peaceful neo-Maoism. Party
statements made at this meeting and in subsequent months underline
the ascendancy of this latter policy with their emphasis on the need
for a broad united front and a strong peace movement and their
repeated condemnation of sectarianism.

Adherence to peaceful neo-Maoism was made explicit in April 1951
when a statement of policy specifically rejected the Chinese model of
peasant guerrilla warfare for the CPI (though not the use of violence
in principle in the more distant future) while retaining the essential
four-class approach of the neo-Maoist strategy. From that point on,
after at least a year and a half of divergence, CPI policy has again
coincided with the Moscow line. During the next few months the
change of policy was confirmed by a change in the CPI leadership,
which placed the Party's present General Secretary, Ajoy Ghosh, in
power, and by a CPI directive ending the fighting in Telengana. The
Soviet and international Communist press expressed its approval of

the CPI's new line; and, at a session in November 1951 of the Soviet Academy of Sciences, both Zhukov and Balabushevich stated explicitly that India could not follow the Chinese model of armed struggle but must adhere to the four-class strategy.

The peaceful neo-Maoist strategy in India, 1952–1954. Developments during the post-1951 period, culminating in the CPI's Third Congress in January 1954, both confirmed the Party's adherence to peaceful neo-Maoism and brought out some of the difficulties faced by the CPI in executing that strategy. The most pervasive among these seemed to be "sectarianism," that is, the reluctance of Party members to cooperate with the many non-Communist elements who must be drawn into the neo-Maoist united front. Another was the tendency to form that united front primarily from above, by entering into alliances with various relatively small "left" parties, rather than from below by winning away members from the major anti-Communist parties, the Congress and the Socialists. Still another problem, related to that of sectarianism, was that of continued hostility in the Party towards the broad non-Party peace movement which the Communists have sought to build up since 1951. America being the main target of the peace movement, hostility in the Party took the form of pointing to Britain rather than the United States as the CPI's main enemy at the Third Congress. Since the Party approves and seeks to encourage any anti-American tendencies of the Nehru government, the leadership was prevented from taking too firm an anti-American, as distinguished from an anti-British, stand; it characterized both countries as main enemies—lest it land the Party in a position of supporting Nehru. Much as Moscow may be on the anti-American side in this anti-U. S. versus anti-Britain controversy in the CPI, the situation was not—or not yet—considered ripe for a return to the "right" strategy of the united front from above with Nehru.* The united front from below against the Congress and Socialist Parties was to be as broad as possible and to include capitalists. A return to the "left" strategy seemed therefore in 1954 to be out of the question. The CPI continued committed, as it had been since 1950, to the neo-Maoist strategy.

II. Conclusions

Neo-Maoism—a new Communist strategy. Our study has demonstrated that there are three strategies of Communism, and that what we here call the neo-Maoist strategy is new and different from both the older "left" and "right" strategies. In its beginnings on the inter-

* See pp. 174–175, above, for 1955–1956 postscripts on this point.

national Communist scene, in the years 1947 and 1948, because of the sharp contrast between it and the "right" strategy, which it succeeded, the neo-Maoist strategy was often confused with the "left" strategy. The Zhdanov speech, which heralded the abandonment of the "right" strategy, was widely regarded both by Communists, such as the CPI leaders, and by non-Communist observers as inaugurating a "left" period. Moscow itself did not seem to appreciate the differences between the "left" and the neo-Maoist strategies until 1949. More recently, although there has in fact been no intervening shift in Communist strategy, there has been a tendency to confuse the neo-Maoist strategy with the "right" strategy of the popular front because of the breadth of appeal that both have in common. Two years of bitter open conflict between Ranadive and the Andhra Communists (turning on the nature of the main enemy, the possible allies of the Communists, and, in particular, on the question whether the native bourgeoisie was to be regarded as one or the other) and the continued rejection in recent years of the "left" strategy with its anti-bourgeois appeal prove beyond doubt that the neo-Maoist strategy is not identical with the "left" strategy although both use the approach of the united front from below. The continued antagonism beyond 1950 of the CPI towards the Congress and the Socialists, who would be its allies under the "right" strategy, demonstrates equally clearly that, although both involve cooperation with the bourgeoisie against imperialism and feudalism, the neo-Maoist strategy is not identical with the "right" strategy either.

We have pointed out that the use of violent methods is not a special characteristic of any one of the three strategies but may or may not accompany any of them. The Telengana uprising, which began in 1946, is a case in point. It continued through 1947, when the "right" leadership of the CPI spoke of it as anti-imperialist and anti-feudal but not anti-bourgeois or anti-Congress; through 1948–1949, when the "left" CPI leadership hailed it as a fight against the bourgeoisie and the Congress as well as against imperialism and feudalism; and through 1950, when the neo-Maoist CPI leadership said that it was directed against imperialism and feudalism as well as the Congress but not against the bourgeoisie. It was called off in 1951 when the neo-Maoist strategy began to be applied in its peaceful form. The termination of the Telengana fighting, the CPI's practice since 1951, and Moscow's and Peking's explicit statements to that effect all underline the fact that even the neo-Maoist strategy, which in view of its Chinese origin is so often associated with the use of violence, can, like the "right" and the "left" one, be used peacefully.

Neo-Maoism—the Communist strategy of the cold war. We have examined a sufficient number of Soviet documents to trace the outline of the gradual adoption of the neo-Maoist strategy in Moscow in the period from 1947 to 1949. Further light could be thrown on the process by which this took place and on the motives underlying it by a more thorough study of Soviet documents and by investigations of the strategy changes of Communist parties other than the CPI and of international Communist organizations such as the World Federation of Trade Unions. While this remains to be done, it appears that the neo-Maoist strategy is essentially the reaction of international Communism to the cold war.

In 1947, with the beginning of the cold war, the "right" strategy of cooperation with the principal bourgeois and labor parties and with the governments formed by them was given up, since these were generally pro-American. During the next two years it developed that the "left" alternative to the "right" strategy, which was advocated by some in Moscow and was being fanatically followed by the CPI leadership, had certain disadvantages from Moscow's point of view. By regarding capitalism as an enemy, it unduly limited the range of the Communists' potential supporters to the so-called exploited classes—the workers, the poor peasantry, and some petty bourgeois elements—while in Moscow's eyes there was no reason, except the negligible one of Marxist theory, why exploiters too should not be mobilized on its side. Furthermore, the "left" strategy, though traditionally "internationalist," entailed the serious danger that each Communist party would concentrate, as the CPI did in 1948 and 1949, on the bourgeoisie in its own country as its main enemy, to that extent ignoring Moscow's main enemy, the United States.*

The neo-Maoist strategy, on the other hand, is admirably suited to the needs of Soviet foreign policy. Under it the Communists frankly invite the cooperation of "all classes, parties, groups, organizations and individuals," including capitalists and even feudal elements, the sole test of their eligibility being friendliness to the Soviet Union and antagonism to the United States. While the neo-Maoist approach to other parties is generally one "from below," that is, antagonistic, it can, in conformity with the dominant anti-American motive behind the

---

* Looked at in this light, the condemnation of Ranadive by his neo-Maoist enemies as both a Trotskyite and a Titoist makes some sense, apart from the common Communist tendency to associate all deviationists with both chief devils of Communism during the Stalinist period: internationalist, "leftist" Trotskyism leads to putting one's own enemies ahead of those of the Soviet Union (once the latter's enemy is no longer capitalism) , to a form of nationalism, i.e., to Titoism.

strategy, be changed to one "from above" where a non-Communist party becomes sufficiently anti-American and pro-Soviet, thus constituting a return to the "right" strategy in relation to that party. In any case, the Communist party's direct appeal to the bourgeoisie is likely to continue.

Since the neo-Maoist strategy is the strategy of international Communism for the cold war, it is not surprising that, like its "left" and "right" predecessors, it has found application throughout the non-Communist world. The Communist parties of Southeast Asia have obviously followed the Chinese model, in some instances adopting even the specifically Chinese features of the Maoist strategy—reliance on the peasantry and on guerrilla warfare. The Communists of all underdeveloped countries, notably of Asia and Latin America, have openly based themselves on the so-called four-class strategy which requires an appeal to the "national" bourgeoisie "from below," as against the major "bourgeois" parties, which is the essential characteristic of the neo-Maoist strategy. Even the Communist parties of Western Europe and the United States, however, are following that strategy, for they, too, concentrate on the American enemy and they, too, more or less openly, seek to include sections of the bourgeoisie in their united front from below.

Marxism, Leninism and neo-Maoism. Under the neo-Maoist strategy the Communist party claims to be the true representative of the interests not only of the workers but also of the capitalists. In its propaganda it emphasizes the interests held in common by workers and capitalists as against foreign imperialists. In brief, the cold war has taken the place of the class struggle. It is obvious that this substitution is a complete perversion of Marxism; but it is only a logical development of Leninism. To Marx and Engels the party was, along with the trade unions, only a tool of the working class in its class struggle; and therefore, like the unions, it could not rely on groups which, by Marxian definition, were the enemies of the workers. Lenin, however, sharply departed from Marxism when he divorced the party from the working class and, in effect, made the latter the tool of the former. Once this step was taken, there was no longer any reason why some other class too could not become the tool of the party. It could be the peasantry, as it clearly was in China, or it could even be the capitalists, as is now possible under the neo-Maoist strategy. The end of the Marxian party, the class struggle, has been superseded by the means, the party in its quest for power.

Sectarianism and the peace movement. The top Communist party leaderships have been sufficiently opportunist as well as subservient to

Moscow to adopt the new strategy. However, it is not surprising, in view of a long upbringing on class struggle doctrines, that they have met with some resistance or at least reluctance on the part of some of the rank and file and the subsidiary leadership. Such opposition, referred to as sectarianism by the Communists, is a deep-seated problem for them. By and large, Communists are naturally inclined to be sectarian. The "left" strategy of antagonism to both the entire bourgeoisie and the bourgeois and labor parties, although it has been applied only briefly since 1935 and may never be used again, is undoubtedly more to their liking than either the "right" strategy of cooperation with non-Communist parties or the neo-Maoist strategy of cooperation with capitalists.

The problem of sectarianism has in recent years arisen particularly in relation to the "peace" movement which, with its concentration on the United States as the main enemy and its approach to all elements of the population regardless of class, is closely related to the neo-Maoist strategy. The difficulty arises from the fact that Communists, being totalitarian, basically divide the world into black and white, into friends completely on their side and enemies completely opposed to them. The peace movement, however, is designed as an appeal to neutralists of various shades rather than to Communists. The Communists can bring themselves to make such an appeal only with great difficulty, since cooperation with people who say "a plague on both your houses" is really too much to expect from the inhabitants of one of the houses. The result is a persistent tendency on the part of Communists, forever denounced in party resolutions, either to look down on or ignore the peace movement or to run it as an organization of the Communist party, thus greatly reducing its appeal to non-Communists.

Moscow, Peking, and the CPI. For a Communist party to adhere to the neo-Maoist strategy is by no means tantamount to its acceptance of direction from Peking rather than from Moscow or to its being loyal to the Chinese rather than to the Soviet Communists. The neo-Maoist strategy has been followed by Communist parties in areas far removed from any possible Chinese Communist sphere of influence, such as Latin America. As we have seen in the Indian Party history, not only did Ranadive, who rejected the neo-Maoist strategy, feel that he could publicly insult Mao in 1949 and ignore Liu's policy directives at the end of that year, but the Andhra Communists, who sought to apply all aspects of the Chinese model in India, also paid no attention to advice from Peking. But the voice of Moscow, even if it did no more than repeat what Peking had said earlier, brought about the desired changes in the Party line both at the beginning and at the end of 1950. The evolution of CPI strategy, as we have traced it, demonstrates beyond doubt that the Party's policy in the postwar years has been, as it was before the war, ultimately determined by Moscow's desires. Throughout this period the Chinese Communists were following the neo-Maoist strategy, but the CPI, like Moscow, adhered to the "right" strategy until 1947. The CPI abandoned this strategy after Moscow did, and finally, early in 1950, accepted the neo-Maoist strategy on orders not from Peking but from Moscow, shifting, again on instructions from Moscow, from its violent to its peaceful form early in 1951.

While Moscow's direction of the CPI is obvious, it is by no means clear that Peking has been contesting it. It is a significant fact that ever since 1949, when the Chinese Communists might possibly have begun to show an active interest in CPI affairs, Moscow and Peking have been recommending the same strategy to the Indian Communists, Moscow in fact often speaking through the Chinese Communists, as at the Peking WFTU Conference or by reprinting or quoting Chinese articles. No conflict between Moscow and Peking can thus be established through detecting differences in the strategies recommended by them to the CPI. This does not necessarily mean that there is no conflict between Peking and Moscow over the direction of the CPI, but a study of Communist strategy in India does not reveal any at the present time.

At least until Stalin's death, there did appear some differences between Peking and Moscow on the degree of originality attributed to the Maoist and neo-Maoist strategy. Chinese sources rightly tended to claim it as a creative development by Mao and the Chinese Communist Party, while Soviet writers generally described it as a mere application of Lenin's and Stalin's teachings, supporting this view with quotations from Lenin and Stalin on the need for cooperation with anti-imperialist sections of the bourgeoisie. On closer inspection, however, these turn out to have advocated the united front from above with such "bourgeois" movements as the Kuomintang or the Indian Congress rather than a united front from below, including parts of the bourgeoisie, against such movements, which characterizes the neo-Maoist strategy. The differences between Moscow and Peking were relatively minor and subdued, however, each side even giving some space to the other's point of view; and, whether original or not, the "Chinese path" has, since 1949, been recommended to the Asian Communist parties by Moscow quite as much as by Peking.

The CPI in 1948 and 1949, under Ranadive's "left" leadership, professed to base itself primarily on the Russian example. In 1950, under the Andhra Communists, it sought to apply all of the Chinese Communists' methods in India, openly hailing them as its model. Since early 1951, when peasant guerrilla warfare, the specific Chinese characteristic of the Maoist strategy, was given up, the dangers of the mechanical application of either example to India have been emphasized. Both countries are now recognized as general models, Russia for the entire world and China for the underdeveloped areas, a formulation that conveniently leaves in doubt which of the two is regarded as primary. During no period, however, did the Indian Communists fail to welcome and describe in glowing terms the actual or supposed successes of either the Soviet or the Chinese Communists. Indeed, especially since 1949 when Moscow itself finally adopted the neo-Maoist strategy, there has been no reason at all why the Indian Communists should express any preference or even any noticeably greater degree of admiration for one of the two Communist powers. So long as Moscow and Peking maintain their appearance of complete amity, an Asian Communist party could only lose by following such a course. Facing no conflict between Moscow and Peking, the CPI is not inconsistent in looking up to both and boasting about the supposed achievements of both. It is as if a boy had been and continued to be greatly attached to and proud of his father but was now equally proud of his more recently successful older brother. An analysis of the CPI's propaganda would thus not even reveal that the Party's primary loyalty is to Moscow rather than Peking, as is suggested by our study of the evolution of its strategy, although neither approach can establish the existence of any conflict between Moscow and Peking over the direction of the CPI.

The nature of Moscow's control over Communist parties. We have now stated our conclusion that Moscow is directing the course of the CPI, but something must still be said about the nature of this direction. Certain very tentative conclusions on this subject emerge from our study which, when regarded with due caution, probably throw some light on the interesting question of the relations between Moscow and the various Communist parties in the non-Communist world in general. We can draw our conclusions only from the Indian postwar experience, however, and there is a real question as to what extent one can safely generalize from that experience. It is possible, for example, that Moscow's relations with a Communist party in a crucial area which is planning or immediately engaged in some decisive operation such as a civil war or general strike may be much closer than those with the CPI have been. It is also likely that a party whose top leader or leaders spent years in Moscow may have closer contacts even after their return to their homeland and may at least have a better understanding of Moscow's thinking than is true of the Indian Party, whose leaders have no such background. There may also be connections between certain leaders and factions in each party and certain leaders and factions in Moscow, which may well play a decisive part in determining a Communist party's relations with Moscow. Unfortunately, we know nothing definite about such connections and must therefore simply speak of "Moscow" as if no differences could exist among the Soviet leaders. In the one instance where we have clearly detected a difference of approach in Moscow—between the advocates of the "left" and the neo-Maoist strategies in 1947 and 1948—the difference was much more probably an unnoticed development due to lack of attention and ignorance of the decisive disagreement between the two than a reflection of a factional alignment among the Soviet leadership.

Indeed, lack of knowledge, interest, and attention on the part of Moscow seem to be more important factors in its relations with Communist parties than is generally believed. Perhaps because of some craving for uniformity in totalitarian thought and its inability to comprehend the vast diversity of conditions in the non-Communist world, Communist strategy—in the broad sense of the word as we have used it, distinguishing only among three strategies—is, except during periods of transition from one to the other, always uniformly applied throughout the world regardless of its applicability in each country. It is determined by Moscow's dominant foreign policy needs during any particular period, which, at least until about 1949, Moscow regarded primarily in the light of the situation in the West. The uniform application of a strategy throughout a non-uniform world often results in a particular Communist party's having to follow a strategy seriously detrimental to its own interests, a fact no doubt known to, though not admitted by, both Moscow and the Communist parties and accepted by all in the name of "proletarian internationalism." However, it can also cause a Communist party to pursue a line detrimental to Soviet interests themselves.

Much of the development of the Indian Communists' strategy illustrates such results of Moscow's ignorance of or lack of interest in their area. Thus, when by 1935 Moscow finally recognized fascism as an immediately more dangerous enemy than democratic socialism, hitherto referred to as "social fascism" by the Communists, the "left" policy of opposition to the labor and bourgeois Left was exchanged for the "right" policy of the Popular Front with these groups. In India also cooperation with the Congress and the Socialists now followed upon years of denunciations; but the shift from "left" to "right," which had made sense in the West, where the Communists' new allies were anti-fascist, made far less sense in India where they were more anti-British than anti-Nazi or anti-Japanese. Correspondingly, the return from the "right" to the "left" strategy upon the signing of the Stalin-Hitler Pact in 1939 was a necessity in the West, where Soviet amity with Nazi Germany was incompatible with Communist cooperation with anti-Nazi parties and governments. However, it was quite unnecessarily also executed in India, where the allies whom the CPI now abandoned and denounced were, just like the new Soviet policy, anti-British. The next strategy switch, following the Nazi invasion of Russia, back to the "right" strategy of cooperation with anti-fascist governments and parties in the West was particularly disastrous for the CPI, which was subsequently for years unable to remove the stigma of having been allied with the British national enemy of India during a crucial period of India's struggle for independence. This strategy of the CPI, which, unlike its predecessors, at least made sense in terms of Soviet foreign policy, was no doubt considered necessary in Moscow regardless of the cost to the CPI—but a more subtle approach might have reduced those costs.

The period more fully covered in our study presents essentially the same story. The immediate postwar years furnish a particularly good illustration of Moscow's lack of interest in and ignorance of Indian affairs. Because the Soviet government, at least outwardly, continued cooperation with its war-time allies, and because Communist parties served in coalition governments with other parties, the Indian Party also was expected to follow the "right" strategy in those years. It was to cooperate with the Congress and Socialist leaders who, having just emerged from British jails which they had occupied while the Communists had operated legally with British blessings, had no desire at all to reciprocate the Communists' overtures. In the first few months after the end of the war the CPI was even expected to combine an alliance with the Congress and Socialist parties with a not too un-friendly attitude towards the British; and throughout the period the united front from above was to include both the Congress and the Muslim League, elements bitterly at odds with each other. Moscow never bothered to furnish any guidance to the CPI on how to execute all these incompatible policies at the same time. The CPI was so bewildered and frustrated that for a few weeks or months in 1946 it even made a sudden and temporary switch from this impossible "right" to the "left" strategy, this being apparently the only instance in the CPI's history when it made a strategy change not called for by Moscow.

Moscow's abandonment of the "right" strategy was expressed as early as June 1947 in relation to India; but no one seems to have troubled to call it to the CPI's attention until Zhdanov's report to the founding meeting of the Cominform finally reached the Party, causing it to return to the "left" strategy in December 1947. The composition of the Cominform and the contents of the Zhdanov speech, with its preoccupation with the West, made it abundantly clear that this strategy switch, too, had been a response to developments in the West. Thus the CPI was once again left to its own devices, evoking little interest or advice from Moscow, which itself failed to settle on a definite alternative to the now abandoned "right" strategy. In the belief that it was executing Moscow's wishes, the CPI proceeded to follow a suicidal policy. Only in 1949, when Communist advances in Europe had definitely been stopped but, on the other hand, the Chinese Communists had won decisive victories, Moscow's attention shifted to Asia and the neo-Maoist strategy was unanimously adopted and, with the cooperation of Peking, proclaimed as obligatory for all Asian Communist parties. Moscow also recognized that for its own good as well as that of the CPI the violent form of that strategy was inappropriate in India.

The neo-Maoist strategy, like its predecessors, is now being applied on a world-wide scale; and it, too, has proved to be not equally suitable to conditions in all countries. Being the Communist strategy of the cold war, above all an anti-American strategy, it is most appropriate for use in countries where the government or major parties are pro-American. Where they are neutralist, the united front from below against them may be out of place, and some problems and doubts on this score have arisen in the CPI in relation to Nehru. Whether Moscow will be able to adjust to this situation remains to be seen. In India it has so far steered an indecisive course between the alternative extremes represented by Guatemala under the Arbenz regime and Indonesia, on the one hand, and Burma, on the other. With Moscow more and more inclined to support and foster rather than to look down on neutralism, it is becoming increasingly likely that, if a choice is to be made, the CPI will follow the path of the Communists in Indonesia, where the united front from above was substituted for that from below in relation to anti-American or neutralist parties and their government, rather than that of Burma, where the Communists for years fought a civil war against a neutralist government.*

It is clear, then, that Moscow, utterly opportunist in devising its strategies, has been rigid in applying them, whether they have been suitable or not, in all countries. Moscow practice obviously is not due

* See the 1955–1956 postscripts on pp. 174–175, above, on this point.

to any adherence to principles. It results from concentration at any one time on one particular area of the world where a given strategy may be appropriate and from lack of interest in and ignorance of other areas where the Communist parties are simply expected to follow the general line.

The extent of Moscow's control over Communist parties. The extent to which Moscow directs Communist parties is probably related to the extent to which it is interested in and aware of conditions in their countries. Here, too, it may therefore be dangerous to generalize from the experience of the Indian Communists. Their experience suggests that Moscow prefers to give as little guidance as possible, interfering only when a Communist party is definitely moving in a direction undesirable from Moscow's point of view, and even then not necessarily immediately. We have already mentioned that six months passed between the first indication of Moscow's abandonment of the "right" strategy for India and the CPI's corresponding action. An even longer period intervened between the time when Moscow settled on the neo-Maoist strategy and the point at which it was imposed on the CPI. Moreover, although from the beginning it was proclaimed in its peaceful form for India, the neo-Maoist strategy was carried out in its violent form for nearly another year by the CPI before Moscow directed the CPI to change. Perhaps Moscow wants to avoid responsibility in case of failure and also hopes that factional struggles in a party may lead to the desired course without outside interference; and, where a party, such as the CPI, is in any case of limited usefulness to Soviet policy, Moscow simply does not bother to provide specific guidance.

In any case, the direction furnished by Moscow seems to be largely negative, the party being guided to the desired goal by the gradual elimination of alternative courses. In 1947 the only thing made clear was that the "right" strategy of the united front from above, which international Communism had been following until then, was to be abandoned. What was to be substituted for it—specifically, whether the united front from below was to include or exclude the bourgeoisie —was left undecided. Since that time, although there has been a single relatively smooth evolution of strategy in Moscow, the corresponding development in the CPI has been interrupted by two upheavals, both caused as Moscow pushed the Party onto the "correct" course by eliminating alternative courses which it happened to be following. At the end of 1947 the CPI had chosen the "left" rather than the neo-Maoist alternative (being quite ignorant of the latter) to the "right" strategy; but at the beginning of 1950, after it had ignored earlier hints, the CPI was told by Moscow that it had been wrong and was now to follow the neo-Maoist strategy. Although quite aware this time that two alternatives again presented themselves, Moscow failed to make clear which one—the peaceful or the violent one—it recommended to the CPI. The CPI chose the violent one, only to be told by the end of 1950 that it had again chosen wrongly and was to follow the peaceful one—which necessitated another shift in the Party's line and leadership.

The CPI's choice now had been narrowed down to peaceful neo-Maoism, and only questions within this strategy could arise. The more the Party's choice is narrowed, the less reason for Moscow's interference remains; but it was always possible that on some subsidiary question, for example, whether Britain or the United States is the main enemy, Moscow might again proclaim which course was the wrong one—without specifying which of any remaining alternatives was the right one. The Indian Party furnishes a particularly good example of this type of negative guidance by Moscow. Each time after 1947 when faced with a choice it chose what turned out to be the wrong line. Other parties, choosing the right one, saved Moscow the trouble of interfering, thus justifying Moscow's hopes that negative guidance would be sufficient.

In the Indian case, at least, the negative direction of policy has its parallel in Moscow's negative influence on the selection of the leadership. The leader following the wrong course is removed, perhaps not so much directly by Moscow as by his rivals, who can attack him once he is deprived of Moscow's support. But his successor is not always enthroned by Moscow. He may simply be the leader of the strongest rival faction in the party. Not having been chosen by Moscow, the new leader may not follow the Moscow line either. This has happened twice in postwar CPI history: when Ranadive, the leader of the "left" faction, succeeded Joshi, after the latter's "right" strategy had been discarded; and again when Rajeshwar Rao, the leader of the Andhra Communists' neo-Maoist opposition during the "left" period, succeeded Ranadive. Whether the present leader, Ajoy Ghosh, came to power when violent neo-Maoism was disavowed by Moscow for India because he had headed the peaceful neo-Maoist faction earlier or because he was simply picked by Moscow is not so clear.

The transmission of strategy directives from Moscow to Communist parties. Finally, our study permits us to draw some partial conclusions as to how directives from Moscow are actually transmitted to a Communist party. There must be as many ways of doing this as there are ways of sending any message; and we do not know all of those used or the role they play. So far as general strategic guidance by Moscow is concerned, however—and this is the only type of guidance we have been able to trace in the postwar history of the CPI—it is clear that openly published directives are of primary importance. The clearest examples are Zhdanov's speech of September 1947, published in the Cominform journal of November 10, 1947, which caused the CPI to change from the "right" to the "left" strategy, and the Cominform editorial of January 27, 1950, which brought about the CPI's switch from the "left" to the neo-Maoist strategy. Other openly published documents that played a large part in the formation of postwar CPI strategy were reports to the Soviet Academy of Sciences, Liu Shao-chi's speech at the Peking WFTU Conference of November 1949 and probably also his "Internationalism and Nationalism," and Palme Dutt's open letter of December 1950. This conclusion is not drawn simply from the fact that CPI strategy has shifted in line with the ideas expressed in these writings. Indian Communists themselves have occasionally mentioned these documents as sources of their strategy, and they have constantly referred to the Zhdanov speech and the Cominform editorial as such.

Personal contacts, such as were afforded by the Calcutta Youth Conference of February 1948, the Peking WFTU Conference, and Harry Pollitt's presence at the Third CPI Congress in January 1954, undoubtedly play their part in keeping the Party informed of Moscow's thought; but, unlike some of the documents just mentioned, none of these three meetings brought about any change in CPI strategy—in two instances because the strategy desired by Moscow was already being followed, and in the case of the WFTU Conference because the CPI seemed unwilling to follow directives or unable to understand them. What the personal contacts there could not do was shortly afterward accomplished by the Cominform editorial of January 1950.

The written, publicly available directives are never actually worded as orders from Moscow to a Communist party. At most they state that a party would be guilty of a mistake if it did not follow a certain policy, or, perhaps, even that it has already been mistaken in pursuing its present course. More often they are statements describing as already existing a situation that is, in fact, the one desired by Moscow. Such statements can easily be recognized as directives and are certainly recognized as such by the Communists. Thus, if a party following the anti-bourgeois "left" strategy suddenly reads in the Cominform journal that the working class in its country is forming a broad united front including sections of the bourgeoisie, it knows that the time has come for a shift to the neo-Maoist strategy. Even a studied omission may imply a directive. For example, beginning in 1949 India was consistently omitted from the list of Asian countries in which armed Communist violence was hailed or merely described, even though such violence was actually going on in India. This turned out to be a directive to the CPI to follow the neo-Maoist strategy in its peaceful form. Finally, articles, especially in the Cominform journal, not dealing at all with a particular country may yet be tantamount to broad directives to the Communist party of that country.   The uniformity of Communist strategy throughout the world is so much taken for granted that each party realizes that every other party is following its strategy not because it is particularly applicable to its country but because it is the Communist strategy that should at that time be followed by all Communist parties.   Thus, for instance, articles in the Cominform journal by Latin American Communist leaders describing the strategies of their own parties are, and have been held by at least one Indian Communist leader to be, directives to the Indian Communist Party.

Although Moscow's directives are somewhat camouflaged, the question still arises as to why they should be issued in a form as freely available to the enemies of Communism as to the Communist leaders. It seems almost incredible that so secretive and conspiratorial a grouping as international Communism should operate in such a way; yet there can be no question that it does—as well as in many other ways, no doubt.   There are not only the instances in the CPI's history but also similar instances elsewhere, for example, the ouster of Earl Browder from the leadership of the American Communist Party through a letter by Duclos in the French Communist periodical *Les cahiers du communisme,* and the repudiation of Nosaka's peaceful tactics in the Japanese Communist Party through the Cominform editorial of January 6, 1950.   A possible and probably partial explanation may be derived from a conclusion that we have reached earlier.   If it is correct, as we have suggested, that Moscow often prefers to secure a party's compliance with its wishes through the factional struggle in that party rather than by direct interference, then its policy directives must, indeed, be widely enough distributed to reach not only the party's leadership but also the leaders of the other factions and even to some extent the rank and file.   Only by thus publicly discrediting a party's current leadership or depriving it of Moscow's support can another faction be sufficiently strengthened to take control of the party and to institute the new policy.   It is also possible that in some instances, whether the new policy is executed by a new leadership or by the old one, Moscow's prestige must publicly be placed behind the change in order to gain for it a party's support when its own leaders may not be able to command that support.   Finally, if it should be true that Moscow likes to interfere as little as possible for fear of assuming too much responsibility, it is even conceivable that it may prefer a public article in obscure language as a medium of direction to a secretly transmitted directive which would necessarily have to be much more specific.

BIBLIOGRAPHY

This bibliography contains only writings cited in this book. It does not, therefore, pretend to be a guide to further reading. The subject of this study is sufficiently specialized to permit the citation in the footnotes of all material of immediate relevance known and available to the author. To go beyond this and present a bibliography on international Communism or Indian affairs in general would far exceed the scope of this work. In a bibliography of this nature there would be little point in listing the very great number of articles of widely varying significance which constitute the primary sources on which this study is almost exclusively based. Complete references to these will be found in the footnotes; only the newspapers, periodicals, and collections containing them are given below.

I. Primary Sources

A. On the Indian Communist view of Communist strategy

1. *Communist,* monthly, Bombay.
2. Communist Party of India, *Political Resolution* (New Delhi: Jayant Bhatt, 1954).
3. Communist Party of India, *Political Thesis,* adopted at the Second Congress, Calcutta, February 28–March 6, 1948 (Bombay, 1949).
4. Communist Party of India, *Statement of Policy of the Communist Party of India* (Bombay: Jayant Bhatt, November 1951).
5. *Cross Roads,* weekly, 1949–May 1952, Bombay; June 1952–September 1952, Madras; September 1952–September 1953, Delhi. (Successor to *People's Age.*)
6. Democratic Research Service, *Communist Conspiracy at Madurai* (also published as *Communist Conspiracy in India*) (Bombay: Popular Book Depot, 1954).
7. Ghosh, Ajoy, *On the Work of the Third Congress of the Communist Party of India* (New Delhi, Jayant Bhatt, 1954).
8. Joshi, P. C., *For the Final Bid for Power!* (Bombay: People's Publishing House, no date).
9. Joshi, P. C., *Views,* Calcutta, May 1950.
10. Karanjia, R. K., *China Stands Up; the Wild Men of the West* (Bombay: People's Publishing House, 1952).
11. *New Age,* monthly, 1952, Madras; 1953–   , Bombay. (Successor to *Communist.*)
12. *New Age,* weekly, Delhi. (Successor to *Cross Roads.*)
13. *People's Age,* weekly, Bombay.
14. Ranadive, B. T., *Nehru Gov't. Declares War against Toilers* (Bombay: M. B. Rao, April 1948).

B. On the Soviet view of Communist strategy

1. Akademiia nauk SSSR, *Krizis kolonial'noi sistemy; natsional'no-osvoboditel'-naia bor'ba narodov Vostochnoi Azii* (Moscow, Leningrad, Izdatel'stvo Akademii nauk SSSR, 1949).

2. Akademiia nauk SSSR, *Uchenye Zapiski Tikhookeanskogo Instituta,* Tom. II, Indiiskii Sbornik (Moscow, 1949).

3. Astafyev, G., *China from a Semi-Colony to a People's Democracy* (Bombay: People's Publishing House, 1950).

4. *Bolshevik,* Moscow.

5. *Colonial Peoples' Struggle for Liberation* (Bombay: People's Publishing House, 1950).

6. *Crisis of the Colonial System, National Liberation Struggle of the Peoples of East Asia.* Reports presented in 1949 to the Pacific Institute of the Academy of Sciences, USSR (Bombay: People's Publishing House, 1951).

7. *Current Digest of the Soviet Press* (Washington: Joint Committee on Slavic Studies).

8. Dyakov, A. M., *New Stage in India's Liberation Struggle* (Bombay: People's Publishing House, 1950).

9. *For a Lasting Peace, for a People's Democracy!,* organ of the Cominform, 1947–1948, Belgrade; 1948–   , Bucharest.

10. International Union of Students, *Hands off South East Asia,* Conference of the Youth and Students of South East Asia Fighting for Freedom and Independence (No. 1, Special Bulletin of the Colonial Bureau of the I.U.S.), Prague, April 1948.

11. *Izvestia,* Moscow.

12. *Izvestia Akademii nauk SSSR,* Moscow.

13. *Mirovoe Khozia'stvo i Mirovaia Politika,* Moscow.

14. *Neue Welt,* Berlin.

15. *New Times,* Moscow.

16. *Ost-Probleme,* Bad Godesberg, Germany.

17. *Pravda,* Moscow.

18. *Soviet Press Translations* (Seattle: University of Washington Press).

19. *Trud,* Moscow.

20. *Voprosy ekonomiki,* Moscow.

21. *World Trade Union Movement,* organ of the World Federation of Trade Unions with headquarters in Vienna.

22. Zhukov, E., *Sharpening Crisis of the Colonial System after World War II* (Bombay: People's Publishing House, 1950).

C. On the Chinese Communist view of Communist strategy

1. Brandt, Conrad, Benjamin Schwartz and John K. Fairbank, *A Documentary History of Chinese Communism* (Cambridge: Harvard University Press, 1952).

2. *China Digest,* Peking.

3. Liu Shao-chi, *Internationalism and Nationalism* (Peking: Foreign Languages Press, written November 1948).

4. Mao Tse-tung, *The Fight for a New China* (New York: New Century Publishers, 1945).

5. *People's China,* Peking. (Successor to *China Digest.*)

6. *People's Daily,* Peking.

7. U. S. Congress, House of Representatives, Committee on Foreign Affairs, Subcommittee No. 5, National and International Movements, *The Strategy and Tactics of World Communism,* Supplement III, Country Studies (House Document 154, 80th Congress, 2nd Session) , Washington, 1948.

8. van der Sprenkel, Otto, ed., *New China; Three Views* (London: Turnstile Press, 1950).

D. *Other Communist sources*

from which Indian, Soviet and Chinese Communist views on strategy can be gleaned.

1. *Communist Review,* London.
2. *Labour Monthly,* London.
3. *Political Affairs,* New York.
4. *World News,* London. (Successor to *World News and Views.*)
5. *World News and Views,* London.

II. SECONDARY SOURCES

1. Atreya, "Indian Communists Plan for Revolution," *The New Leader,* XXXVII, No. 10 (March 8, 1954) , 3–5.

2. Beloff, Max, *Soviet Policy in the Far East, 1944–1951* (London: Oxford University Press, 1953) .

3. Bhargava, G. S., "Communists change their tactics," *The Manchester Guardian Weekly,* January 12, 1956, p. 3.

4. Borkenau, Franz, "The Chances of a Mao-Stalin Rift," *Commentary,* XIV (August 1952) , 117–123.

5. Bowles, Chester, *Ambassador's Report* (New York: Harper & Brothers, 1954) .

6. Bowles, Chester, "The Odds on Communism in India," *Harper's Magazine,* Vol. 208, No. 1244 (January 1954) , 41–48.

7. Carr, Randolph, "Conflicts Within the Indian CP," *Problems of Communism* (Washington, D. C.) , IV, No. 5 (September–October 1955) , 7–13.

8. Chanakya, *Indian Revolution* (Bombay: National Information and Publications, 1951) .

9. Curran, Jean A., Jr., "Dissension Among India's Communists," *Far Eastern Survey,* XIX, No. 13 (July 12, 1950) , 132–136.

10. Das, S. R. Mohan, *Communist Activity in India (1925–1950)* (Bombay: Democratic Research Service, 1950) .

11. Fischer, Ruth, "The Indian Communist Party," Russian Research Center, Harvard University, Minutes of the Seminar Meeting, July 11, 1952 (mimeographed).

12. Fischer, Ruth, "The Indian Communist Party," *Far Eastern Survey,* XXII, No. 7 (June 1953) , 79–84.

13. Frankel, Joseph, "Soviet Policy in South East Asia," Chapter VIII of Beloff, *Soviet Policy in the Far East.*

14. Graham, W. Gordon, "Communism and South Asia," *The Pacific Spectator,* V, No. 2 (Spring 1951), 215–231.

15. Hurd, Volney D., "Peking-Vietminh Rift Rumored," *The Christian Science Monitor,* March 9, 1954, p. 1.

16. "Indian Communist Order: Avoid Terrorist Tactics," *The Christian Science Monitor,* December 28, 1953, p. 4.

17. "The Indian General Elections," *Indian Press Digests*, Berkeley: Bureau of International Relations of the Department of Political Science, University of California, I, No. 4 (September 1952), pp. 45–85.

18. "India Reds Choose Leaders," *The Christian Science Monitor*, January 4, 1954, p. 10.

19. "India's Reds Mapping Non-Violence Policy," *The New York Times*, December 27, 1953, p. 5.

20. Kautsky, John H., "Indian Communist Party Strategy Since 1947," *Pacific Affairs*, XXVIII, No. 2 (June 1955), 145–160.

21. Kautsky, John H., "The New Strategy of International Communism," *The American Political Science Review*, XLIX, No. 2 (June 1955), 478–486.

22. Levi, Werner, *Modern China's Foreign Policy* (Minneapolis: University of Minnesota Press, 1953).

23. Limaye, Madhu, *Communist Party. Facts and Fiction* (Hyderabad: Chetana Prakashan, 1951).

24. Limaye, Madhu, "Indian Communism: The New Phase," *Pacific Affairs*, XXVII, No. 3 (September 1954), 195–215.

25. Masani, M. R., "The Communist Party in India," *Pacific Affairs*, XXIV, No. 1 (March 1951), 18–38.

26. Masani, M. R., *The Communist Party of India. A Short History* (London, Derek Verschoyle, 1954; New York, Macmillan, 1954).

27. Ministry of Home Affairs, Government of India, *Communist Violence in India*, September 1949.

28. Moraes, Frank, "Can Communism Conquer India?," *United Nations World*, VII, No. 7 (July 1953), 24–27 and 63.

29. Morris, Bernard S., "The Cominform: A Five Year Perspective," *World Politics*, V, No. 3 (April 1953), 369–376.

30. Morris, Bernard S., and Morris Watnick, "Current Communist Strategy in Nonindustrialized Countries," *Problems of Communism*, IV, No. 5 (September–October 1955), 1–6.

31. Mosely, Philip E., "Soviet Policy and the Revolutions in Asia," *Annals of the American Academy of Political and Social Science*, Vol. 276 (July 1951), 91–98.

32. North, Robert C., *Moscow and Chinese Communists* (Stanford: Stanford University Press, 1953).

33. Overstreet, Gene D., *The Soviet View of India, 1945–1948*, Columbia University, unpublished M.A. Thesis in Political Science, February 1953.

34. Park, Richard L., "Indian Democracy and the General Election," *Pacific Affairs*, XXV, No. 2 (June 1952), 130–139.

35. Park, Richard L., "Indian Election Results," *Far Eastern Survey*, XXI, No. 7 (May 7, 1952), 61–70.

36. Park, Richard L., "India's General Elections," *Far Eastern Survey*, XXI, No. 1 (January 9, 1952), 1–8.

37. "Reds Back Nehru on Foreign Policy," *The New York Times*, June 30, 1955, p. 4.

38. Sacks, Milton, "The Strategy of Communism in Southeast Asia," *Pacific Affairs*, XXIII, No. 3 (September 1950), 227–247.

39. Schwartz, Benjamin I., *Chinese Communism and the Rise of Mao* (Cambridge: Harvard University Press, 1952).

40. Schwartz, Morton, "The Wavering 'Line' of Indian Communism," *Political Science Quarterly*, LXX, No. 4 (December 1955), 552–572.

41. Watnick, Morris, "The Appeal of Communism to the Underdeveloped Peoples," Bert F. Hoselitz, ed., *The Progress of Underdeveloped Areas* (Chicago: The University of Chicago Press, 1952), pp. 152–172.

42. Watnick, Morris, "Continuity and Innovation in Chinese Communism," *World Politics*, VI, No. 1 (October 1953), 84–105.

43. Windmiller, Marshall, "Indian Communism Today," *Far Eastern Survey*, XXIII, No. 4 (April 1954), 49–56.

44. Wofford, Clare and Harris, Jr., *India Afire* (New York: John Day Co., 1951).

INDEX